MOSCA

In memory of my parents
Giovanni and Giusy Albertoni

MOSCA
and the Theory of Elitism

Ettore A. Albertoni

Translated by
Paul Goodrick

Basil Blackwell

English translation by Paul Goodrick © Ettore A. Albertoni 1987

First published in Italian as *Dottrina della classe politica e teoria delle élites*
© Ettore A. Albertoni, Milan, Giuffré Editore, 1985

English translation of the revised and extended edition first published 1987

Basil Blackwell Ltd
108 Cowley Road, Oxford, OX4 1JF, UK

Basil Blackwell Inc.
432 Park Avenue South, Suite 1503
New York, NY 10016, USA

All rights reserved. Except for the quotation of short passages for the purposes of criticism and review, no part of this publication may be reproduced, stored in a retrieval system, or transmitted, in any form or by any means, electronic, mechanical, photocopying, recording or otherwise, without the prior permission of the publisher.

Except in the United States of America, this book is sold subject to the condition that it shall not, by way of trade or otherwise, be lent, re-sold, hired out, or otherwise circulated without the publisher's prior consent in any form of binding or cover other than that in which it is published and without a similar condition including this condition being imposed on the subsequent purchaser.

British Library Cataloguing in Publication Data

Albertoni, Ettore
  Mosca and the theory of elitism
  1. Mosca, Gaetano   2. Elite (Social sciences)
  I. Title   II. Dottrina della classe politica e teoria delle elites. *English*
  305.5'2'0924   JC330
  ISBN 0–631–15254–7

Library of Congress Cataloging in Publication Data

Albertoni, Ettore A.
  Mosca and the theory of elitism.

  Translation of: Dottrina della classe politica e teoria delle élites.
  Bibliography: p
  Includes index.
  1. Mosca, Gaetano, 1858–1941—Contributions in political science.   2. Elite (Social sciences)
  3. Power (Social sciences)   4. Political science—Italy—History.   I. Title
  JC265.M65A813   1987   306'.2'0924   87-10320
  ISBN 0–631–15254–7

Typeset in 10½ on 12pt Ehrhardt by
Opus, Oxford
Printed in Great Britain by T. J. Press Ltd, Padstow

Contents

Foreword viii
Introduction to the English edition xi

PART I: Gaetano Mosca and the Doctrine of the Political Class 1

1 The life and times of Gaetano Mosca, 1858–1941 3

2 Birth of the doctrine of the political class 12
  The three periods of Gaetano Mosca's political thought
  Elucidation of terminology: political class and ruling class

3 The concepts of the open system, 1879–1895 19
  Formation and structure of the political class
  Access to the political class: military valour, wealth, birth, individual merit
  A political formula for each political class
  Mosca's early political philosophy
  The parliamentary system and the bourgeoisie in nineteenth-century Italy
  The political class and the bourgeoisie in Italy: an uncharacteristic nineteenth-century bourgeoisie state

4 The bourgeois myth of the middle class as the political class 33
  The aims of the political class
  The middle class and political democracy
  Elections and organized minorities
  An ideological framework for the new social forces with the capacity to renew Italy politically

Contents

5 The development of the scientific system as a comprehensive ideology, 1896–1922   46

The first edition of the *Elementi di scienza politica*: a complete synthesis of Gaetano Mosca's thought
History of individuals and history of institutions
The juridical defence as an ethical basis for the relationship between rulers and ruled
The new significance of the political formula
The results of the scientific and ideological system
From the science of counter-revolution to ideological anti-socialism

6 From the nineteenth to the twentieth century – political commitment and parliamentary experience   65

Against universal suffrage, 1912
The great crisis in the Italian liberal political system, 1919–1922
Gaetano Mosca, Senator of the Kingdom of Italy – the polemic against syndicalism, 1921
Mosca and Mussolini, 1922–1926
Rejection of the Fascist regime

7 Codification of the doctrine, 1923–1941   85

Ruling classes and civilization
The codification of Mosca's doctrine as his response to the political crisis of the 1920s
Aims and results of Mosca's new political and historical research
Dialectics in the doctrine of the political class – science, ideology and ethics

8 Legitimacy and power during the European crisis of the 1930s   98

The role of ideology in Mosca and Ferrero
The balance of ruling forces and the principle of legitimacy
In the heart of the European crisis

PART II: Elitism, Neo-elitism and Democracy   107

9 The 'Italian school of elitists' – between myth and reality   109

From Mosca's political class to Pareto's elite
The influence of the first research into political parties: Ostrogorskij and Michels

The specifically Italian quality of the 'Mosca–Paretian paradigm' and its progressive internationalization

10 The development of elitism in the English-speaking intellectual political tradition . . . 120

A new democratic conception based on elites – Schumpeter and Burnham

Scientific reformulations of elitism and the development of neo-elitism

Neo-elitism as an instrument for understanding the contemporary world in political terms

11 Gaetano Mosca and the intellectual political tradition in Italy after the Second World War, 1945–1985 . . . 131

The rediscovery of the liberal meaning of Gaetano Mosca's thought

The return of the 'theory of elites' from the Anglo-American world to Italy

The 'Mosca-Paretian paradigm' and the contemporary crisis in the Italian intellectual political tradition

12 Towards a critical conclusion . . . 145

Elitism versus Welfare-statism: Lowell Field and Higley

An attempt to go beyond the theory of Schumpeter: Otto Stammer

A critical interpretation of corporate elitism: José L. Orozco

Marxism and ethical elitism: Aleksandar Sekulovič

Elitism and the intellectual political tradition in the French-speaking world

Between past and future

Abbreviations	165
Notes	168
Select bibliography	186
Name index	192

Foreword

The theory of elites was first expounded towards the end of the nineteenth century and in the early part of the twentieth century in the writings of Pareto, Mosca and Michels, and it then came to be widely used by sociologists and political scientists as a framework for studying social stratification and political power in terms other than those of the prevailing democratic theory or of Marxist thought. From the outset indeed the theory displayed two aspects: on one side it was intended to provide a more scientific and realistic account of political rule, while on the other side it functioned as a political doctrine or ideology which questioned and criticized the wider claims that were being made for an extension of democracy and in particular the socialist (especially Marxist) conceptions of a future classless, egalitarian society.

But the formulations of the theory were quite diverse, and as Professor Albertoni makes clear in this excellent study it is an uncritical oversimplification to focus attention upon a supposedly distinctive 'Italian school of elitism'. His own aim is, first, to provide 'a documented reconstruction of the life and work of Gaetano Mosca', who was a central figure in the elaboration of the theory; and secondly, to show how Mosca's doctrine of the 'political class' could be developed into a valid theory of the permanent existence of competing elites in a modern democracy, which may modify profoundly our conceptions of political democracy as well as the original, widely divergent formulations of Pareto, Michels and Mosca himself.

Mosca's concept of the 'political class', as the organized minority which effectively imposes its rule, in all societies, on the unorganized majority, was first introduced in his book *Sulla teorica dei governi e sul governo parlamentare* (1884) and was then expounded more systematically in *Elementi di scienza politica* (1896, 2nd edition with a new section 1923). Albertoni traces in detail the development of this concept, setting it in the context of Italian society and politics in that period and shows how deeply Mosca's 'realistic' account of politics was infused with ideology, so that it became a veritable 'political doctrine' which was intended to aid the organization and rise to power of a new class. From this aspect, however, it was in important respects 'unrealistic', for the bourgeoisie which Mosca saw as a class 'already comfortably well-off [and] gradually acquiring that other important prerequisite by means of which . . . a class is able to impose itself on society and achieve the capacity to rule it: knowledge' was in reality, as Albertoni observes, largely descended from the notorious 'band of rogues and rabble scum' which Mosca himself describes in another context. Albertoni goes on to argue that 'the limits to Mosca's analysis are to be found in his instinctive conservatism, the inability to grasp . . . the real differences between the classes, and the consequent erroneous identification of the bourgeoisie with the educated class.'

Yet Mosca was a moderate, even liberal, conservative who desired gradual social reform and the ultimate advent of a 'middle-class' society and state, dominated by the values of the intellectuals within the bourgeoisie and regulated to a large extent by moral norms (social mechanisms which he analysed with the aid of a new concept, 'juridical defence'). These last two concerns, with intellectuals and with moral/ cultural influences, which are crucially important for constructing a 'political formula' or principle of legitimacy, are evidently close to the preoccupations of Gramsci, whose critical evaluation of Mosca played a significant part in the development of his own theory of the intellectuals and 'hegemony'.

There were, as Albertoni shows, several different and even contradictory strands in Mosca's thought, ranging from conservatism and a strong emphasis on 'realism' to a kind of critical Utopianism, although he tried persistently to reconcile them, especially in his later writings, and at the same time to give due attention to the contradictions in society itself. Thus, in a letter to Guglielmo Ferrero in the 1930s he describes as the biggest anomaly existing in the modern world the contradiction between political equality and economic inequality, and at the end of his *Storia delle dottrine politiche* (1936, revised and corrected edition 1939) he advocates 'mixed regimes' in which 'neither the autocratic nor the liberal system is totally predominant and there is a slow but continual renewal of the political class.' Earlier, unlike Michels who was converted to Fascism, Mosca was openly critical of Mussolini, rejected the Fascist regime and urged the restoration of representative government.

Far more than the other early elite theorists Mosca developed a comprehensive and complex theory of political rule in modern societies, and he did so with the practical intent of influencing the course of politics, in Italy and more widely in Europe (especially in the turbulent period following the First World War, and during the economic and social crisis of the 1930s), not only through his writings but more directly as a member of the Chamber of Deputies (1909–13), an Under-Secretary, and from 1919 a Senator. In the second part of this book, therefore, Albertoni considers the significance and influence of Mosca's thought in the development of elite theory and 'neo-elitism' since 1945. His main theme, which also incorporates an illuminating account of the development of elitist ideas in the English-speaking world and within the Italian intellectual-political tradition, as well as a wide-ranging review of recent thought and research, is the relation between the theory of elites and democratic theory, and he gives particular attention to the doctrine expounded by Schumpeter in *Capitalism, Socialism and Democracy*: 'the most complete and convincing modern formulation of elitism [presented] in an exemplary manner as a true political doctrine which has the capacity to go beyond the limits of the classical "theory of elites" '. Schumpeter's work was indebted perhaps more to Max Weber than to the Italian thinkers (which is why he uses the terms 'leaders' and 'leadership' rather than 'elites'), but it poses very sharply the problem that is addressed by many other recent writers, which is summarized by Albertoni in his critical conclusion as being 'to move on from the now somewhat static position into which theoretical and practical neo-elitism has now rigidified, to the formulation of elitist political doctrines that are feasible within the context of the substantially participatory and mass form of democracy in contemporary societies'. It is indeed the confrontation between 'participatory democracy' and 'political leadership' – and the analysis of their forms and limits – which dominates recent and current debates and will constitute in my view the crucial issue in democratic doctrine and practice for the foreseeable future.

In Albertoni's book we are given an unrivalled introduction to Mosca's thought, based upon much new research, and at the same time an incisive and wide-ranging account of how the ideas of Mosca and other earlier thinkers have entered into, and been modified by, the subsequent elaborations of elite theory. It will be an invaluable guide and source of ideas for all those – social scientists, political philosophers, active politicians – who are engaged in analysing and interpreting the meaning and potentialities of democracy in the large-scale, complex societies of the present day, bound together in one world system yet infinitely diverse.

Tom Bottomore

Introduction to the English edition

Gaetano Mosca and his relevance to the present age

This book represents the synthesis of a comprehensive study which I have been carrying out for several years into the 'doctrine of the political class' by Gaetano Mosca (1858–1941), and into its subsequent development and interpretation. In this work I have re-elaborated and summarized the data, results and methodology contained in my more extensive and systematic study *Gaetano Mosca. Storia di una dottrina politica. Formazione e interpretazione* [*Gaetano Mosca. History of a Political Doctrine. Its Development and Interpretation*], which was extensively modified and presented under a different title in 1985 as a research proposal:[1] one that concerned more than just the history of ideas. However, as Karl Popper has rightly pointed out, 'research is a never-ending process' and so this present work brings together several new elements not found in the previous study. These new elements are also the result of the detailed research which an international group of scholars has been conducting for some time into the themes treated in this book on the initiative of the 'Gaetano Mosca International Committee for the Study of the Political Class', which I have the honour of chairing and which publishes the series of studies and research results known as *Archivio Internazionale Gaetano Mosca per lo studio della classe politica* [Gaetano Mosca International Archive for the study of the Political Class].

The 'Committee', which has organized two 'Gaetano Mosca International Seminars' in Italy (in 1980 and 1981) is a body interested in research and scientific collaboration in the field of the formulation of doctrine and ideology in Italian political thought. Its aim is to propose a more general multidisciplinary and interdisciplinary reconsideration not only of Mosca's doctrine of the political class, but also of the various formulations of the theory of elites and of political systems, with particular reference to the system of political parties and the theoretical-practical relationship between democratic political conceptions and elites. Its commitment and interest in these themes is further demonstrated by its participation in the organizing of the international congress on 'Political Class, Political Elites and Political Parties', held at La Trinidad-Tlaxcala near Mexico City in July 1984 in collaboration with the Universidad Autonoma Metropolitana (Unidad Xochimilco) and with the *Centre de recherche sur les élites* in Paris. In terms of content and method, this seminar represented the third in the Mosca Seminar series. The themes dealt with were then examined in more detail at the fourth Mosca Seminar, organized in Mexico City in October 1986 by the *Universidad Nacional Autonoma de México (Facultad de Ciencias Políticas y Sociales – División de Estudios de Posgrado)* and the Mosca Committee.[2] To complete this survey of the various initiatives in this area of study, I will mention the conferences held on the theme of the masses organized in Paris and Quebec by Jacques Zylberberg and Michel Maffesoli (1984–5) and the *Round Table* dedicated to the question of elites during the XIII World Congress of the International Political Science Association (Paris, July 1985), as well as an explanatory analysis of the connection between political class and ideology in a single Italian town, Cremona, during a period spanning the nineteenth and twentieth century.[3] Finally, one should also consider the research work being conducted along similar lines by Moshe M. Czudnowski at DeKalb University (Northern Illinois, USA) to coincide with the celebration in 1981 of 'The Centennial of Mosca's Theory of the Ruling Class' and the publication, since 1982, of the various volumes of the *International Yearbook for Studies of Leaders and Leadership*.

Before entering into the heart of the subject, I would like to state in advance – borrowing a phrase from Jean Starobinski – that 'the choice of which subject to study is not an innocent one'; it 'already implies a preliminary interpretation and is inspired by our present interests'. The formation and the circulation of the political class are everywhere, today more than ever, central themes not only in political debate, but also in the life of societies and states. I wish to make it clear that, as far as I am concerned, the reconsideration of Mosca's work within the context of political studies in Italy tackles a series of problems to do with research and historiography and satisfies a precise requirement in terms of political science. The former problems are those which I have highlighted in the successive studies dedicated to Mosca from 1968 onwards;[4] the more purely political-scientific requirement is to verify the theoretical and practical utility of the results obtained from a reflection on the thought of this Italian writer and on all the questions related to it.

Introduction

My interest in Gaetano Mosca was stimulated by and is based on two achievements which ensure the relevance for today of the questions he dealt with: his adoption of the theoretical-practical concept of political class as a criterion for interpreting different forms of government as well as political events, and the close connection he established between the political-doctrinal system, juridical institutions and conditions of social and cultural life in the formation, development and circulation of ruling groups. But besides the scientific importance of Mosca's work and the internal evolution of his thinking, I hold that it is correct to bring out the fundamental ideological coherence of his overall political conception, the substantial identity between his position as a critic of the liberal-parliamentary system as it had developed and functioned in Italy from the nineteenth to the twentieth century, and his stance as a defender of the liberal state when triumphant Fascism was radically altering the political-constitutional order in the 1920s and 1930s. This meant introducing a precise link between the purely historiographical analysis and a series of contemporary ideas of topical interest.

With the publication in 1978 of the above-mentioned *Gaetano Mosca. Storia di una dottrina politica* I had exhausted all the possibilities of my own personal study of this subject from a historical perspective. I then set about devising and organizing the 'Gaetano Mosca International Seminars'. These seminars form an instance of essentially multidisciplinary and interdisciplinary research, which in the six volumes of the 'Archive' published so far has met the need for more detailed investigation; a need which I have indicated and illustrated in this book. The results thus obtained, updated and summarized in my subsequent work, *Dottrina della classe politica e teoria delle élites*, show that more is now known about the writer's life and there is a more precise awareness of the different scientific inspirations behind the work of a scholar interested in many different fields (constitutional law, political science, political economy, the history of political doctrines and institutions). Considerable importance must also be attached to the extensive research that has been carried out on an international scale (ranging from Europe to the Americas, from a communist country like Yugoslavia to Japan). It has shed light for the first time in a systematic manner on the propagation and, sometimes, misunderstanding of Mosca's thought outside of Italy. After a careful and systematic investigation – carried out in the various volumes of the *Archivio Internazionale Gaetano Mosca per lo studio della classe politica*, and received positively especially in international circles[5] – it has turned out that Mosca's work has been read and studied much more than might be imagined, above all through the translations of the *Elementi di scienza politica* and *Storia delle dottrine politiche*. It should not be forgotten that in 1984 Gaetano Mosca's doctrine of the political class celebrated its first one hundred years of existence. It is therefore time to draw up a balance sheet. The first thing to take into account are the results obtained from the many studies which have been dedicated not only to Mosca, but also to Vilfredo Pareto (1848–1923) and Robert Michels (1876–1936). In particular, the volumes of the 'Gaetano Mosca International Archive for the Study of the Political Class' – collected works written with the help and participation of 50 scholars from Italy and nine other countries – form a very useful series of documents regarding the fundamental theme which has emerged from the research. We are aware, however, that the definitive structuring of the extensive theoretical area explored so far is still far from complete and not only in terms of its effective use, but also from a purely conceptual point of view. The theme in question concerns the development of the doctrine of the political class into a true theorization of the permanent existence of competing elites in a modern democracy based on pluralism in society and a multiparty system. Such a theorization modifies profoundly both the conception of political democracy and also the different formulations of Mosca, Pareto and Michels.

Taking all of this into account, I must add that this present work is divided into two parts for reasons of practicality and in order to make the exposition clearer.

In the first part my aim has been to provide a documented reconstruction of the life and work of Gaetano Mosca. I set forth in a critical manner the characteristic elements of the doctrine of the political class and in doing so, I refer to the results achieved in all my previous research mentioned above. Furthermore, I am particularly concerned in this part of the work to oppose a deep-rooted prejudice regarding the ideological significance of the doctrine of the political class. By way of example, I shall mention my participation, during 1984 and 1985, in the two previously mentioned seminars on the masses held at the Sorbonne (University of Paris V) and the Laval University in Quebec City. The theme of my two papers was the relationship between the masses and elites in the thought and work of the classic Italian writers. The event was also of interest for the undoubted fact that in the French and French-speaking intellectual political tradition, the uncritical classification of the doctrines formulated by Mosca and the other Italian theorists under the generic and ideological heading of 'Italian school of elitists' prevails over the scientific nature of their theoretical elaborations. To put it plainly, these doctrines are too often considered to be, and condemned as, authoritarian and even Fascist or semi-Fascist. This is certainly not only an ideological prejudice, but also an error which can be avoided by introducing a historical dimension, that is, by setting such studies within the context of Italian history. Applied to Mosca, this means a knowledge of the writer's life, a philological analysis of his writings and an awareness of the political-historical context. The entire first part of this study aims to achieve this objective by explaining the real meaning of Mosca's thought.

In the second part, on the other hand, importance is given to reconstructing, above all at a conceptual level, the significance and perspective of Mosca's work by comparing it, though in a summarized form, with the theories formulated by Vilfredo Pareto and Robert Michels.[6] What emerges clearly is the deep divergence in inspiration between the three theoretical approaches and the clean break made by all three with the dominant political climate in Italy during the 1920s and 1930s, the period of the Fascist dictatorship.

However, what is chiefly investigated in the second part of this study is the passage of political thinking from the classic formulations of Mosca, Pareto and Michels to the particular conceptions of present-day elitism and neo-elitism. The implications of such a tricky process have still not been explored and made clear. Yet there is no doubt that within the historical sequence of the several liberal-democratic models of organization of the state and society – analysed and discussed, for example, with great acumen by the Canadian political scientist Crawford Brough Macpherson[7] – Mosca's theoretical formulation and that of the classic Italian school of elitists constitute only partially recognized but fixed elements in that model of a pluralistic equilibrium of elites which was given a definitive form by the Austro-American economist Joseph Schumpeter (1883–1950) at the beginning of the 1940s. Thus the thought of Mosca and the other classic elitists forms part of the complex interweaving of both theoretical and practical problems which concern the development of liberal-democratic ideas and the institutions to which they have given rise. These are problems which go beyond the simple aim of a historical reconstruction and they extend from the last decades of the nineteenth century up to the present day with its evident signs of crisis in political thinking and in politics in general.

A clear continuity can be discerned between the classics, like Mosca, who wrote in the years spanning the last part of the nineteenth and the first part of the twentieth century and scholars active during the last fifty years. What they have in common is their rigorous and deeply felt meditation on the effective possibilities for establishing a democratic political order, its methods of self-preservation and its limits. They also share an approach which is particularly significant: the close connection made between speculation about power and its inflexible logic and the ethical-political aspiration to construct institutions able to resolve the most difficult problem of all times. This is the ever-increasing need to govern those particularly complex systems that are modern societies and states with the consent and participation of their citizens, while guaranteeing these citizens independence and freedom. From this general research there clearly emerges the still uncertain and contradictory features that were characteristic of the doctrines of the classic writers; the eclectic development of elitism based on the work of Mosca, Pareto and Michels in the Anglo-American world during the 1940s; and subsequently the present-day neo-elitism of an essentially methodological and empirical nature. The latter forms the basis for several proposals of doctrines which, despite their still uncertain and vague outlines, none the less deserve specific critical attention. As a consequence, the research on Mosca constitutes the core of these central themes, which I believe should be known about and discussed to a greater extent beyond the confines (and limits) of Italian intellectual circles.

The overall approach of this work, therefore, is characterized by an attempt to stimulate research and by the affirmation of a more precise methodology in this field of studies; several little known lines of research have also been indicated. It does not follow from this that I presume the present study has exhausted the many questions dealt with. On the contrary, I would like to think that I have gone some way to demarcating the themes and organizing the most reliable data, and that I have proceeded without any preconceived notion or prejudice in order to help face some of the central problems in contemporary political thinking.

Acknowledgements

In the twenty five years that I have been researching in this field I have accumulated many scientific debts. Apart from the grateful recognition due to my academic mentors – Renato Treves, Norberto Bobbio, Luigi Firpo and Alessandro Passerin d'Entrèves, the list of people to whom I owe thanks is too long for me to name them all. I shall therefore mention only the following for their valuable and stimulating suggestions when I was writing *Dottrina della classe politica e teoria delle élites*, which is the third volume in the 'International Archive' (Italian series) and, extensively revised and modified, forms the basis of the present English translation: Tom Bottomore, José Luis Orozco, Mattei Dogan, John Higley, Moshe M. Czudnowski, G. Lowell Field, Aleksandar Sekulovič, Walter Euchner, John G. Gunnell, Rafael Perez Miranda, Filippo Sabetti. However, to talk of a translation is too limiting and to a large degree inexact. Through a very intensive cultural exchange with scholars of politics in the English-speaking world, I have been made aware of the great interest shown in this area of research and its problems. So although the original Italian text of *Dottrina della classe politica e teoria delle élites* clearly provides the basis for this edition, new ideas and interests generated by various scientific encounters and comparisons led me to rewrite practically the whole of the second part – as I also did for the French edition – as well as to adapt extensively the first part for the benefit of the English reader.

There have been and still exist for the non-Italian reader quite a few problems relating to terminology. Those who study the history of political thought, political science or political philosophy are aware that problems of terminology are in every case also problems of a conceptual kind. For an important aspect of Mosca's terminology relative to the key concepts of 'political class' and 'ruling class', I refer the reader to chapter 2 in which a precise clarification is given.

Then there is the use of the term *'scuola italiana delle élites'* which has been rendered in English by 'Italian school of elitists', the intention being to indicate a line of thinking which encompasses – without cancelling, however, the basic differences between them – the studies carried out by Mosca, Pareto and Michels. The term 'elitism', on the other hand, indicates a further stage which in conceptual, practical and even ideological terms goes beyond the formulations of the classic Italian writers and in which the possibility of new doctrines has been opened up.

In addition, I wish to thank most cordially Tom Bottomore to whom I am doubly indebted: first, for the fruitful path opened up by his fundamental text *Elites and Society* (1964), and secondly, for his generous help in getting my book published in an English version.

Compared with the Italian edition the present text has a much reduced critical apparatus and fewer notes for reasons of space and to avoid unwieldiness. Anyone wishing to see the now very extensive Italian and international bibliography should consult the Italian edition. I must also warn the reader that in quoting writers and works that have been translated into Italian, I have in part referred to the Italian edition; wherever this is the case, the date of publication of the original language edition is indicated in brackets after the title.

Finally, I would like to express my warmest thanks to Paul Goodrick, Lecturer in English at the State University of Milan, for his patient and intelligent collaboration in discussing and going over the text with me. This has made possible the improved version in English of a difficult work.

Facoltà di Scienze Politiche
Università degli Studi di Milano
April 1987

PART I

Gaetano Mosca and the Doctrine of the Political Class

1
The life and times of Gaetano Mosca, 1858–1941

Gaetano Mosca was born in Palermo on 1 April 1858 during the very last years of Bourbon rule over the southern half of Italy and the island of Sicily. His family, originally of Piedmontese descent, occupied a modest but respectable position on the social scale. The only information we have about the first years of his life is a short autobiographical sketch, contained in the Preface to *Sulla teorica dei governi e sul governo parlamentare. Studii storici e sociali* [*The Theory of Governments and the Parliamentary System. Social and Historical Studies*] (1884).

In 1877 Mosca enrolled in the Faculty of Law at Palermo University, where in just under four years he completed his degree with a thesis on 'The Factors of Nationality', published the following year in the Florentine *Rivista Europea*. In this first piece of research Mosca put forward a programme which would remain unchanged throughout his entire life of intellectual and practical activity: to be a realist at all times, explode myths and tirelessly reveal the truth hidden by ideology and metaphysics. This was a declaration of loyalty to Machiavelli and his method, from which the Sicilian scholar would never deviate.

The fact that Mosca rejected any metaphysical or a priori approach also implied a condemnation of the general climate produced by the Age of Romanticism. The emotive and religious atmosphere in the liberal nineteenth century was strongly pervaded by a sense of nationality, while at the same time it was very open to the reciprocal influence of renascent national cultures. Mosca's thought and personality can only be understood by comparing them dialectically with both the contemporary cultural background in Sicily and a certain mystical enthusiasm, which became a prominent ideological element of considerable political as well as emotive force during the national-bourgeois revolutions.

His involvement in political journalism, however, dates back to 1879, when he wrote for the *Rassegna Palermitana*, a fortnightly review of the sciences, letters and arts, published in Palermo from January to August of that year.

After taking his degree, Mosca spent a year in Rome attending the complementary course in political and administrative sciences. Here his teachers were: Francesco Protonotari (1836–88), editor of *Nuova Antologia di Scienze, Lettere ed Arti*, the most intellectual quality review of the Right; Luigi Palma (1837–99), one of the founders of modern constitutional law and a keen student of electoral systems; Antonio Salandra (1853–1931), lecturer in economic and financial legislation in Rome and a future Prime Minister; and Angelo Messedaglia (1820–1901), the head of the course, who, in 1851, had begun working for the creation of separate university faculties for the study of political administration as distinct from law. The intellectual environment certainly influenced the young Mosca, whose keen and learned interest in law was mingled with a strong leaning towards history and politics.

In 1884 *Teorica* was published with the subtitle 'Historical and Social Studies' by Loescher of Turin. It formed the first complete formulation of the concept of the political class, and placed Gaetano Mosca among the great thinkers and innovators of political science. This work clearly states that there exist 'effective organized minorities' which are the real protagonists of history: an assertion which was in stark contrast with the often genuine, but over-rhetorical ideal of liberty inherited from the very recent struggle against absolutism. In this respect, however, *Teorica* aims to demonstrate the human face of the 'immortal principles' by examining critically the foundations of freedom and power.

On 26 July 1885 Mosca obtained a university teaching qualification in constitutional law from the University of Palermo where, in 1886, he was appointed to give a course in that subject. The year 1887, in which he was appointed editor of the proceedings in the Chamber of Deputies, marked a break with his Sicilian background. After his marriage to Maria Giuseppa Salemi in Palermo on 11 February 1888, he moved permanently to Rome and, in June of the same year, had his teaching qualification transferred to the university in this city. Very few documents exist regarding his stay in Rome and his activity in the Chamber of Deputies (an exceptional vantage point for a mind like Mosca's, intent on analysing men and institutions 'in the field'). The Chamber's archives contain no data with which to reconstruct his political career between 1 November 1887 and 31 January 1897.

In this period, therefore, Mosca spent his time between Palazzo Montecitorio and the university. Furthermore, he established a very close personal and political relationship with Antonio Starrabba, Marquis of Di Rudinì (1839–1908), who was Prime Minister in 1891 and 1896, and this may explain the reduction in his scholarly and journalistic activity. In fact, it was during these years that the involvement of the scholar in politics took a more practical turn. His friendship with the Marquis of Di Rudinì played an important role in this respect, and it certainly helped him to be elected, in 1909, to the Chamber of Deputies for the constituency of Caccamo in Sicily. This event took place, however, in rather different political circumstances after the death of the Marquis.

On his arrival in Rome, Mosca was already an accomplished figure with a respectable scholarly output, who was in the process of elaborating a scientifically organic and original work: the *Elementi di scienza politica* [*Elements of Political Science*]. Although uneventful, the years spent in Rome also saw Mosca consolidate his methodology. This consisted in combining in various ways theory and practice, ideas and experience, and doctrines and facts. It was at this time that through considerable theoretical generalization, involving the skilful use of very incidental data, the scholar defined and perfected his overall view of politics and its related problems. Moreover, in this period Mosca, whose outlook was never tainted by provincialism, succeeded in broadening his perspective by moving away from a too exclusive concern with Italian (or even, at times, Sicilian) matters. Although the latter were of value as social and historical facts, they also formed an obstacle to a more broad-based theory.

This turning-point was confirmed by the publication in 1896 of the *Elementi di scienza politica* (it actually appeared between 1895 and 1896), which Mosca submitted in April 1896 with his successful application for the chair of constitutional law at Turin University. Thus Mosca began a long period of teaching at this university, having given up the editorship of parliamentary proceedings in the Chamber of Deputies following his academic appointment. Between 1898, when he became a full professor of constitutional law, and 1924, the year he settled permanently in Rome, he led a complex, intense and varied intellectual life. He was able to combine fruitfully his scientific and didactic activity with his political role as a member of the Italian parliament and, later, Under-Secretary of State.

The city of Turin, where Mosca took part in university life, had been a lively centre for scientific activity not only in national, but also European terms throughout the entire period of the Italian Risorgimento, the movement for Italian unification in the nineteenth century. It is true that the general atmosphere in late nineteenth-century Turin was no longer that of the epoch of national heroism; nevertheless, it still enjoyed a vigorous cultural life. In this city Mosca befriended the great socialist criminologist Cesare Lombroso (1835–1909), with whom he established a relationship based on a constant exchange of political and intellectual ideas. This link with Lombroso is one of the keys to a full understanding of Gaetano Mosca's positivism. During the same period he became a firm friend of the economist Luigi Einaudi (1874–1961), and developed close ties of mutual respect with other colleagues engaged in political studies and law, such as Francesco Ruffini (1853–1934), Giuseppe Carle (1845–1917) and Gioele Solari (1872–1952). He also developed a respect and personal liking for Robert Michels, which was returned by the young academic towards the mentor-like figure of Mosca. Michels had been given a teaching post at the University of Turin in 1907, following a period of political, journalistic and intellectual experience in the stimulating area of international affairs and inside the socialist movement.

In 1901 Mosca began writing for the *Corriere della Sera* of Milan, the most important daily newspaper in northern Italy and edited from May 1900 by Luigi Albertini (1871–1941), who attempted to introduce English-style journalism into Italy. This significant new experience in journalism provided a further demonstration of Mosca's increasing integration into the life of this part of Italy and also sheds light on the scholar's political horizons.

One of Mosca's very first articles appearing in the *Corriere*, entitled 'Guardando avanti' ['Looking ahead'] (7 August 1901), is highly revealing in terms of his political position, which, in our opinion, can be defined as undoubtedly conservative, but also openly reformist. The really significant aspect of this article is to be found, above all, in the assertion that an aristocracy of workers 'has already been formed or is being formed in England, the United States, France, Germany and Switzerland, and closer examination shows that it is everywhere an inevitable result of modern industrial society', and that there is a need to find 'the practical means which will enable the State, capitalists and proletariat to give official recognition of this new labour aristocracy by legalizing it, while at the same time curtailing its power'.

A confirmation of Mosca's new cultural and political interests is given by the lectureship in political economy which he held at the University of Turin from 1902 to 1904. In addition to this, he was also appointed to teach constitutional and administrative law at the Luigi Bocconi University in Milan, a private institution specializing in business studies, which was set up in 1902 to help create a class of commercial and industrial entrepreneurs by providing a modern and scientifically based education. He continued to teach at the Bocconi until 1923, as a professor in administrative and constitutional law from 1902 to 1917–18 (interrupted during the war years 1914–16) and in political science between 1918–19 and 1922–3. His involvement with this private university also fulfilled a twofold aspiration. On the one hand, it offered him the possibility of working at a practical level inside a private academic institution which had close links with the most advanced entrepreneurs in Italy: those who were active in the region of Lombardy. He experienced at first hand, therefore, the formation of a new ruling class. In terms of theory and research, on the other hand, his teaching involvement at the Bocconi provided the scholar with a framework in which he was able to develop gradually and perfect his courses in political science. His interests in law and constitutional matters were to take a permanent second place to this side of his activities.

In 1907 there arose a controversy between Gaetano Mosca and Vilfredo Pareto over which of the two writers had first formulated in a scientific way the concept of the minority foundation of power. It turned into an argument which went beyond a strictly scientific dispute. Nevertheless, aside from the resentment felt by both men, the reason behind the controversy requires some explanation. There is, in fact, little point in discussing the merits of the dispute itself which is now no longer relevant. Neither is there any doubt that the concept was formulated according to scientific criteria: using quite distinct methodologies, both Mosca and Pareto made original contributions to scientific knowledge. What concerns us at present is to restore integrity to the Moschian doctrine as compared with the more general theory of elites. Accordingly, the polemic between the two scholars should be considered concretely within a more directly political context. It occurred at a time when Mosca was already an established academic figure and about to enter public life. He certainly felt slighted by Pareto's disrespect, accusing him of 'a lack ... of scientific courtesy'. However, there also exists a clear divergence in theoretical and practical aims between the two formulations, which are only superficially similar. In fact, great care must be taken when placing together under the common heading of 'Italian school of elitists' three such different areas of research as those of Mosca, Pareto and, later, Michels.

In December 1923 the Law Faculty Council of Rome University decided to offer Mosca the vacant chair of public law, having moved Vittorio Emanuele Orlando (1860–1952) – the father of the 'Italian school of public law' – to the chair of constitutional law. Their express intention was to change the title and subject matter of the chair in question; and, in fact, this decision and the start of Mosca's teaching activity in Rome marked the birth in Italy of a new academic discipline: the History of Political Doctrines. In this new capacity Mosca was able organically to link the new subject to historical and juridical culture and, above all, to the rise and development of those institutions belonging to the modern representative state. Thus, at the very moment when political science faculties were being set up in Italy, Mosca's approach met the longstanding desire for a professional education from those seeking careers in the bureaucracy and public administration. This demand, put forward with convincing arguments throughout the whole of the nineteenth century, had been taken up by Mosca in person and given clear expression in an article of 1914 entitled *'Burocrazia e concorsi'* ['Bureaucracy and Entrance Examinations'].

For some time, in fact, the scholar had been aware of bureaucracy as one of the central phenomena in the political life and organization of the state. However, any kind of abstract analysis was excluded by Mosca's realism, and bureaucracy was too important an aspect in the affairs of the political class to escape his attention. This turning towards new horizons of scientific thought and research demonstrates his clear awareness of the human dimension in every political structure and, at the same time, the realization that purely legal means cannot adequately discipline and organize the many tensions and aspirations inherent in politics. A precise declaration along these lines is contained in Mosca's inaugural lecture at Rome University, given on 26 February 1924 in the presence of well-known authorities in politics and law. The theme chosen, 'The ancient city-state and the modern representative state', is highly significant and the lecture itself is a remarkable fusion of theoretical and institutional, and scientific and ideological elements.

In particular, Mosca analyses the concept of political liberty and tends to attach less importance to the theoretical element in the interpretation of the historical process. He sees the real course of social and economic development as being accompanied, rather than preceeded, by the formulation of doctrines, which are then used to justify the very results of such development. It is difficult to avoid the impression that, alongside his scientific and didactic aims, Mosca wanted to use this lecture to underline the most typically political facts of his day. In that very same year the crisis of the liberal state in Italy had reached its climax. The murder of the socialist deputy Giacomo Matteotti (1885–1924) and the withdrawal from Parliament of the anti-Fascist opposition (the so-called 'Aventine secession') paved the way for the adoption of a hard line by Fascism, which culminated in Mussolini's speech of 3 January 1925 marking the demise of the representative-parliamentary state and the birth of the new regime. The conclusion to the inaugural lecture reflects the leitmotiv in Mosca's various theoretical and political writings: the essential element of his teaching, which, from 1925–6 onwards, would be developed in an exclusively academic environment. According to Mosca, it is the task of 'the new generation, born in the last decades of the previous century and the first of this century', to provide a political response to the great crisis in theory and practice which was having a devastating effect on public life in Italy and the rest of Europe. There emerges from this extremely terse conclusion an imperative, both ethical and juridical in nature: the call not to abandon certain principles of 'public law' which formed and continue to form the basis of political civilization in the ancient *polis* and in the modern state respectively. Mosca maintains in particular that these principles 'can be summed up in the idea that the law must emanate from the consciousness of the people on whom it is imposed, or at least from its better part, and be respected especially by those responsible for its application'.[1] Seen in this light, Mosca's inaugural lecture is also a document of great political and biographical interest, which links up with his previous research and that undertaken from the beginning of the 1920s in the specific field of the History of Political Doctrines.

The year 1925, in which Mosca organized his entire previous research into a more or less definitive system, was of crucial importance. The situation in general was one which required the need for theoretical reflection to be combined with decisions of a practical political nature. This was, in fact, the year during which he made a speech in the Senate against the Fascist transformation of the state. Moreover, he also stopped writing for the *Corriere della Sera* at a time when the freedom of the press in Italy was on the decline, and decided to abandon political activity altogether. Already in May of the same year, Mosca had added his name to the 'Counter-Manifesto' drawn up by Benedetto Croce (1866–1952) in opposition to the 'Fascist Intellectuals' Manifesto', written by Giovanni Gentile (1875–1944). It was a very important political act arising out of his declared loyalty to the liberal system and his political commitment. It must be especially remembered that, on 19 December 1925, Mosca made an important speech in the Senate where, together with Benedetto Croce and Francesco Ruffini, he led the liberal group until political parties were liquidated by Fascism in 1926. This speech referred to the bill concerning 'the powers and prerogatives of the Head of Government', introduced by Mussolini with the declared aim of radically altering the Italian Constitution. At the time of the Fascist March on Rome in 1922, like most other Italian liberals he had made no attempt to oppose Mussolini. He now had the opportunity of closely linking his experience as a scholar with his role as a politician. 'I would never have thought', he explained to the Senate, that I would be alone in pronouncing the funeral oration for the parliamentary system. When I was in the Chamber of Deputies, I remember being surprised at the common practice whereby, when a former Deputy died, his funeral oration was nearly always delivered by his successor in the constituency, who in many cases had been the one to unseat him; so it happens that someone who had previously spoken ill of his opponent was then obliged to sing his praises. Similarly, I who have always been sharply critical of parliamentary government must now almost regret its fall. I admit that this system has been in need of considerable modification, but I don't think the time is right for a radical transformation, and now that the system is being renounced we should remember its merits.[2]

This outburst of sincerity served, on the one hand, to confirm the liberal intention behind his criticism of parliamentary government and, at the same time, to censure rapid radical change, given his conviction that the parliamentary system should be modified 'with greater prudence and moderation'.[3]

At this point Mosca's awkward, yet deeply felt, position appeared detached from the dramatic events of Italian political life. However, it was leading him to search for a meaning and purpose which could underlie a creative form of politics, radically different from and, we might even venture to say, beyond existing institutional forms. In fact, it should not be forgotten that, in addition to his scientific and cultural activity as a scholar and political historian (which we have attempted to trace in broad outlines), Mosca was deeply involved in politics as a twice-elected Deputy (1909–13), Under-Secretary in the Salandra Government from 1914 to 1916 and Senator from 1919 onwards. As has already been mentioned, alongside his parliamentary duties Mosca was also an effective political journalist, contributing to both the Milan daily *Corriere della Sera* and, from 1911 to 1921, the Rome daily *Tribuna*. The main concerns to which the scholar dedicated his efforts on both fronts were essentially those regarding the Italian conquest of Libya and the workings of parliamentary institutions.

During the Fascist dictatorship Mosca continued to teach at Rome University until May 1933, working in successive stages on his *Storia delle dottrine politiche* [*History of Political Doctrines*], which was first published in France in 1936. In spite of the fact that it contains some errors and gaps, this work made an important contribution to contemporary historical-political studies. It showed how the study of political thought could be freed from a too restrictive juridical framework, though still very usefully combining the history of political doctrines with that of institutions. In fact, if Mosca's *political science* constitutes a forceful and genuine attempt to interpret and organize the fixed data of political life, then his *Storia delle dottrine politiche* certainly represents a vigorous approach to politics seen as the history of the philosophical systems, ideas and institutions which have inspired it. In other words, Mosca's research reflected that psychological and spiritual element which an authoritative interpreter of Moschian thought, Mario Delle Piane, has identified, within the 'dramatic transition from certain modes of thought and action to others of a completely different kind', as the 'need to look back into the past for an example, sign or word which can be transformed into a certainty'.

The combined theoretical and historical approach adopted by Mosca meets this demand for knowledge, certainty and concrete facts. His merit consists in having based his historical research on the principle that

we cannot understand a given theory without considering the kind of political organization to which it refers, whether we wish to defend or to attack it. In other words, without a clear idea of the political organization of a given people in a given age it is very difficult to have a clear idea of the theories which were formulated by that people in that age.[4]

Today the history of political doctrines as a branch of learning is increasingly characterized at an academic level by the philosophical approach and the detailed examination of the ages, places and contexts which gave rise to different political doctrines. If this is so, then the pioneering work carried out by Mosca throughout his entire scientific career (which took a clearly historical turn from the mid 1920s) should be viewed as a by no means negligible, but rather a concrete and dialectical contribution to this field of interest and study.

Mosca died in Rome on 8 November 1941 as the Second World War was casting its sinister light over the lives of men and reawakening their dreadful urge towards death and destruction, which almost two centuries of dominant bourgeois civilization had been unable either to eradicate or transform. In fact, this long and dramatic stage in history was to reach incredible new heights of barbarity.

2
Birth of the doctrine of the political class

In *Sulla teorica dei governi e sul governo parlamentare* Mosca states the following:

In all societies established on a normal basis in which there exists what is called a government, as well as the fact that its authority is exercised in the name of the whole population or a dominant aristocracy or a single monarch ... we repeatedly discover a further fact: that the rulers, those who hold and exercise State power, are always a minority, and that below them lies a numerous class of people who never participate *in real terms* in government and are subject to the will of the former; we may call them the ruled.[1]

This social division, which Mosca deduces from the experience of history, provides the foundation, the 'factual premise', on which his entire doctrine is developed.

The three periods of Gaetano Mosca's political thought

The three distinct periods in which the scholar formulated, developed and modified his theoretical approach towards politics will now be examined in detail. They are:

1 that of the *open system* from 1879, the year in which he started out as a political journalist, to 1895. In this period he published, among others, two such important and complete works as the above-mentioned *Teorica* and a study of different aspects of law and politics, *Le costituzioni moderne* [*Modern Constitutions*] (1887);
2 that of the *scientific system*, which was fully formulated during the entire period from the publication of the first edition of the *Elementi di scienza politica* in 1896 to 1922;

3   that of the *codified doctrine*, stretching from the second edition of the *Elementi* (1923) to the writing of *Storia delle dottrine politiche* over a long period of time (1933–7).

It must be pointed out that in this attempt at periodization, which has been widely accepted by other scholars, alongside the major works various other writings have been examined: essays, lectures, speeches, and articles in newspapers and journals.

The division of Mosca's work into three periods will now be considered in the light of his main concepts. The first period was designated 'open system' so as to indicate that the work published in 1884 already contained a theoretical formulation of his early ideas. Here we find the organically interrelated concepts of the doctrine of the political class. These are the *political class*, understood as the organized minority of rulers which has always existed and imposed its will on the unorganized majority of the ruled, and the *political formula*, by which is meant the abstract principle serving both to legitimize power and bind the rulers and ruled together through common values and sentiments.

If this theoretical basis to Mosca's 'system' – which would remain the same throughout his entire life – is taken together with the empirical data obtained through the young writer's political experience and his criticism of parliamentary institutions in Italy, the picture emerges of a doctrine which is not dogmatically rigid, but open to further development. In fact, *Teorica* is far from being an organic body of ideas and analysis. A true evaluation of the open system can only be carried out by also taking into account several of Mosca's other writings: namely, *Del Parlamento e il potere giudiziario* [*On Parliament and Judicial Power*] (Palermo, 1885); *Sulla libertà di stampa. Appunti* [*Notes on the Freedom of the Press*] (Turin, 1885); *Studi ausiliari del diritto costituzionale* [*Studies Supplementary to Constitutional Law*] (Palermo, 1886); and in particular *Le costituzioni moderne* (Palermo, 1887) which further develops and completes *Teorica*. Also worth mentioning is the short article *Intorno al parlamentarismo* [*On the Question of the Parliamentary System*] (1895) in which Mosca discusses the pamphlet *Contro il parlamentarismo. Saggio di psicologia collettiva* [*Against the Parliamentary System. An Essay in Collective Psychology*] (Milan, 1895), written by the positivist psychologist Scipio Sighele (1868–1913). The period of the open system is also very interesting for an understanding of Mosca's early ideological viewpoint: his declared objective was the formation in Italy of a new political class, originating in the middle classes and economically independent (neither rich nor poor), with a good cultural background and firm ethical convictions. The task of such a political class, according to Mosca, would be to represent a wider range of social values than that resulting from the electoral system; its emergence should be based on individual merit and guided by the values of social order, political liberalism, and social and economic reformism.

The term 'scientific system' is intended to indicate that the years between the first edition of the *Elementi di scienza politica* and the second edition in 1923 form the writer's most mature period. Publication of the *Elementi* revealed that his 'system' had been further developed by the introduction of a new concept, *juridical defence*, closely linked to the concepts of political class and political formula, which formed the basis of the early theoretical formulation. Besides a more logical and systematic definition of the political class, the *Elementi* also gives a consistent and scientific expression to certain ideological tensions and inclinations always present in this writer. At the centre of the reorganization of his earlier ideas, in which the emotional involvement in contemporary political issues has given way to a genuinely scientific approach, lies the concept of juridical defence. Inspired by political liberalism, this concept is used by Mosca to try and reconcile the harsh realism behind all political actions with the ethical needs of individuals, of a society wishing to avoid the blind rule of force and a power structure which is absolute and oppressive.

The main concern of Mosca during this period was to lay the foundations for a scientific conception of politics, which he calls either 'political science' or 'scientific politics'. In short, he used the concept of juridical defence to modify and complete his original theory. What we have here is nothing less than a doctrine of the state with a highly prescriptive content; it is derived from his more general doctrine of the political class. Founded on the principles of realistic, non-religious humanism and on a deeply felt ethical-political conception of power, it is a doctrine in which the state and law are conceived essentially as instruments for harnessing the selfish impulses of individuals and groups in the true interests of society: they must serve the real ends for which society continues to exist. It should also be said that this overall vision of Mosca's has nothing particularly optimistic to say about the nature of man; rather, it is inspired by a very clear awareness of the need to defend the interests of both the individual and society within the state. Although carried out in a scientific manner, the theoretical application of these ideas was evidently influenced by the writer's ideology. Responding to the difficult period of transition between the nineteenth and twentieth century, Mosca expressed his conservative liberalism in explicitly anti-socialist tones and showed increasing hostility towards organized trade-union power.

Birth of the doctrine

Mosca's scientific system is to be found chiefly in the *Elementi* and is only complemented to some extent by his *Questioni pratiche di diritto costituzionale* [*Practical Questions of Constitutional Law*] (Turin, 1898), which also includes the important essay, *Sopra due possibili modificazioni del sistema parlamentare in Italia* [*Two Possible Ways to Change the Parliamentary System in Italy*]. Other works of notable interest are his lectures on the Mafia in Sicily held in Turin and Milan and later published as articles in the *Corriere della Sera* (1900), his contributions to Ercole A. Marescotti's survey of socialism (1902–3), and the lecture he gave on 'The Aristotelic and Democratic Principles in the Past and in the Future' to inaugurate to the 1902–3 academic year at Turin University. Finally, it should be borne in mind that this second period coincided with the establishment of his reputation not only as a scholar and university teacher, but also as a politician and, more generally, as a public figure, speaker and journalist.

The term 'codified doctrine' covers the whole period from the new edition of the *Elementi* (1923) to the reprinting of *Teorica* and to Mosca's death. There is no implication in the use of this term that the last phase in the writer's life was of less intellectual and political importance. It is true that the theory of the political class is laid out in full in the first chapter of the new second part of the *Elementi*, significantly entitled *Origini della dottrina della classe politica e cause che ne ostacolano la diffusione* [*Origins of the doctrine of the political class and the obstacles to its dissemination*]. However, it must be stated at once that the term codified system has a double meaning. First, it is in the writings of this period that Mosca gave a final definitive form to his political doctrine, and we consider the new edition of the *Elementi* to be his fully worked out response to the new political situation created in Italy by the First World War and the Triumph of Fascism. On the other hand, it was in this period that Mosca developed in an especially acute and original manner a series of ideas contained in his earlier works. Analysing the connection between political institutions and political doctrines, he gradually adopted a different approach and arranged his subject matter into a more complex system. The codification of Mosca's system of thought was the result of a sincere and vigorous effort to interpret and organize what he considered to be the permanent facts of political life. Yet in the way it treats the history of political theory and institutions, it also revealed a new, determined approach to politics, seen not as the mere occurrence of events behind the mask of political formulas, but as the strictly interrelated history of philosophical systems, political ideas and institutions. This new approach was founded on the realistic observation of institutions, and important evidence to this effect is contained in the only recently published correspondence between Mosca and Guglielmo Ferrero (1871–1942), edited by Carlo Mongardini of Rome University.

An important aspect to be considered at this stage is that the ideological element in Mosca's thought makes it difficult to reconstruct and interpret. In his classic study, Thomas B. Bottomore makes some very interesting points about this problem, referring to the analyses carried out by Gyorgy Lukacs and Karl Mannheim among others.[2] It is this English scholar in particular who has examined in some detail those general interpretations of the 'doctrine of elites' which, as Mannheim asserted, acted 'an an irrational justification for "direct action" and unconditional subordination to a leader'.[3] Taking his cue from the classic work by James H. Meisel (which also contains a faithful description of Mosca's doctrine), Bottomore states that several questions are raised when considering 'the ideological elements in elite theories'. The most important question concerns the attempt 'to reconcile the idea of elites with democratic social theories'; and in fact according to Bottomore – with whom we agree – it is clear that 'the elite theorists themselves have had an important influence in producing the new definitions of democracy . . . which are then held up as being compatible with the notion of elites'.[4]

The comprehensive approach which we have adopted in interpreting the development of Mosca's thought can be used as an aid to understanding the specific working out of his political theory. Following the theoretical rejection in his early period of the possibility of 'democratic government', he gradually moved towards accepting and defending a form of government in which the free exchange of ideas and interplay of interests is an expression of the people's will. Thus Mosca's ideas converged with the mainstream of liberalism in the 1920s and 1930s, a period of great uncertainty for democratic and liberal political doctrines under strong attack from both the Left and the Right.

Elucidation of terminology: political class and ruling class

Having indicated the chronological development of Mosca's concepts and how they were modified through time, we consider it useful at this point to clarify the difference between the terms 'political class' and 'ruling class'. Whereas in *Teorica* Mosca uses the term *classe politica* (political class), in his next major work, the *Elementi di scienza politica*, he adopts the expression *classe dirigente* (ruling class), especially in the later second edition. The reason behind this change is not mere lexical variation, but rather indicates a fundamental rethinking.

Birth of the doctrine

In his now classic study of the Italian Parliament Giovanni Sartori (Professor of Political Science at Columbia University, New York) has explained in precise terms that by 'ruling class' he means 'all ruling minorities: political, economic, social, religious, intellectual, technological, military, bureaucratic and so on. The political class is therefore a sub-species of the ruling class: that section of the ruling class whose task it is to exercise power.[5] Sartori's clarification also provides a good interpretation of the progress achieved by Mosca and subsequent writers in the choice and use of terminology. Mosca in fact moved away from the emphasis placed in the last century on the role of government (discussed at the beginning of the present chapter) and towards a more subtle consideration of the different strata and groups which make up the ruling class in the twentieth century. None the less, there is still a problem for the English reader who since the appearance in 1939 of the English version of the *Elementi*, edited by Arthur Livingston, is accustomed to the two different Italian terms both being translated as 'ruling class'. Livingston had a legitimate reason for adopting the single term in English: first, it was derived from the Italian text of Mosca's main work[6] and, secondly, the English translation was read and approved by Mosca himself.[7] However, in order to stick more closely to the author's actual thinking, the term 'political class' is expressly used in this present translation. We are aware of the novelty it introduces, and wish to point to both the original use which Mosca made of the term in his early research and to the specific social group which engages in politics permanently and in a professional capacity. This last aspect is a thoroughly modern phenomenon and of great importance both in Italy and the rest of the world. The term 'ruling class' is used to translate the Italian *classe dirigente*, the two expressions having the same meaning and connotation in both languages. This term belongs more to Mosca's mature phase in the working out of his ideas and is given the meaning attributed by Sartori's definition, which we believe to be quite clear and precise.

It can be stated with certainty that 'political class' and 'ruling class' are concepts derived from real phenomena which go beyond differences in regimes and states and which today are found in all theoretical discussions about politics. What we have here are invariable facts that form part of our common knowledge, basic axiomatic data for understanding political systems in the contemporary world, which are much more complex than in the past. In this way one of Mosca's old dreams has been realized: to root a realistic interpretation of politics in the facts of common sense and provide it with a basis in scientific methods and convictions – scientific in the way they are tied to human rationality and the rejection of all mystification and idealism.

It must be also be said that Mosca's analysis has a much more complex structure compared to the simplifications introduced by a schematic interpretation. As it developed the doctrine of the political class was more and more closely linked to the underlying social reality and to political institutions. Without a clear awareness of these multiple links the richness of Mosca's intuitions risks petering out in an abstract game of verbal formulae, because such intuitions would be disconnected from the social context which generates social groups and forces, from the real substratum of the political class and the ruling class. In fact, nearly a century ago, Mosca's research showed an awareness of all this, even though it was not presented in a systematic form. In the formulation of the scholar's doctrine the political class (he invented the term and was the first to investigate the essential nature and role of this class) is clearly derived from the existing social forces, in particular from the middle classes, which he improperly calls the bourgeoisie.

Since this present work of interpretation aims to examine the ideological and political aspects in Moschian thought, we consider it fruitful to start from the heart of his theory. We therefore begin with the concept of political class as formulated and put forward by Mosca, a concept which he derived from a systematic examination of the constant features of power, and we link it with the corresponding concept of the bourgeoisie.

3
The concepts of the open system, 1879–1895

The unifying element in Mosca's research was provided by the 'discovery' of the doctrine of the political class, which was adopted as the basis for all further elaboration of his ideas. But as we have already seen, his interests were closely tied in the first period to his cultural background and to his responsiveness to questions of law and history. It is therefore reasonable to try to link together the themes in his various writings with a view to organizing the results of his research and the initial conclusions drawn.

It is immediately evident from an analysis of *Sulla teorica dei governi e sul governo parlamentare* that Mosca was far from interested in problems of philosophy and methodology. In the first chapter he sets out in very concise terms the criteria which guided his research. In his view, the unchanging data which form the laws governing the organization of society can only be identified by observing and ordering the facts, and by acquiring a wide-ranging knowledge of history; it is essential for the researcher to proceed 'calmly and cautiously'. The Moschian approach is thus inspired by the need to 'construct' political science using the observed facts of real life in opposition to a process of a priori deduction.[1] The aim of his research was essentially a practical one; in fact the connection between political science and political action, defined in a way which remains constant in all of his thinking, is already present in this first work. In short, his approach is a realistic one based on a pragmatic view of history and free from legal abstractions and concerns lying outside the realm of politics. It could be said that the empirical method and political realism are the fundamental convictions underlying his early writings.

Formation and structure of the political class

Teorica already contains Mosca's rejection of the classification of governments derived from Aristotle, which divides them into 'democratic, aristocratic and monarchical according to whether supreme authority lies with the majority of citizens, a restricted class or one man'.[2] Accepted by most political theorists before Mosca, it went against the grain of his realistic approach; and like the similar system developed by Montesquieu, repeatedly criticized by Mosca on many counts, it does not start from the precondition of discovering where real power lies in the state. Whether the state is nominally in the hands of a monarch, an oligarchy of nobles or a group claiming to rule in the name of the people is of very little significance. Mosca insists on the fact that power is of necessity diffused within an articulated system; history shows us that it is divided up among a larger number of persons than those who, on the surface, symbolize a particular regime or than that group of men who are commonly identified with power.

The first theoretical division introduced by Mosca is that between the *rulers* and the *ruled*, that is, between those who control and exercise state power – always a minority – and that 'numerous class of people who never take any *real* part in government and thus do nothing other than submit to it'.[3] This is the idea he starts from and represents an 'absolutely invariable, general fact', which he simply infers by observing society 'not from a scientific but from a practical perspective'.[4] He rejects the historical preconception which, in his view, has existed since Aristotle, pointing out that those who were 'clearly aware of the secret inner workings of absolutist government knew very well that, except in the very rare case of a strong personality on the throne, the sovereign was generally the principle on which the government's authority rested. Personally, however, he had no or very little authority over the government'.[5] Alongside the historical preconception there is also what he calls the contemporary preconception. This is the belief that governments based on popular sovereignty really express the will of the majority and that, consequently, 'the majority does actually govern or, at least, is able to'.[6] Mosca, on the contrary, maintained that in all regimes everywhere there must needs be 'a government machine, an organization naturally consisting of a fairly large minority, which puts into effect all government decisions'.[7] Given that this is the case, he then went beyond the Aristotelian definition and the general distinction between rulers and ruled in order to identify a special class of individuals assigned to carry out all public duties: he called this the *political class*.

Historically speaking, this class is seen as being made up of the barons, clergy and heads of the corporations during the Middle Ages, and of the bureaucracy and court nobility under 'Enlightened Despotism'. In modern times it is composed of civil servants and the so-called 'people's representatives'. Mosca tends therefore to define society in its different historical manifestations according to the basic principle that

> everything in government which concerns decision-making, the exercise of authority, command and responsibility is always a function of a special class; it is true that the elements which make up this special class may vary according to country and historical epoch, but whatever its exact composition, it is always a tiny minority compared with the ruled mass on which it imposes its will.[8]

This is, in a nutshell, the most original element of the Moschian doctrine; the rest of *Teorica* is nothing more than an exposition of the facts in support of the initial intuition. These facts were derived from a thorough study of history, ranging from very remote ancient history to the Graeco-Italic city, the Hellenic city-state, the Republic of Rome, the Roman Empire, and reaching as far as the modern era.

In Mosca's time the question of the political class was a complex one; nowadays this is even more the case. Nevertheless, his method of approach – which has unjustly been seen as polemical – is clearly defined and characterized by its aim of political education. In a kind of theoretical demonstration of political truths, the existence of the political class is the premise to the thesis that its continual emergence is visible throughout history. But before demonstrating his doctrine, Mosca provides some further explanation. First of all, he deals with the question of the relationship between the political class and the ruled, the masses which act as the support for the former's actions. Then there is the principle of the moral superiority of the political class as against 'the superiority of number and brute force'.[9] He makes the further observation that since the political class acts as an *organized minority*, it will always dominate the unorganized minority, which has 'neither the will nor the urge to take concerted action'.[10] Moreover, the fact that the political class has a cohesive force is almost inevitable and this implies that government will naturally be run by a minority. According to Mosca, this is the unavoidable result of certain general principles, but it is mitigated by the fact that 'those who belong to the political class cannot be forced into it'.[11] The stimulus to become part of this class comes solely from the desire to dominate, which is an expression of 'man's natural thirst for power and its privileges'.[12] The masses obey their rulers not out of any natural inclination, but because they 'sense their superiority' and 'submit to the influence of power'. In more specific terms, Mosca states that '. . . precisely for this reason, apart from the immeasurable prestige conferred on the political class by its co-ordinated organization, the elements of which it is composed must stand out through a kind of innate superiority'.[13]

Access to the political class: military valour, wealth, birth, individual merit

There are many examples to show how the conditions and requisites for entry into the political class vary from country to country and in different historical periods. In primitive societies 'the political class originates in the assembly of chiefs, and in the barbarian state it is the strongest and bravest of men who are the leaders; thus the criterion for recruiting the dominant class becomes military valour'.[14] Then as society gradually becomes more civilized, 'the development of an intellectual culture and increasing wealth create other means by which the few impose their will on the many'.[15] Mosca believes that the composition of the political class has never depended on a single criterion of selection, but rather on a combination of different requisites; for example, during the 'most cruelly violent phase' of the Middle Ages in Europe, ecclesiastics were placed on exactly the same level in the social hierarchy as the class of feudal lords, recruited according to the criterion of military valour. Although the political importance of this criterion continues to diminish in the more economically and culturally advanced modern societies, nevertheless it still plays a quite significant role even here: to make use of it is the only way 'to halt the slide to ruin' whenever there is 'anarchy and the threat of social collapse'.[16]

Wealth starts off by being a legal requirement for the formation of the political class and 'is then maintained as an objective element in well-ordered societies'.[17] Mosca points out that many peoples have chosen to confer special privileges of power on wealth, granting civil rights only to the economically well-off; but these privileges can also be taken away at a later stage. The real political influence of wealth comes from those advantages 'which it inevitably bestows on those who possess it'.[18]

Birth is another important factor in becoming a member of the political class: 'no longer an exclusive and legal criterion for the formation of the political class, it is still of some importance in real terms'. Birth means wealth, ease in making social acquaintances, the acquiring of knowledge and culture and even 'the habit of command and occupying an important position in society'.[19]

Lastly, there is the fourth factor: individual merit, which encompasses those 'special abilities that permit one to fulfil a given political function'. It is a criterion peculiar to 'civilized societies at an advanced stage of development'.[20] Consequently, this aspect of class cohesion is found specifically in modern societies; it forms a particular requirement on the part of such societies and does not arise from an ideology inspired by equality and social justice. Individual merit, however, does not automatically guarantee inclusion in the political class, as is the case with military valour or wealth; 'it has no value apart from its more or less official recognition'.[21] It is interesting to note that Mosca specifies the ways in which individual merit allows entry into the political class: by examination and professional qualification. Those who decide on who is to be admitted into the political class are 'the top people who are presumed to be legally recognized as possessing the special knowledge and cultural background required for membership of the political class'.[22] By modifying the drastic assertion that the political class is a special class of persons which 'forms the government, and the government consists solely of this class', Mosca succeeds in linking his presuppositions dialectically. He achieves this through clarifying the fact that the different criteria listed for recruiting the various political classes 'are almost never applied exclusively; they are taken together, combined and altered in a thousand different ways according to the different levels of a people's civilization'.[23]

A political formula for each political class

As set out so far, the concept of the political class comes across as a rigid idea lacking in complexity. Mosca therefore proceeds to correct this by asserting that

the entire political history of mankind in all epochs, in all nations, and in all civilizations can be summed up in terms of these two main perspectives: the degree of co-ordination between the various political classes, the amount of resources under their control, the force of their collective action, the various elements which enter into these classes; and the different ways in which they impose their will, the rivalry and struggles between them, their mutual transactions and combinations.[24]

From this he makes the deduction that the dynamic of human societies always results from the way in which these two central aspects are held in a state of balanced tension. Furthermore, Mosca's early programmatic statement contains the firm conviction that any political class, whatever its make-up, 'never admits that it is in command for the simple reason that it is composed of elements which are, or have been up to that moment in history, the most suitable to govern; instead, it always finds justification for its power in an abstract principle which we shall call the political formula'.[25]

From an historical examination of many different political formulas Mosca derives two main types:

those which are based on supernatural beliefs, and those which are founded on a principle which is, at least on the surface, rational. Thus, for example, the belief that all power derives from the sovereign who, in turn, received it from God is a formula of the first kind; to the second kind, on the other hand, belongs the principle which locates the source of all legitimate power in the will of the people.[26]

So there is a strong connection between political class and political formula. However, he specifically states that 'it is not the political formula which determines the way in which the political class is formed, but on the contrary, it is the latter which adopts the formula most suited to it'.[27] This assertion that there exists a one-way causal connection appears to be groundless. How, in fact, is it possible in a complex society for an entire ruling class in a truly hegemonic position to acknowledge the same monolithic principle at all times, accepting or modifying it to its own convenience? In its so far loosely defined sense of 'principle of legitimacy' and 'ideology', the concept of the political formula clearly strikes Mosca himself as ambiguous. As a consequence, he proceeds to explain that the political formula is by no means a 'pure and simple mystification'[28] and that, on the contrary, it is justified by unchanging human nature; people prefer to believe that 'we obey an abstract principle rather than an individual who is in command because of his natural abilities'.[29] The concept still remains somewhat imprecise, however, despite Mosca's systematic effort at describing the various types of past and present political formulas.

First, there are the formulas which are based on a belief in the supernatural; they tend to endure because of their origin and the faith they inspire in people. Then there are the rational formulas which, as such, should in theory be refutable; instead, they have become indisputable values which are like a 'sacrosanct truth. This demonstrates that it is possible for someone to abandon completely or in part the capacity to reason, even without believing in the supernatural'.[30] In addition there are complex formulas such as those which combine the supernatural and the rational (for example, in the Kingdom of Italy where the Monarchy existed by the 'Grace of God and the Will of the Nation'); but as Mosca observes, 'in these governments too only one of the principles is in reality truly respected, whilst the other is usually a left-over from the past, a phrase preserved for the sake of tradition'.[31] Derived from this type of historical survey, the political formula appears at this stage in the development of Mosca's theory to be nothing more than the principle of legitimacy which serves as a reference point for the political class.

The above statements by Mosca provide us with a key to understanding his scientific approach and the practical-political aims of his doctrine. His starting-point is the recognition of: a) the permanent existence of a ruling political group, however the government may be formally classified – the dichotomy between rulers and ruled is a given fact which is immediately evident; b) the continued existence of a political class as a result of this dichotomy: a special class which runs the state machine and is more extensive and complex than the visible power structure that formally governs the state and society in general; c) the existence of social values (military valour, wealth, education, birth, merit) around which a political class is formed into a cohesive body; d) a certain mobility resulting from the conflict between this class cohesion and the striving for inclusion by individuals from the ruled mass; and e) the existence of a principle of legitimacy which guides the actions of the poltical class and expresses a body of values and ideas accepted by the ruled (the *political formula*).

Mosca's early political philosophy

Having fully stated his approach and theoretical premises, Mosca holds that the next step must be to define what we would call his 'political philosophy'. First of all, he denies that man has 'certain rights – it goes without saying they are innate – called political rights, such as freedom, equality, etc., and the standard by which governments are judged is the extent to which they respect such rights'.[32] Although not acknowledged as such, this is unmistakably a refutation of that political philosophy which is rooted in the Enlightenment and the French Revolution. Mosca maintains that it is a mistake to see political progress as the final goal of social life, in the sense of an end which different societies should strive to attain through applied social science and which should constitute 'the complete triumph of those so-called political rights of man over the obstacles placed in their path, now and in the past, by ignorance, violence and barbarism'.[33] In his opinion, innate rights are nothing more than an abstract hypothesis; the task of a scientific study of politics is not to discern 'what the political rights of man are – we can dream up as many as we like – but rather what he can and does do politically by observing the facts of past and present societies'.[34]

We shall now examine how the core of Mosca's political philosophy is presented in *Teorica* and, at the same time, try to understand the more incidental or political aims of his doctrine. A guideline for this analysis is provided by Mosca's polemical criticism of the 'new political formula', that is, of

that new political and philosophical school whose doctrines were derived partly from an imperfect study of classical antiquity and partly from a priori abstractions and concepts, which in truth had very little to do with real facts; nevertheless, these doctrines were most appropriate for attacking and destroying the beliefs that were used to justify the *ancien régime*'s political structure.[35]

Liberty, equality and fraternity, 'the so-called immortal principles of 1789', form the basis of this new political formula, which has served as the premise 'for all revolutionary legislation and, in fact, provided the revolution itself with a political formula. Moreover, the influence of this new formula can be felt more or less in all current constitutional arrangements, and it has inspired the political systems and ideas of most politicians, but not true statesmen, in Europe today'.[36] Against these principles and this particular formula Mosca underlines the fact that 'they are impossible to put into practice'. In this respect, moreover, he explains that his political formula is nothing other than the principle of legitimacy of power and that it always has a counterpart in the *political mechanism*, that is, the state; it is due to the latter that the ideas and political principles contained in and expressed by the formula are able to achieve practical results.

Although it is sometimes described in different terms, this concept of political mechanism now becomes a permanent feature in Mosca's work and forms an essential link in the complex relationship between rulers and ruled, and between these and the formula understood both as a principle of legitimacy and as a synthesis of moral and cultural values which serve to unify the beliefs and sentiments of an entire society. The relationships of power and duty between the different classes in society are structured in the concrete reality of the state through the mediation of a principle of legitimacy which permits the political class to rule and ensures the obedience of the ruled. The state is the point at which the multiple interconnections between rulers and ruled are ultimately formed. Mosca's interest in different constitutional forms, especially the case of England, should be viewed in this light.

His critical attitude towards the French Revolution is now expressed in precise terms: it had tried to put the formula 'liberty, equality, fraternity' into effect at the level of constitutional arrangements and of the political mechanism in particular. The scholar considers the French experience, a recent event full of significance for the Italian situation, as the first step in the complex transformation of the parliamentary system which had come about in England at the end of the seventeenth century with the formation of the first representative government. He thus embarks on a painstaking study, inspired by great admiration for English institutions, which aims to demonstrate the impossibility of putting into practice a constitutional model torn from its historical, social and cultural context, and to praise the concrete example of a regime that is able constantly to renew itself over a long period of time without violent upheaval. He also takes the opportunity to underline his strong criticism of the revolutionary and Jacobin formulas thrown up by the French Revolution.

First of all, he attempts to grasp the specific element in the fundamentally important English experience. It is seen to lie in the fact that despite the aristocratic aura surrounding most of its institutions, there nevertheless existed in seventeenth- and eighteenth-century England a principle which had been 'applied in practice, that of a community being represented by those it had elected on the basis of a majority vote';[37] and this is a principle which lends itself to the putting into effect of revolutionary ideals. According to Mosca, its adoption outside of England has been particularly unsuccessful due to

the hostility of the old privileged classes; the anarchical outbursts of the common herd as soon as they sense the old order of government weaken and before the new one has been consolidated; civil and foreign wars; and lastly the excessive dogmatism of the great majority of revolutionary leaders, their blind presumptuous faith in principles, and the contempt they display for anything smacking of moderation, study and accommodation to the practical necessities of political life.[38]

So the revolutionary application of the English constitutional mechanism ends by undermining several of Mosca's most cherished values in that it leads to the ruinous collapse of the body politic, the unleashing of the ignorant and indifferent masses, the dogmatism of doctrinaire Jacobinism, and the adoption of drastic solutions instead of the subtle and carefully arranged balance which must always characterize the dialectical relationship between society and the political class. Neither the sword nor the sceptre of Napoleon were subsequently able to resolve positively the inherited situation, because within the Napoleonic system 'the military as well as the administrative and judicial bureaucracy, though... controlled by severe legal regulations, in reality also formed the sole elements of the political class, and any political activity was strictly prohibited to other social classes, though they too might be inclined towards such activity'.[39] In Mosca's view, what actually took place was that a negative situation was replaced by an equally negative state of absolute bureaucracy (which may be defined as imperial Bonapartism); and whereas behind the first lay the Montagnard Terror and the Vendéan revolt, behind the second was the omnipotent police with its widespread organization and limitless powers, a recently created and effective instrument of tyranny.

These observations give some further indications as to the writer's attitude and inclinations. First, there emerges the profoundly political sense of his moderate conservatism when he extols study and the practical compromises inevitable in public life as the best way of achieving a prudent, rational form of politics which respects a society's historical and cultural complexity. Secondly, he repudiates dogmatism which he sees as coinciding with 'the art of stirring up the blind and brutal masses and directing their chaotic actions with daring and fanatical decisiveness'.[40] Lastly, his reason for rejecting individual dictatorship (by which he means bureaucratic dictatorship) is that it leads to a complete bureaucratization of the political class. The inevitable effects of this on a political system are in the long run disastrous, since the rulers gradually lose all touch with the ruled, causing the latter to feel indifferent and even to hate the former; such a situation also 'brings about the narrowing down of the rulers to an oppressive caste, which not even the most strong-willed sovereign is able to influence or change'.[41]

The parliamentary system and the bourgeoisie in nineteenth-century Italy

Having established the premises mentioned above, Mosca begins his examination of the parliamentary system, especially the concrete form it assumed in Italy. It must be remembered at the outset that the objective of *Teorica* is at the same time both political and juridical. In fact, law and history were inextricably linked in his cultural background.

In *Teorica* Mosca does not use the term '*parlamentarismo*' (the parliamentary system), as he would do later on, as a catch-all for every deficiency and imperfection of parliamentary government; this is also true of the varied and wide-ranging journalism of the time. Essentially a liberal, Mosca's analysis of the parliamentary state does not attempt to confirm an ideological prejudice against representative government, but rather to ascertain its effectiveness and how far it corresponds in reality to the principles which have inspired it. Mosca focuses his attention, from both a theoretical and historical perspective, on two examples of a 'pure parliamentary system' as practised in France and Italy. His analysis is particularly interesting if we consider that it was the work of a very young scholar. Twenty-three years after the birth of the first unified national state on Italian soil, Mosca proceeds to dissect its parliamentary institutions. First of all, he contrasts the 'actual government' (the government as it really is) with the 'legal government' (the government as it should be) provided for in the Constitution of the Kingdom of Italy; but he goes beyond the legal-constitutional aspect and applies the theoretical instrument of the political class to make some very relevant criticisms of the way in which the administrative structure of the Italian state had been set up: the seven different state structures into which Italy had been divided previous to 1861 were merged into a single whole. As well as the country's institutions and bureaucracy, the way in which the group of elected representatives is formed by means of clientelism and power cliques is also heavily criticized. The conclusions he draws are especially severe, both in political terms ('the Chamber of Deputies is thus becoming increasingly a partial and fictitious representation of the country') and in social terms ('our masses are among the most wretched and miserable in Europe, suffering in squalor especially in the countryside; and in the twenty-three years since our Nation was established their condition, instead of improving, has in some cases even worsened').

So, in the early Mosca, a genuine sense of protest is to be found, which is combined with an intelligent examination of the real relationship between the country's economic and social base, legal institutions and political class. None the less, what is lacking is a precise awareness of the effective status during the second half of the nineteenth century of the bourgeoisie in Italy, a country which was still quite backward in terms of social and economic development. The following observation by the Russian revolutionary Populist Alexander Herzen (1812–70), who knew the Italy of that period very well, is most fitting in this respect:

The Italian bourgeoisie has evolved in a completely different way to that of the bourgeoisie in France [and] England... In Italy, it was a particular section of the population which emerged with the first revolution (brought into Italy by the French army); using a geological metaphor, it can be called the Piedmontese stratum. Its distinguishing characteristic is that it is invariably liberal on many single issues but, on the whole, fears the people and speeches about work and wages which are too outspoken. Moreover, it is always ready to give in to its enemies above, but never to those below.

Given such a situation, Mosca's description of the emergence of the bourgeoisie is completely unrealistic; he saw it as that class which 'being already comfortably well-off, was gradually acquiring that other important prerequisite by means of which ... a class is able to impose itself on society and achieve the capacity to rule it: knowledge'.[42] The bourgeoisie to which Mosca refers was, on the contrary, descended for the most part from that notorious 'band of rogues and rabble scum' which – as he himself describes – used the radical change taking place in Italy as a means of conquering political power to match the social power acquired in opposition to the old nobility and the Catholic clergy. Another point to bear in mind about this class is that it adopted a constitutional approach: finding itself under pressure on several fronts, it introduced parliamentary government and limited the powers of the restored monarchy. On a political level, the only way it could consolidate its recent gains was to have adequate instruments of government at its disposal. In social and economic terms, the principle of unfettered freedom in industry and commerce – that is, the sweeping away of the feudal restraints which had been removed by the French Revolution and Napoleon but restored, at least partially, at Vienna – represented the precise political formula for attaining its ends: the possession and accumulation of wealth.

As was to be expected, the Italian bourgeoisie had difficulty in relating to the emerging movement of the lower classes, which had also been thrown into ferment by the French Revolution; this problem existed rather more in the towns than in the countryside. However, in this classic example of a transitional period the bourgeoisie professed an ideology of social co-operation. It was not until the crisis of 1848 that the different sectors of society which had brought about the 'revolution' split apart. This lead to a clearer ideological division between *moderates* and *democrats*. The moderates (or conservatives) believed that economic progress and political freedom would result from a policy of *laissez-faire* implemented with a firm hand by the aristocracy and the upper bourgeoisie; the democrats, to be found in all classes of society, were strongly motivated by a common ideal: to destroy unacceptable legal and political privileges and constraints in line with an ideology derived not only from the example of the Great Revolution of 1789, but also from the new bourgeois social structure and state established by Napoleon.

The political class and the bourgeoisie in Italy: an uncharacteristic nineteenth-century bourgeois state

The limits to Mosca's analysis are to be found in his instinctive conservatism, the inability to grasp the underlying sociological significance of his research and the real differences between the classes, and the consequent erroneous identification of the bourgeoisie with the educated class. He was unable to understand the dialectical relationship between the classes which was taking shape during his formative years and while he was writing his first book. These were the years of peasant revolts, the destruction of the class of urban artisans and in which the new liberal political regime came up against a still highly static social reality. On the other hand, these years witnessed the passing of huge amounts of real estate into the hands of the bourgeoisie as a result of the expropriation and sale of church land and the conversion of state property; the first expansion in capitalist-based agriculture and the establishing of a growing manufacturing industry; and finally, the rise of that new aristocracy of capitalists and political dealers which thrived on speculation in public works, the building of the railways and the construction of the first main components in a nationwide infrastructure. Mosca's view of the heterogenous and contradictory bourgeoisie which was then developing in all of Italy was too distorted by its particular Sicilian variant. The latter was made up of families the oldest of which

have their origins in the class of lawyers, some of them going back perhaps a hundred or a hundred and fifty years; but these are an exception. The others are of more recent origin, and more recent still in the small towns of the interior than in Palermo and Messina. In such small towns a family of well-off landowners which can trace its lineage back seventy or eighty years without coming across – as they say in those parts – 'a peasant's cap', may justly boast that it is the most aristocratic in the district.[43]

As a consequence of his limited vision, he was unable to comprehend the most important upheaval which occurred in the Italian bourgeoisie during the nineteenth century. The social reality of the bourgeoisie in his native Sicily eluded him. This class was not only represented by the descendents – who were few in number – of former peasants, but was still firmly rooted in that mixture of the medieval and the modern described by every visitor to and student of the island. This race of former peasants, grown rich for the most part through plunder and parasitical exploitation, did not give birth to a bourgeoisie in the modern sense of a class engaged in risky industrial and commercial ventures, as was the case in other parts of Italy. What took place was a simple shift of economic power from the old nobility (parasitic absentee landlords *par excellence*) to the new rich: a symbolic relationship of intermarriage and the selling-off and repurchasing of estates. This explains why, alongside the men of learning produced by this particular bourgeoisie of whom Mosca himself is a typical example, there also continued to exist the much more numerous layer of semi-illiterate former tax and duty collectors, mining contractors, stewards on the large estates and all those who subjected the resources of Sicily to intense exploitation, not in opposition to but in symbiosis with the old, and in some cases more educated, class of nobles. This is a period of history which is narrated in an exemplary fashion by Giuseppe Tomasi di Lampedusa (1896–1957) in his posthumous novel *The Leopard* (1958) on which Luchino Visconti's famous film of the same name is based.

4

The bourgeois myth of the middle class as the political class

In *Sulla teorica dei governi e sul governo parlamentare* Mosca's aim is not only to clarify and develop his ideas about the political class but also about more general questions. He maintains that before proceeding to analyse the existing *de facto* institutions in Italy and to study the ways in which the political class is formed, one must first establish what its precise objectives are. To the accusation of wanting to destroy something without knowing what to put in its place he retorts that with regard to political institutions, it is the task of the man of action, not of the theoretician, to be constructive in a practical way. The former follows step by step those temporary, changing circumstances 'to which every political concept must of necessity be adapted', whereas the latter can 'neither foresee them nor take them into account'. In Mosca's opinion, 'it is evident that no individual can ever build something on his own, when this means creating out of nothing a whole new system of ideas, institutions and instruments of government; when it means completing a task which at present has hardly been outlined and which requires the energy of a whole people, an entire generation'.[1] He concludes, therefore, that his goal has been to carry out 'the search for this truth which no-one told us of, this end which no-one pointed out to us'.[2] He believes the result of his research has been to acquire a core of basic certainties, arrived at by identifying the principal laws which regulate the organization of governments (political class, political formula, political mechanism), and to develop criticism of the existing political order so as to 'throw some light on the course of political events, whether actual or in the near future'.[3] Although he states that it is 'highly unlikely' that the type of parliamentary regime set up at that time in Italy and France could survive in the long run, he nevertheless maintains that his own society, 'except in the Government', showed no signs of decadence and imminent collapse. This implies that there was substantial acceptance on his part of the values of the representative state, an awareness that it would last and a sceptical attitude towards the government's daily political practice.

This part of *Teorica* is characterized by its tendency to over-describe and theorize and by a polemical and moralistic tone, in spite of which it is very useful as documentary evidence; a fact which was noticed by Antonio Gramsci (1891–1937), a severe critic of Mosca and his work. In fact, for Gramsci, 'the concept of the political class is very imprecise and is neither worked out nor justified theoretically' and, furthermore, it is hard to understand exactly what Mosca meant in precise terms by political class, 'given that the notion is so elastic and variable. Sometimes he appears to mean by political class the middle class, at others all of the propertied classes, and on still other occasions what is called the educated part of society, or the State's personnel (the parliamentary class).' He concludes by stating that 'Mosca's so-called political class is nothing other than an intellectual category for the dominant group in society'.[4] In our opinion this judgement needs revising. The communist theoretician was intent, of course, on using any element in his country's cultural experience which might be of use to nascent Italian Leninism. In this respect, Mosca's doctrine appeared to be of limited value given its contradictory combination of realism and ethical demands, the vague practical consequences and often rigid confinement within a conservative view of the world. However, it should also be pointed out that the doctrine of the political class appears to have been shaped originally by a bourgeois class concept of politics, of some interest and importance in the political life of the unified Italian nation. In this early period, the essential elements of Mosca's political ideology were the above-mentioned bourgeois class concept of politics, the myth of the middle class and the myth of order.

The scholar's own bourgeois class position derives from the fact that he was an intellectual belonging to the southern middle bourgeoisie of the first decades of national unity. His political convictions were then merged with the vision, deeply motivated by authentic utopianism but pursued coherently, of a rationally organized State able and ready at all times to take the initiative in defence of society, if necessary adopting radical measures. It is important to realize that his utopianism has a conservative as well as a revolutionary side to it. In this light and within these limits, Mosca succeeds – as has been already indicated – in getting to the root of the 'sacred' right of property and the wealth-creating process, both of which are seen to derive their legitimacy from the state alone. The reason for this is that if the government 'is that which ensures the inviolability of private property and, so to speak, infuses it with life', this same government must be able to 'modify and even limit it when necessary so as to maintain social order: otherwise it would represent the association of the rich against the poor, and not the organizing of the most intellectually valid elements in the country, the controlling brain which is able to identify society's interests and follow the best course for attaining them'.[5] Thus, by linking the more avowedly scientific requirements with those of a contingent political nature, Mosca's thought also developed a Utopian strand intended, above all, to express a sharply critical attitude towards existing society and its political order. This criticism constitutes a medley of, at times disparate, philosophical and cultural notions applied to the still very contradictory reality of Italian society at that time. Moreover, his answer to the eternal question of how doctrine should be put into practice is to appeal to the new generation to understand that its task consists in gaining time: 'this is what, at the present, a peaceful solution to the several problems swamping us depends upon: to gain time, to attain a clear vision of the social situation in which we find ourselves, to know how to take the right steps and avoid catastrophe before it plunges down on us.'[6]

This conclusion to *Teorica* points to the fact that a different generation was emerging, far more critical and pessimistic than the generations of the great patriots who had united Italy. In carrying out this task, they had differed in their use of the ideological, cultural and social elements at hand, but had sought a minimum common denominator in an ideology based on social co-operation, an economic philosophy of *laissez-faire*, religious tolerance, a not unreasonable mistrust of the modern state's tentacular growth and, lastly, a blind faith in the principles of parliamentary government. Mosca can be seen as one of the most important representatives of the new emerging generation; a fact which has been highlighted in our analysis up to this point, while at the same time the ambiguities and contradictions in the elaboration of his thought have also been underlined. A realistic reading of Mosca, therefore, completely contradicts Gramsci's assertions. It was in fact at a later date, in the agitated climate of the 1920s, that an exponent of progressive liberalism and anti-Fascism, Piero Gobetti (1901–26), saw in the doctrine of the political class one of those intuitions which open up new and extremely fruitful areas of research. Read historically in the context of its own time, the Moschian doctrine is indeed very interesting and stimulating; there is nothing at all vacillating about it. As we have shown, the ambiguities and contradictions are a result of the unintegrated combination of scientifically based elements and ideological motives. The constant dichotomy established by Mosca between the governed classes and the political class, the demystifying use of the political formula and the very myths contained in his doctrine are obviously factors which cannot be neglected by anyone wishing to understand the social and political reality in Italy during the passage from the nineteenth to the twentieth century: a reality forged in the melting-pot of the many contradictions arising from the experience of being a united country after centuries of separate, regional histories. Once freed of its accompanying and qualifying elements, the Moschian doctrine is a powerful instrument for completing the Marxist interpretation of political struggle, institutions and history. Consequently, it can be seen that Gramsci's evaluation of Mosca's ideas passes over the scientific core and focuses exclusively and in negative terms on the ideology inherent in the doctrine. His overall rejection of Mosca's ideas is open to much criticism.

Published in 1884, *Teorica* is both a 'manifesto' of Mosca's political and ideological thought and a statement of his basic convictions and scientific premises. Closer inspection of this work reveals a whole series of wide-ranging and contrasting aspects. There is the criticism of the principles of 1789 and the praise for the essential elements in Enlightenment philosophy (summed up in the modern saying: '*le mérite au pouvoir*'); the refutation that parliamentary institutions are appropriate for the ultimate ends which inspired their creation and can serve as mechanisms for the advancement of the political struggle; the extolling of the bourgeois class and its state, while at the same time putting forward the alternative demand for a state which is truly impartial with respect to all classes and also able to effectively limit the principle of property for strictly social – not ethical or philanthropic – reasons (an 'impartial' state administered by the educated sectors of the bourgeoisie, capable of imposing their will on the new breed of capitalists as well as on the plebian masses). Finally, there is the conflict between the prevailing strand of realism and the desire for the political class and the state to be founded on ethical principles deeply rooted in experience: a contradictory coexistence of realism and utopianism. How far Mosca was aware of this last aspect is not clear. It would be possible to continue adding to this list of contradictions in Mosca's thinking. Seen in their historical and political context, they must be understood as a consequence of his endeavour to grasp the contradictory situation of a country like Italy. During these years it was still struggling with the initial problems of capitalist development, but was also feeling the effects of a trend which had already been sweeping across the whole of Europe for some time; a trend which led Italy away from the *laissez-faire* enthusiasm of the first years of the nineteenth century and through to the protectionist period following the Franco-Prussian War, the prelude to the great upheavals which would result from the struggle for markets in the next century.

It would be incorrect to say that these dynamic elements are present in Mosca at a conscious level. He makes few references to political economy, going no further than to restate some standard notions. Nevertheless, if Mosca's repeated appeal to a new generation has any meaning, it is because there was a new generation which was sensitive enough to grasp intuitively several facts not immediately visible that were bringing about a radical change in the economic, political and social climate.

The aims of the political class

What has been said above confirms that Mosca's thought is characterized by the contrast between the ideological tension behind his research and the realistic approach adopted. The latter is expressed in his acceptance of existing social reality: there is no hint of a desire to turn back the clock, to reinstate absolutist government, which is how he defines the *ancien régime*. As regards the ideological aspect, this is clearly shown in his declared intention to aim at a new and more effective political solution, because

if it is true that the duty and destiny of man is to aspire continually for improvement and to attain a greater good, we do not see why the struggle should be renounced on this occasion; it could lead to useful and lasting results in the future and would undoubtedly improve the present situation by providing a goal, a purpose, a direction for those with the most energy and intelligence. At present, due to the absence of such a specific aim these individuals are left idle, and this is especially the case among the younger generation.[7]

The new political class desired by Mosca has the same values and tendencies as certain strata within the Italian bourgeoisie during the last decades of the nineteenth century. But as has been already pointed out, the term 'bourgeoisie' is still too generic when applied to a society like that of Italy which, at that time, was mainly based on agriculture and in which conditions varied greatly from one region to the next. This term has ideological and polemical overtones which make it difficult to obtain a precise and differentiated picture of the class itself. In this respect, the following observation by the sociologist Renato Treves is very true: 'few sociological studies have been carried out on social classes in Italy, the little research that has been done is mostly fragmentary in character and scientifically speaking the methodology varies greatly in quality'. This evaluation applies to an even greater extent when we consider Italy as it was a hundred years ago. It certainly applies in the case of the Italian bourgeoisie, a class which developed along complex and contradictory lines and spread its influence over the whole of the country without interruption from the moment it succeeded in setting up its own state in 1861.

A question which arises with regard to the patriotic Italian bourgeoisie during the period of the Risorgimento is whether it can be seen as a class conscious of itself or whether the term 'bourgeoisie' covers essentially different social, cultural and ideological experiences and values. We agree with Stanislaw Ossowski that a social class cannot exist without there being the awareness of belonging to it and, above all, the awareness of the position of the class to which one feels attached. In the years following the unification of Italy, the lower and middle bourgeoisie consisted of a miscellany of widely varying social strata for the most part under the hegemony of the upper bourgeoisie and the liberal and monarchical nobility; despite such a subservient position the more numerous sections of the former attempted to create a role for themselves within the system of power. This is demonstrated by the entire history of Italian politics during the said period, which was especially marked by *trasformismo*: a term coined to describe the parliamentary practice of deputies who without further ado deserted the ranks of the Right to join those of the Left. Generally speaking, this phenomenon meant that the domination of governments of the Left after 1876 was accepted by deputies who belonged to the other forces in the Chamber. Moreover, it was not a transitory event and would characterize the Italian political scene for a long time. Although it produced conservative government, it was by means of this formula that some power was transferred from the upper bourgeoisie and the nobility, represented historically by the Right, to the professional and white-collar, lower and middle bourgeoisie politically active among the Left. It is also true, however, that the revolutionary minority which existed then and still exists today – its influence on the class as a whole being marginal – was of bourgeois origin. In this respect, Mosca typified that part of the lower and middle bourgeoisie of southern origin which was deeply divided by the fundamental contradiction between its attempt at integration into the system and its desire to change it substantially. In resolving this contradiction, Mosca took a distinctly conservative line. This politically sterile choice of approach had its origin in a premise of a precise social nature, which is worth analysing. The acute observation has been made that Mosca believed in the vocation of the Italian middle class to become the country's real ruling class. Consequently, he acted as the ideologue of the bourgeoisie; the linchpin – the 'social myth' – of his scientific and political positions was formed by the middle class. It can therefore be assumed that Mosca's scientific activity expressed an intellectual, cultural and practical attempt to show that by applying a moderate political methodology capable of discouraging 'anarchy' and 'social democracy' as well as absolutist 'reaction', it was possible to construct a model of the middle-class state in Italy which could integrate on both a political and a socio-economic level all the individual 'values' expressed by society. If it is true that Mosca's convictions have a historical-juridical basis, clearly derived from the constitutional doctrine of his time, it is also a fact that their ideological roots are embedded in a sociological vision of politics and society.

The middle class and political democracy

It is clear from the above considerations that Mosca's view of the bourgeois class is fragmentary and unsatisfactory. Surprisingly, he failed to understand the necessary relationship between the class nature (bourgeois) of Italy's ruling stratum and the political-constitutional arrangements adopted. When Mosca wrote *Teorica* the political-constitutional, social and economic reality of the country was entirely bourgeois, and it is difficult to see what more he could have wished for. An evaluation of this aspect of Mosca's thought throws light on his ideology, already apparent in this first work, and leads us to consider how he applied his own doctrine and the reason for the antithesis which he saw between liberalism and democracy. He was not alone in suggesting such an antithesis: the greatest philosopher of Italian liberalism, Benedetto Croce, was still insisting in 1923 that the liberal State and the democratic state are not the same thing. It must also be said that the theoretical and practical hostility between liberalism and democracy is a fixed point of reference in Mosca's work. However, we must remember that he was in all respects a man of the nineteenth century; this can be seen in the strong influence exerted on him by the most recent historical developments.

In the second half of the nineteenth century monarchical and theocratic absolutism – and its political formula – was still a reality, threatening in some cases and of very recent memory in others; Mosca could not, of course, neglect such a fact. Thus the democracy against which he engaged in much polemic was nothing other than the direct democracy of Jacobin inspiration, the theoretical and ideological roots of which are to be found in the thought of Jean Jacques Rousseau (1712–78): a political doctrine which turns 'majority government' into an absolute value. He used his own ideas about the political class to demonstrate the impossibility of such a doctrine. Democracy in this case meant that 'democracy' which was somewhat rhetorical and vague in its political and ideological impact and of which Piero Gobetti would remark in *La rivoluzione liberale* that its reformism marks 'the logical culmination of our revolutionary impotence', the illusion expressed in terms of governmental action by the prophetic optimism of Giuseppe Mazzini (1805–72), the great Republican patriot of the nineteenth century, who 'had believed the revolution could be achieved through propaganda'. Mosca held that he had shown how 'democracy', understood in terms of an organized political group, fails to lead to the government of a state by the people; on the contrary, it is forced to adopt demagogic and anti-scientific formulas in order to achieve a consensus. This was obviously a polemical thrust in the direction of nineteenth-century democratic radicalism in Italy and the rest of Europe.

From this perspective the significance of the scholar's criticisms of the parliamentary system can be more fully appreciated. We may say that from when he started working on *Teorica* Mosca was in a precise sense a non-democratic, conservative liberal. He was already conscious of belonging to an independent class distinct from the upper bourgeoisie and the proletariat. On closer inspection, Mosca's middle class turns out to be none other than the sum of the middle strata in Italian society, a gathering point for widely differing social groups ranging from the lowest levels of the white-collar petty bourgeoisie in the North (whose problems were the same as those of the plebeian masses) to the petty bourgeoisie of the southern countryside (the source for state employees); from the intellectual and professional middle bourgeoisie, which supplied the upper class with a permanent personnel of considerable cultural and technical experience for running its affairs, to those intellectuals of the same class origins who took up a critical position towards society to the extent of using culture to break through class boundaries and form a permanent factor of unorthodoxy and opposition in the country. It is clear that in the Italian situation such a social base was not sufficient for the middle strata to achieve class independence: the conscious unity of different groups linked by common interests. On the contrary, the middle classes of that time were characterized in the lowest strata by the psychological and social attitude of distancing oneself from the masses; by the aspiration of the most advanced sections to be promoted to the upper bourgeoisie; and by the not easily definable state of mind of the more numerous middle strata.

We now have sufficient elements with which to attempt a first, general critical judgement. Notwithstanding the fact that he had correctly grasped the significance of the social change behind the establishment of the parliamentary system and had attempted to provide as well a sociological interpretation of the educated sector of the bourgeoisie,

Mosca was in fact unable to go beyond the historical reality of Italy and consider the problems he dealt with in a more general context. His analysis has a fragmentary character of which he himself was aware; this was especially the case when he was studying the parliamentary and administrative organization of the Italian state. It is clear that at this stage in his thinking Mosca's aims were basically very generic, often inconsistent and stimulated by youthful impetuosity. There was an obvious unbridgeable gap between his scientific premises and political conclusions. The objective he set himself, which forms the dominant element in his subsequent work, was 'to see to what extent these types of governments, arisen as a result of a real and tangible change in social conditions but devised according to theoretical abstractions and mechanical imitation, are then able to satisfy those needs for which they were created'.[8] In other words, it remained to be seen how the new political formula and constitutional arrangements derived from the English experience could be put into practice and to verify whether

the problem has been resolved of substituting individual merit for birth and, as far as possible, knowledge for wealth in the formation of the political class. It remains to be seen if by being scrupulously applied, all the political elements and all the social values in a country really become part of political life and are not already for the most part excluded therefrom; and finally if the principles of public law on which they are based allow them to be interpreted and applied in such a manner . . . or whether in order to achieve this end, they have to be totally repudiated.[9]

Here the basis for Mosca's own political theory was laid, and the subsequent analysis served as a prelude to a description of the relationship of the various strata in society to the political struggle and existing institutions. This analysis of the way in which the Italian state was *materially constituted* is extremely interesting not only for understanding this period of Mosca's thought, but also for an objective picture of the social climate and cultural background in and against which it evolved. His research into theoretical, historical and constitutional matters took on a particularly political colouring from his inclination to search behind legal forms for the real facts, to uncover manipulation, mystifying language and ideas, the corruption of theory and practice, the harnessing together of truth and falsehood, and the assertion of a principle and its negation. These are all elements which characterize this part of *Teorica* and form the premise for further theoretical and practical elaboration.

Elections and organized minorities

Mosca's next published work after *Teorica* was *Le costituzioni moderne*, which appeared in 1887. This new work provides a basis for further examination of the themes contained in the first. It shows in more detail how social forces are organized in modern collective society – a subject of particular interest to Mosca. Through greater conceptual precision and a more critical analysis Mosca is now able to depict the state as a balance between 'the interests, passions and *raison d'être* of present-day society' and

that class which having the benefit of higher education, occupies all the scientific professions. Numerically and materially weak, it imposes its will by the sheer force of its superior knowledge. It disposes of neither the capital nor the labour to create wealth, but represents reason and science amid the interests and passions of those who produce it. Without this class it would be impossible for the entire economic and social structure of modern civilization to function; any noble conception of law and social justice would disappear and a large part of the outstanding cultural achievements in the nineteenth century would be erased.[10]

The ethical ideal of this collaboration between the different social forces in the administration of the State is represented, in Mosca's eyes, 'by the development of that sentiment of social justice, free from any religious creed and national or class prejudice, which we believe will provide the future basis for regulating political relations between citizens, and between them and the State'.[11] Although expressed in his usual pessimistic tone, he nevertheless asserts more resolutely than in *Teorica* that these are the kinds of considerations that can lead 'if not to the solution, then at least to a clarification of 'the intricate social and political problems besetting the doubtful future of troubled European society'.[12]

Another theme developed in *Le costituzioni moderne*, which had been touched on in *Teorica*, is Mosca's interpretation of political elections. According to Mosca, political struggle always results from the purposeful activity of 'an organized minority, which dedicates much effort [to the political struggle] and is therefore motivated by its own reasons and interests, almost always more effective than platonic benevolence which is usually reserved for public affairs'.[13] This is a restatement of his thesis in which the idea that an elected representative is always chosen by a minority is held to be a 'scientific principle'. In this regard, however, after a careful examination of both electoral systems and the organizing of election campaigns he formulates the opinion that institutions can be judged as good or bad according to the extent to which they satisfy some fundamental requirements:

The bourgeois myth 43

the protection of the law, that is, the safeguard in all cases and for every individual of certain principles of morality and social justice universally recognized according to the country and the times, and genuine representation in the Government of the various social forces; that is to say, the running of society's political affairs is placed in the hands of those elements which, depending on the particular historical moment and the level of civilization, are the most important.[14]

Though declaring his lack of confidence in the present state of society's institutions and in their capacity to 'develop', that is, to become a stronger, more effective and rational structure, Mosca none the less reaches some interesting conclusions. In the first place, he specifies through his interpretation of elections that the concept of organized minority indicates a constant feature in the formation of that sector of the political class which is an expression of the electorate. All those elements which are influential inside the state, whether they come from the bureaucracy or the electorate, are held in a state of equilibrium within the political class. So the concept of organized minority, referred to the political class, means no more or less than the coexistence of the different values present in the representative state. It is clear that differences and checks and balances are possible within this minority, which in actual fact and by law runs society; they guarantee that the different sectors and individual members of the political class control one another. To speak in this regard of organized minority means, basically, to affirm a concept which corresponds to the structure of the modern representative state in which the effective disposition of the several elements making up the governing group does not depend on an exclusivist attitude, but is rather the recognition of a *de facto* situation which finds full expression in the organization of the state and its division of labour. The election committees, on the other hand, constitute the organized minority which succeeds in imposing its own candidate on the unorganized, atomized majority of voters who

remain more or less passive spectators of the struggle, their participation being minimal because they have little interest in the result. And the reasons are evident; at the moment they exercise their right to vote – as if redeeming their share in popular sovereignty – they have only three alternatives: to abstain from voting, to cast their vote for whom they think is the best man, which is almost always the same as wasting it; or lastly, to choose from among the two or three likely candidates and vote for one of them.[15]

Finally, Mosca still talks of selected and organized minorities in terms of protagonists in the great 'moral and social regenerations and revolutions'. If we take *Le costituzioni moderne* and *Teorica* together, we may say that these three definitions of organized minorities meet three precise objectives: the scientific definition of the minority governing group; the study of how the electoral system functions in reality as against the claim that elections are a moment of real choice for all citizens; and the determining of Mosca's ideological ends in matters of political reform.

An ideological framework for new social forces with the capacity to renew Italy politically

When dealing with this question, Mosca reconfirms some well-known concepts but is careful to invest them with his own particular meaning. He recognizes that the basic defect in previous criticism of the parliamentary system lies in the fact that it came from the supporters of absolutist regimes in the past. Consequently, the idea of parliamentary government 'has always triumphed; it has been seen more or less as a part of the general trend and taken on the aura of invincibility attributed to it by many'.[16] On the other hand, he maintains that adequate study can make it possible to avoid 'terrible upheavals', the 'periods of civil war and anarchy', and that however rudimentary the stage reached by such study, it still has something to offer. At this point Mosca puts forward a very interesting and original proposal. In a different tone than that adopted in *Teorica*, he asserts that real change can only come about when 'behind all political reform and supporting each new institution' there exists 'a new social force'.[17] Present evils can be made less acute by temporary intervention, but a radical change will only be possible when 'the moral regeneration of society has taken place: in other words, when the new morality is fully formed and widespread and, at the same time, the new social forces are thoroughly organized. These are the labouring classes which will have acquired that prestige and political power to which they are summoned by the new civilization'.[18]

It is in this respect, in our opinion, that Mosca's proposal is also innovatory politically speaking: he equates the new social forces with the labouring classes by which he means not only 'those who live by manual labour, but also those whose work requires the use of the intellect'.[19] Although he predicts a 'great future with heavy responsibilities' for the latter, he also outlines the hypothesis of a real alliance between these two components of society that might possibly reduce the influence of wealth, which – as is stated frequently in the chapter on elections – represents an element tending to upset the balance of society. The way to bring about such an alliance is through the reorganization of local government, which must be taken out of the hands of 'the centralizing, all-embracing bureaucracy of red tape that makes possible the monstrous despotism of

The bourgeois myth

the few who control and run it',[20] but also of the elected official, 'almost always the instrument of a local group or clique';[21] through reform of the Senate so that it becomes an expression of provincial assemblies and the different social classes; and by changing the system of national elections, first of all through the introduction of measures for checking both the electoral rolls and the counting of votes. Here Mosca's rethinking is stretched to the utmost in his attempt also to overcome the limits of a bourgeois class position which had a strong conditioning effect on him. He thus addresses himself to a series of problems, not dealt with in *Teorica*, which correspond to the real situation of society's institutions and of the political struggle. When he presses for the 'organization of new social forces which are fully aware of what the future requires, namely, the classes involved in both mental and physical labour',[22] Mosca is also appealing to an ethical ideal which verges on utopianism. He declares that what is needed is

to end that state of scepticism and listlessness in which the destruction of past ideals has left us, and to replace the old moral sense with a new entirely reformulated one; it should no longer be inspired by supernatural beliefs or religious fears, but by those lofty sentiments of impartial altruism and social justice which, if human progress is not a Utopia, must unfailingly grow stronger and more widespread.[23]

What we have here is the fully systematic expression of Mosca's first ideas within a conception of society which is highly class-collaborationist and dominated by the values of the intellectuals within the bourgeoisie rather than the values of those concerned with money, trade and industry. Aside from any contradictions and immature features, the general lines along which the writer's thought developed in the early period are underlined by his political and cultural awareness of the fundamental values of the 'middle class', understood as a social group which upholds universal values; by the advocacy of class collaboration in declared opposition to wealth and plutocratic power; by the assertion that order is a primary civil and ethical value; by an irreverent polemical attitude; by the emphasis on the need for state intervention also in the economic sphere; and by demands relating to ethics and freedom.

5
The development of the scientific system as a comprehensive ideology, 1896–1922

During what Henry Stuart Hughes has described as the 'intellectual revolution of the 1890s', Mosca's thought developed further and reached full maturity. The cornerstones of his doctrine of the political class remained firmly in place and the arguments supporting them were still the same. What changed was the value which the author attributed to the results of the doctrine formulated by him. In fact, it was at this point that Mosca passed from youthfully vigorous criticism (with the many contradictions already indicated) to a *scientific system* which is much less dependent on political and social contingencies and has a clearer historical and theoretical perspective. In this way the doctrine was turned into a more practical tool for research and made a concrete contribution to that 'social science' dreamt of by the 20-year-old Mosca. Stripped of much of its polemical tone, the doctrine of the political class now appeared in an entirely new form without its original controversial simplications, no longer 'anti-democratic' but 'non-democratic'.

The first edition of the *Elementi di scienza politica*: a complete synthesis of Gaetano Mosca's thought

The fundamental changes in Mosca's approach can be ascertained by paying particular attention to his intellectual output in the years between 1896 and the second decade of the twentieth century; all the ideas expressed in this period are linked together systematically in the first edition of the *Elementi di scienza politica*. What this amounts to is a new system: one which moves towards unifying two equally important moments in the critical and scientific exposition of all his previous work and towards making the conservation of political forms the openly declared objective of his intellectual activity.

It must be remembered that in the 1890s the Italian political scene was very different to what it had been in the first two decades of the new state's existence. The two leaders of the country in this later period, Francesco Crispi (1818–1901) and Antonio Starrabba, Marquis of Di Rudinì – both Sicilians like Mosca – operated in a political context characterized by growing social tension, which would reach a climax on the eve of the new century with the assassination of King Umberto I. The birth of the Socialist Party and the growth of the labour movement heralded the appearance on the scene of new social and political protagonists in a country where, for some time, even conservatives had been denouncing the gap between institutional power and its social base. On the international scene, the new state was placed in a difficult and sometimes dramatic situation by the diplomatic rupture with France, a traditionally friendly country. It had been brought about by Crispi who was also responsible for the extraordinary alliance with the Austrian Empire, an old enemy, as well as with the recently formed German Empire, and for the first attempts at colonial expansion into Africa. As we have already seen, Mosca's position was very close to that of the Marquis of Di Rudinì who, after the Italian defeat at Adua (1895) in the war against Ethiopia, was entrusted with liquidating the colonialist policy of Crispi; thus Mosca's political conservatism can be seen as a response to a particularly stormy moment in Italy's history. In fact, the social and political situation worsened considerably as the end of the century drew near: Italian politics took a reactionary turn in 1898 with the nomination as Prime Minister of Luigi Pelloux (1839–1924), a Piedmontese general. His method of governing was to proclaim martial law, use the army against the civilian population of Milan, and arrest and put on trial Democrats, Republicans, Socialists and even politically active Catholics. But despite all this, despite the new state's restricted economic base and the fact that millions of peasants were emigrating from the most backward regions, the new state managed to survive the crisis. Immediately following the murder of King Umberto I a new Prime Minister was chosen, Giuseppe Zanardelli (1826–1903) from Lombardy; and he was succeeded by the more important figure of the Piedmontese Giovanni Giolitti (1842–1928), who remained at the head of the government until the First World War. The leadership given to the country by these two men enabled it to go through a process of renewal in a liberal and sometimes progressive direction, opening up the way for real social and economic modernization.

This was the climate in which the first edition of the *Elementi di scienza politica* was elaborated and its core was to remain unchanged in all subsequent editions. In this period Mosca worked out a system of political thought that is both scientific and loaded with ideological implications. Those features which appear to be more interesting for a sufficiently thorough evaluation of Mosca's thought can be traced precisely to the interconnection between cultural, scientific and practical-political themes; no claim is made, of course, that our examination exhausts all the problems brought to light and studied by the author. In addition to the more rigorous definition of the concept of political class, this work contains several new features which provide a focus for the author's ideological and polemical tensions. First of all, there is the doctrine of juridical defence; but Mosca also provides a clear statement of his convictions regarding the aims of a 'positive political science' on both a scientific and political level. In this respect, what he writes in the final chapter of the *Elementi* is significant:

Now democratic doctrine has rendered undeniable services to civilization. Embodied in the representative system, for which England set the pattern, it has contributed to important improvements in juridical defence, which have been attained through a system of debate and political progress that has been established in many parts of Europe. But now that we have come to its last logical implication, and men are trying to realize the principles on which it was based down to their remotest consequences, the same doctrine is disorganizing the countries in which it prevails and forcing them into a decline. And this must necessarily be the case, since under its pseudo-scientific appearance this doctrine is really purely metaphysical.[1]

So among the results of the *Elementi* is to be found a synthesis of Mosca's political and scientific programme, which the contemporary Italian philosopher Norberto Bobbio has summed up in the scholar's two main commitments, one negative and the other positive: 'the first consisted in sweeping away mistaken doctrines of society and the state which at one time had a corrupting and inciting influence' and, in the language of positivism, in setting 'a complete positive system' in opposition to 'a complete metaphysical system'; the second consisted in formulating scientific doctrines, that is to say, based on the facts so as to lead the governed majority to ask for, and the governing minority to concede, only reasonable reforms'.[2]

These aspects of the *Elementi* were those which provided Mosca's research in this period with clearly determined objectives both in the scientific field and, through attempts to give them practical expression, in the scholar's political-parliamentary activity. Whereas the 1880s had formed the framework for research in which Mosca developed the original formulation of his ideas (political class, political formula, study of the political mechanism), the 1890s were the years which allowed him to work his way out of the stimulating, but sometimes confusing, complications of the early system by elaborating in a positive way the 'new concept' of *juridical defence*. This concept is a *leitmotiv* throughout the whole of the new period which was then just beginning; it gives his work a sense of ethical, ideological and political completeness and, above all, represents the point at which the writer synthesized theoretical study and political praxis.

History of individuals and history of institutions

We shall now examine more closely how Mosca came to extend the range of basic problems treated and to formulate more fully the concepts and perspectives, hopes and concerns which the open system of his *Sulla teorica dei governi e sul governo parlamentare* had not only had failed to clarify, but had jumbled together in polemical, pessimistic declarations and in a Utopian desire for radical social change.

In the *Elementi* Mosca starts off by analysing methodology in the science of history. His initial premise is that 'a science is always built upon a system of observations which have been made with particular care and by appropriate methods on a given order of phenomena, and which have been so co-ordinated as to disclose incontrovertible truths which would not have been discovered by the ordinary observation of the common man'.[3] On this basis Mosca states that his intention is to make a contribution to the development of political theory founded on a scientific approach; the backwardness of the subject in this respect is evident. The fault does not lie with those minds which have made great efforts in studying the relevant problems but, on the contrary, is due to

the greater complexity of the phenomena involved in this subject and, especially, in the circumstance that, down to a few decades ago, it was virtually impossible to get accurate and complete information about the facts on which we are obliged to depend in trying to discover the constant laws or tendencies that determine the political organization of human societies.[4]

By making a comparative study of the historical documents available, the writer proposes to determine *constant laws* which should make it possible for politics to become an exact science. 'In other words', he concludes, 'if political science is to be based on the study and observation of political facts, then we must go back to the old historical method'.[5] This is the fundamental principle of Moschian methodology, which had been more or less anticipated in an integral form in *Teorica*. In this regard, Bobbio has correctly explained that 'in order to understand what Mosca, who was no lover of philosophical niceties, meant by the term "historical method", we must avoid attaching some deep significance to it, as is often the case: to use the historical method simply means to build up political science by observing facts rather than deducing it from a priori principles'.[6]

The different strands of Mosca's thought exist side by side in the *Elementi*, underlining the ideological significance of his research even in this most successful and mature synthesis of his ideas. For example, there is the claimed *neutrality* of research: the ability of political science 'not to justify this or that existing State, but to explain how States come into being, are organized and decline'.[7] He also expounds his own personal conception of history, which underlies his analysis and according to which the theoretician must direct his attention not so much to the actions of important historical individuals as to 'those details of social custom and political and administrative organization in different peoples which are of far greater interest to the study of political science than the personal feats of great warriors and rulers'.[8] History as Mosca understands it is more 'history of institutions' than 'history of individuals'; by way of example he says:

The historical facts which are and always will be shrouded in the greatest uncertainty are ancedotal, biographical facts, facts which may involve the vanity or profit of a man, a nation, a party. It is chiefly in regard to such facts that the passions of a writer may be the cause, be it unwittingly, of error. Fortunately, that type of fact is of scant interest to the student of the political sciences. It makes little difference to him whether a battle has been won through the merit of one commander or lost through the fault of another, or whether a political assassination was more or less justifiable. On the other hand, there are facts that concern the social type and organization of the various peoples and the various epochs; and it is about such facts, which are of the greater interest to us, that historians, spontaneously and without bias, often tell the truth. At any rate, more enlightening than the historians are the documents themselves.[9]

This history of institutions is open to criticism and it has been rightly observed

that Mosca does not tell us what lies behind the distinction between history of individuals and history of institutions; also the examples he puts forward are more likely to raise than allay any doubts. I think that he had in mind the difference between small-scale and large-scale history, between micro-history and macro-history – if I am using the terms correctly – and wanted to suggest that only the latter could furnish enough material for revealing general tendencies or laws, the discovery of which was precisely the task of political science.[10]

The scientific system

These are the types of problems treated by Mosca as he develops his overall thought. He declares that his intention is to do away with all forms of dilettantism, which amounts to separating politics and science; the formulation of his doctrine is to have both a practical and a scientific end. Thus we have come to that specific conception of *scientific politics* which he intended to be put into effect by 'men of government' who would be inspired in their decision making by 'the methods and results of the social sciences, in particular political science. And since science taught caution in procedure, circumspection about presuppositions, distrust of definitve results, political science was synonymous with moderate politics, in favour of reform, certainly, but in gradual stages; and a bitter enemy of too sudden and precipitate change.'[11] The fusion of the different elements in Mosca's thinking now appears also in its full political light: his conservatism emerges in the period of peak maturity precisely from this close link between scientific and political motives, from his lifelong pursuit of 'the mirage of a counter-revolutionary science'.[12] Therefore, the clarification of Mosca's method allows us to understand better the precise structure of his doctrine, which in the *Elementi* adds to the concepts of political class and political formula the wholly ideological notion of juridical defence.

The juridical defence as an ethical basis for the relationship between rulers and ruled

We shall now look at how Mosca rearranges the concept of political class within the system adopted for the *Elementi*. This concept still remains, however, the starting-point of his work and is linked dialectically to the 'new concept' towards which his entire research is directed: that of juridical defence.

As is the case in *Teorica*, he starts from the distinction – verifiable in 'the practice of real life' – between rulers and ruled and draws two conclusions: first that

in every political organism there is one individual who is head among the leaders of the political class as a whole and stands, as we say, at the helm of the State. That person is not always the person who holds supreme power according to law. At times, alongside of the hereditary king or emperor there is a prime minister or a major-domo who wields an actual power that is greater than the sovereign's. At other times, in place of the elected president the influential politician who has procured the president's election will govern. Under special circumstances there may be, instead of a single person, two or three who discharge the functions of supreme control.[13]

The doctrine of the political class

Secondly, even though there is a clear distinction between these supreme rulers of the state and the ruled, none the less 'pressures arising from the discontent of the masses who are governed, from the passions by which they are swayed, exert a certain amount of influence on the policies of the political class'.[14] In reality, according to the Moschian scheme, between the extremely limited group of those who control 'the helm of the State' and the ruled masses there exists a special class: the political class, whose function is to carry out and enforce the commands handed down from the top of the social pyramid.

Mosca is acutely aware of the influence which the various social strata exert on one another and of their tendency to intermingle. Thus the head of the state could not possibly govern without the support of the political class. He is able to exert some pressure on it as well as on one or more 'individuals belonging to this class', but 'he certainly cannot be at odds with the class as a whole or do away with it. Even if that were possible, he would at once be compelled to create another, without the support of which action on his part would be completely paralyzed.'[15] On the other hand, the ruled can exert pressure on the political class; however, 'granting that the discontent of the masses might succeed in deposing a ruling class, inevitably ... there would have to be another organized minority within the masses themselves to discharge the functions of a ruling class. Otherwise all organization, and the whole social structure, would be destroyed.'[16]

In the scientific system adopted by Mosca for the *Elementi* the analysis contained in *Teorica* is reproposed, the distinction between at least two layers of the political class being made clearer. The element of stability and continuity is to be found in the second of these layers: it is not located at the top of the state hierarchy but could be described as intermediary, a true 'conveyor-belt' for power, used to transmit commands downwards and requests and complaints upwards.

Another concept which recurs in the *Elementi* is that of organized minority. In our opinion, it should not be interpreted as a diabolical contrivance, the conspiracy of a minority to impose its will on the majority. In some parts of Mosca's work the concept does in fact take on this particular connotation; however, careful analysis shows – as we have already seen – that the expression is used by Mosca, in the sense it has here, to refer in particular to minorities which organize elections. Although this aspect is linked to the formation of the political class, nevertheless it does not fully explain how the latter came into being. More precisely, the concept of organized minority must be related to that organization of society in which the intermediary layer, by nature bureaucratic, occupies most of the power structure. In this regard, there

The scientific system 53

are a series of references in Mosca's analysis in which the concept of political class is closely tied to that of the state. In so doing, Mosca brings about that identification between political class and state which allows him to investigate more thoroughly the ideological justification put forward by the political class to support its own rule: an ideological justification which is always based on a more general moral principle. Leaving aside the origin of the different values which converged historically in the new conception of an actual ruling class (much more complex and socially heterogeneous than the political class described in the first phase of Mosca's research), this moral principle consists in identifying the qualities, carrying out the functions and developing the personal and moral characteristics which justify both some elements of the political class being combined with those of different origins and functions and the exercise of power on the part of the political class. He gives this example to support his line of argument:

Political classes inevitably decline when they cease to find scope for the qualities through which they rose to power or when they lose in importance in the social environment in which they live. So the Roman aristocracy declined when it was no longer the exclusive source of higher officers for the army, of administrators for the Republic, of governors for the provinces. So the Venetian aristocracy declined when its nobles ceased to command the galleys and no longer passed the greater part of their lives in sailing the seas and in trading and fighting.[17]

Compared to the somewhat peremptory empiricism and often simple positivism of *Teorica* the analysis contained in the first edition of the *Elementi* has undoubtedly a more scientific basis. The marked political approach of *Teorica* is filtered and perfected in the first edition of the *Elementi* through the juridical writings of Mosca's early period. Although these appear slightly forced with respect to the author's political vocation and also in some respect 'heretical', from the viewpoint of method and content they none the less form, within the context of the more highly technical discussions by writers on constitutional matters, a very important link in the construction of the Moschian system understood in both political and juridical terms. Thus the work of most importance for Mosca's thinking: the *Elementi di scienza politica*, is enriched by cultural references which are more wide-ranging and systematic; the methodology adopted by Mosca in his approach to politics uses in a modified form several concepts from the theory of evolution by Charles Darwin (1809–92). Perhaps the most typical in this regard is the concept of the 'struggle for pre-eminence', which Mosca applies as an invariable fact in the history of societies and which he almost interprets as a kind of tough but necessary training in the art of civilization for nations and individuals.[18]

In the *Elementi* the concept of political class is seen to be synonymous with real power, with effective government, and should be located and interpreted within the context of that dichotomy which, from this work onwards, is a permanent feature in Mosca's formulation of his doctrine. In line with this dichotomy only two 'types of State' are identified in history (the *feudal* and the *bureaucratic*); they act as archetypes which allow one 'to classify all political organisms'.[19] Furthermore, compared to *Teorica* the *Elementi* introduces the notion of juridical defence which, as we have stated above, forms almost a special body of doctrine in itself within Mosca's more general doctrinal system.

The fifth chapter of the first edition of the *Elementi* outlines the new doctrine, which starts from a careful consideration of the moral sense understood as 'that mass of sentiments by which the natural propensity of human beings to develop their activities and capacities, to satisfy their appetites and impulses, to command and enjoy oneself, is curbed by a natural compassion for the pain or harm that other people may experience from an indulgence of that propensity'.[20] For Mosca the juridical defence consists, above all, in the 'social mechanisms' that regulate the discipline of the moral sense[21] and permit one to reach an understanding of 'a great psychological law which alone can explain why the moral instincts of a people are now more, now less, embodied and developed in its political constitution'.[22] The significance he ascertains in this is that 'the greater or lesser force of moral restraints in all manifestations of social life' forms a genuine standard for assessing a people's level of civilization. So the entire treatment of the theme may be readily approached and read as a mature and very stimulating analysis of the real conditions of governability in modern societies, and as a code of both political and ethical behaviour for the political class.

From our present perspective we are predisposed to view the concept of juridical defence in terms which are too modern relative to the period in which the *Elementi* was published; Mosca is read as a pluralist in whom the juridical-constitutional element is not posited as a presupposition but as the final outcome of that 'balance of the social forces' which James H. Meisel has very appropriately evoked in this respect. But an analysis of this kind, despite its appeal, would take us to far beyond our present concerns. It is sufficient to emphasize that the lines of interpretation which connect, in the writer's heart and mind, his more mature and consciously scientific requirements with the ever present need to be in tune with the political affairs of his age allow us to indicate an element of clear continuity between the two, otherwise distinct, periods of Mosca's thought.

Moreover, in the conclusion to the *Elementi* Mosca also takes the opportunity, with the nineteenth century drawing to a close, to point out

The scientific system

the ideal objectives of an effective government and a tenacious capacity to organize and run society, both now founded – also ethically – on the new doctrine of juridical defence. The adversary to be subdued is no longer the day-to-day degeneration of the parliamentary system against which he polemicized in *Teorica*, but rather the *democratic metaphysics* which risks leading to 'socialism' and eventually 'anarchy',[23] thereby undermining any basis for juridical defence and rendering any notion of government void.

At this point it would be out of place to examine more closely the clearly ideological content in these assertions; they probably form the weakest and most incidental side to the formulation of his ideas in this period.[24] Consequently, we shall limit ourselves to stating that in the Mosca of the *Elementi* the doctrinal element which was taken over from traditional liberalism is still antithetical to any theoretical-practical development in a democratic direction. In fact, the opposition between freedom and equality is here more inflexible than ever. Nevertheless, the concept of political class in the *Elementi* is now developing into the more articulated concept of ruling class,[25] while the function of government and its effective realization finds in the juridical defence its most complete formulation in terms of principles and method as a moment of ethical balance in the relationship between rulers and ruled.

The significance of Mosca's ideas has at this stage been revealed to its full extent and import. We no longer have the indeterminate theoretical-practical system of the 1880s, that is, the open system in which his firmest presuppositions are not general principles of philosophical, ethical or economic origin, nor a generally valid liberal conception of the new Italian state; the 'discoveries' of his early period are now considered to be fixed principles arrived at empirically. We have seen how the young scholar combined different elements and requirements into an original but basically contradictory interpretation of politics. In the *Elementi*, on the other hand, the inspiration and the intention are quite different: the political class is situated in the dialectical reality of social life and the state; power is no longer founded in a reality viewed exclusively as a series of facts and mediated solely by the political formula; and the basis on which power is justified is still a political formula, but this is now what philosophers of law generally call 'principle of sovereignty'. As a result, in this later work Mosca identifies the political formula more clearly with this principle, which is not, however, the abstractly ideological and mystifying principle which he claims to have noted on several occasions.

The new significance of the political formula

Basically, Mosca's intention is to put right a deficiency in *Teorica*, above all by means of the political formula and its multiple layers of meaning. As we have indicated, the deficiency emerges at that point where, pointing to the reciprocal nature of the connection between political class and political formula, he nevertheless maintains that it is always the political class which determines the values expressed by the formula and not the formula which determines the formation of the political class. By institutionalizing the political class within the state (it is no accident that Mosca here uses a variety of terms: ruling class, dominant class, governing class, *ceto civile*: the latter a ruling group conceived on the model of the English gentry, and so on) and making a connection between the formula in the sense of a real instrument of ideological homogeneity and social classes, as well as through the formula being understood as a principle of legitimacy and sovereignty for the hegemonic group within the political class, a close link is established between all these different elements. In fact, each political class has its origin in a social structure which expresses one unified culture and morality (today this would be seen in anthropological terms) deriving from common beliefs and ideas, that is, from a common ideology.

In this way, Mosca breaks down the formal one-dimensional rigidity of political class and political formula, recasting them in a dialectical relationship between social groups and ideologies which objectively pinpoints the most characteristic facts about the life of society. Always keen to point out that he has never failed to make a clear distinction between the *art of politics* (which in his opinion inspired Machiavelli) and the *science of politics* (which guided him in his research and writing), Mosca takes great pains to link this varied dialectical relationship to the historical and juridical reality of social organization; its stability and order constitute a guarantee that there will be an effective improvement in people's lives. In Mosca's view, the political class should not look for points of reference in a 'culture that is wholly abstract and conventional'[26] but pursue 'a sound and accurate knowledge of human nature'.[27] The political class must not fall into the error of being 'closed, in actual fact if not legally, to elements rising from the lower classes. In the lower classes the hard necessities of life, the daily bitter scramble for sustenance, the lack of a humanistic education keep the primordial instincts of struggle and the unfailing ruggedness of human nature alive.'[28] When the political class is isolated, it loses 'its ability to provide against its own dangers and those of society, which has the misfortune to be run by it'.[29] In other words, when the political class is no longer the expression of a social force, as when the state no longer rests on a consensus which brings together ideological motives and real social forces, society has lost its ability to deal with 'the slightest disturbance'; and 'the changes that a strong and intelligent political class would have carried out at a negligible cost in wealth, blood and human dignity take on the proportions of a social cataclysm'.[30]

The results of the scientific and ideological system

We now have a clear idea of the practical end of Moschian 'science' and the aim of his research as formulated in the *Elementi* is well defined: to outline the development of public life and social struggle as the continuous strengthening of the political class through a permanent process of osmosis with the rest of society. At a methodological and conceptual level the *Elementi* represents the definitive fusing of the facts most closely linked to his doctrine and his more pronounced ideological motives. He gives his convictions definite shape through a historical comparison:

One should note, as an example, that in the course of the nineteenth century England adopted peacefully and without violent shocks almost all the basic civil and political reforms that France paid so heavily to achieve through the Great Revolution. Undeniably the advantage of England lay in the greater energy, the greater practical wisdom, the better political training, possessed by her ruling class.[31]

Furthermore, Mosca's political attitude also emerges in a definitive form in the *Elementi*. This work contains a body of doctrine which brings together not only the elements of his analysis, but also certainties and proposals derived from his conservative instinct. Though he always remained true to this basic trait in his character, he was able to enrich his general outlook by profiting from his personal experience, as well as that of work and academic life, in Rome and Turin.

By way of a general comparison, it could be said that *Teorica* mirrors a political situation in Italy which was static and highly confusing. During the period of the open system (in the 1880s), the scholar carried out an extensive analysis which summarized the themes of a wide-ranging and complex, social and political debate taking place at the time, as well as his theoretical convictions and the results of his empirical research. In the first highly charged decades after the unification of Italy, the early Mosca was able to make out a class (the political class composed of the learned, well-off lower and middle bourgeoisie) which mediated between the numerous rural populace, in many cases still nostalgic for past regimes or ready to give riotous expression to Messianic hopes, and the upper bourgeoisie and aristocracy, the classes that dominated the country socially, economically and politically. In this phase the state is vaguely defined as a mainly organizational and administrative apparatus, effective only in terms of its solidity and iron authoritarianism. In this context, Mosca's ideology is mostly an independent product, derived from personal considerations of daily life – still very provincial – in the Italy of that period. As we have already mentioned, Mosca was never provincial in his outlook; none the less, he expresses the conditions of a provincial Italy compared to the great political and cultural developments in Europe and the world during the second half of the nineteenth century. At a time when the labour movement was beginning to adopt historical materialism as its own class ideology in opposition to the bourgeoisie, few references can be found in his early works to the modern, capitalist, bourgeois economy; the connections he makes between economics and politics are schematic and merely intuitive; his consideration of European history during the last hundred years is quite limited; and lastly, there is no persuasive analysis of the industrial society which was being formed in Italy. As we have noted on several occasions, Mosca's class motivation has a predominantly psychological basis, and this is firmly bound up with his experience as a southern bourgeois intellectual – he belonged to a part of Italy which was still tied to precapitalist economic forms and to a traditional type of agriculture.

In the 1890s, on the other hand, despite the clear continuity with his earlier convictions and language, Mosca felt compelled within a greatly changed political and social framework and on the basis of his own personal development to reformulate his doctrine in a systematic manner. Within the space of a decade Italy went from the confused adventurism of Crispi to the experience of reformist liberalism, to the rise and consolidation of the socialist movement and workers' organizations, and to the adoption of universal suffrage in 1912. This was the social context, profoundly different from the basically static reality of the first years of Italian unity, in which the scholar reformulated the concepts of political class and political formula into an organic system, linked closely to the ethical, theoretical and practical construct represented by the juridical defence. The result from combining these different elements was the formation of the Moschian scientific system, which also takes on the features of a *true political doctrine*, a fully comprehensive ideology based on bourgeois values.

The political goal of this complex intellectual operation is openly declared by Mosca when he points to socialism as the logical development and future projection of mistaken democratic theories and sets political science the clear task of challenging such ideas and establishing the real facts. He says:

In the world in which we are living, socialism will be stopped only if a realistic political science succeeds in demolishing the metaphysical and optimistic methods that prevail at present in social studies; in other words, only if discovery and demonstration of the great constant laws that manifest themselves in all human societies succeed in making visible to the eye the impossibility of realizing the democratic ideal. On this condition, and on this condition only, will the intellectual classes escape the influence of Social Democracy and form an invincible barrier to its triumph.[32]

It is interesting to consider Mosca's approach in the light of what Friedrich Engels (1810–95) wrote, during the same period, in the preface to the Milan edition of the *Communist Manifesto*. Engels maintains that

the first capitalist nation was Italy. The close of the feudal Middle Ages and the beginnings of the modern capitalist era were marked by the giant figure of an Italian: Dante, both poet of the Middle Ages and the first modern poet. Today, as in 1300, a new historical age is dawning. Will Italy give us the new Dante to mark the birth of the proletarian age?[33]

It is a truly singular fact that whereas Marx and Engels had a highly dialectical vision of the rise of the bourgeoisie and of its ethical values, summed up in their recognition that 'the bourgeoisie has played a supremely revolutionary role in history',[34] Mosca's vision is totally absorbed by the anxiety he felt about the relations between social classes. Even where his thinking is most developed, the 'difficult task' of political science is seen as that of resisting the pressures from the most conscious sections of the popular classes to focus attention on the idea of a new political class in a thoroughly reformed society. The optimism of the political forces which relate in different ways to the two dominant social and economic factors, the central protagonists of the modern world: the industrial bourgeoisie and the proletariat, is opposed by Mosca's bitter scepticism rooted in a long-standing, cultural and human experience.

The scholar expresses – as does his culture – a way of thinking typical of and peculiar to the Mediterranean world to which he belonged by birth, education and temperament. Faced with the exciting conquests of modern man it underlines the lasting antithesis between man and society, instinct and reason: an Old Testament vision of social relationships in which evil, destruction and the undermining of all values form an ever present threat and the individual is bound by morality only to the extent that society is able to intervene and, above all, to repress. This is most probably the origin of that fundamentally pessimistic vision of human and political relationships which, although it did not lead Mosca to adopt radical political positions, nevertheless throws a shadow of equivocation over his theoretical work. Even if we can explain the reasons behind it, such equivocation is not an unimportant factor in assessing the real state of confusion not only of one, but of many intellectuals and wide sectors of the middle bourgeoisie. They lived in a country which at that time still had a precapitalist structure and in a society based on scepticism and mistrust. Its educated classes were too accustomed to looking back over the millennia of their ancient and more recent history to be capable of really participating in the everyday events which were laying the foundations in Europe and America of a totally different world.

From the science of counter-revolution to ideological anti-socialism

It is interesting to note that when dealing in the *Elementi* with the spread of socialist ideas in Italy, Mosca refers with enthusiasm to the pamphlet of a democratic radical like Guglielmo Ferrero entitled *Reazione* (1895). It has recently been brought to light that there existed a deep friendship and mutual admiration between the two men for over thirty years in spite of the great differences in their assessments of political phenomena and in their practical activities. Mosca never had a profound and direct knowledge of Marxism and based his judgements about the socialist movement on, above all, the economistic and evolutionary interpretation of Marxist thought provided in Italy by the economist Achille Loria (1857–1943). So he was struck by the way in which the socialist movement was interpreted by Ferrero who, in total contrast, had a direct link with socialism through his mentor and father-in-law, the psychologist Cesare Lombroso. According to Ferrero,

there are always a certain number of individuals who feel the need to get excited about something that is not immediate and personal to them, something that lies at a distance. Their own affairs, the problems of science or of art, are not enough to absorb all their spiritual activity. What else was there for them in Italy except the socialist idea? It came from far away which always has an enticing effect. It was sufficiently complex and vague, at least in certain of its aspects, to satisfy the widely differing moral needs of its many proselytes. On the one hand it brought a broad spirit of brotherhood and international feeling, which corresponded to a real modern need. On the other, it had a suggestion of scientific method that was reassuring to minds educated according to the scientific experimental method. Given all that, it is no wonder that a great number of young men joined a movement in which there may have been the danger of meeting some lowly ex-convict or petty habitual criminal, but in which one steered clear, at least, of speculators, political grafters, professional patriots and the whole crew of unscrupulous adventurers who, having made Italy, were now devouring it. The most cursory examination shows at once that in no part of Italy do the conditions exist for the formation of a genuine and sizeable Socialist Party. Moreover, it is logical for a Socialist Party to find the nucleus of its recruits among the bourgeoisie as happened in Italy. If a Socialist Party has developed under such unfavourable conditions and in so illogical a fashion, it must be because more than any other movement it answers a moral need in a certain number of young people sick of so much corruption, baseness and cowardice; young people who would sell their souls to the devil just to get away from the old parties which are rotten to the core.[35]

Mosca subscribes to this evaluation by Ferrero, which highlights the moral basis (by no means negligible) of the political movement that in Italy took its cue from socialism. Ferrero's approach was very much in line with Mosca's methodology and way of thinking and inspired by very similar sentiments. It would therefore be mistaken to think that Mosca ignored or failed to understand the deep-rooted political and social demands at the heart of the socialist movement. In the conclusion to the first edition of the *Elementi* in particular, he makes a great effort to give an overall interpretation of socialist doctrines not so much in terms of their theoretical foundations, but more in consideration of their political development on a social and psychological level. He believes that the most evident factors which underlie socialist doctrines and ensure their spread and influence are the European revolutionary tradition in the eighteenth and nineteenth century; the 'great current of ideas and passions' which move many generous people to help the most underprivileged classes; the incompetence and corruption of the ruling classes; the weakening of religious feelings; 'the injustices and hypocrisies of parliamentary systems'; public and private poverty 'caused by excessive taxation, large-scale debt and too much unproductive expenditure; and lastly, 'the present arrangements in secondary and higher education that have turned the schools into factories producing misfits'.[36]

Despite the fact that he lacked an analytical knowledge of Karl Marx's work, Mosca nevertheless had a great capacity to grasp its most significant political aspects. A particularly good example is his treatment of class struggle; he believes it to be 'based on an incomplete, one-sided and biased examination of history'.[37] He does not at all deny that men are divided into exploiters and exploited, but passes over the economic basis for such a division; he specifies that 'parasites and exploiters exist in all social strata, just as there are those who are exploited at all levels on the economic and social ladder'.[38] His attempt at interpretation here reaches its limit in a moralistic judgement in which he stresses that

> at one time the exploited were called the good, the honest, the courteous, the decent, the industrious and the temperate, and the exploiters were called sinners, idlers, cowards, schemers, rascals and criminals. One may call them what one will. Perhaps it is not a bad idea to have just two expressions to synthesize the multiple categories that make up the two classes which have always existed and, alas, always will exist in the world.[39]

This judgement summarizes the writer's general human understanding with regard to the matters which the socialist movement was bringing to light not only through its forceful doctrine, but also by means of its moral, political and organizational strength. Given this, however, what Mosca is attacking at the roots are the very assumptions of socialist doctrine. He firmly maintains that 'even granting the fact that collectivists and anarchists may chance to be victorious and gain control of political authority in a number of countries, the carrying out of their programme would still be *impossible*; for the postulates of collectivism, communism and anarchy can never be put into practice'.[40] This is how he expresses his idea that it is a great mistake to take one's cue from political ideas which strive for the impossible: in other words, to try and alter 'the constant laws that regulate the organization of human societies, laws which would inevitably assert themselves in the end and triumph'.[41]

It is also worth noting Mosca's view that rather than from the social and political situation, it is from the moral climate that socialism draws its 'vital strength', a climate 'prepared by all the rancours, ambitions and greeds which are the necessary consequence of a long revolutionary period and the changes in fortune associated with it'.[12] The conclusion drawn at the cultural level is that it is more than anything else a question of 'an intellectual malady of our age',[43] whereas at the political and theoretical level it is clear that the same sort of 'ideas and sentiments which produced parliamentary democracy 'lead inexorably to socialism and eventually anarchy'. Such a conclusion is in keeping with all the presuppositions of Mosca's overall system summarized in this study: one must not only engage in politics and be active in Parliament, but also be conscious of the fact that

> democratic doctrine has rendered undeniable services to civilization. Embodied in the representative system, for which England set the pattern, it has contributed to important improvements in juridical defence, which have been attained through a system of free discussion that has been established in many parts of Europe. But now that we have come to its last logical implication, and

men are trying to realize the principles on which it was based down to their remotest consequences, the same doctrine is disorganizing the countries in which it prevails and forcing them into decline.[44]

This is a telling example which reveals Mosca's convictions; it shows how they were directed towards challenging any *postulate of equality* between men and reasserting that 'absolute equality has never existed in human societies. Political power never has been, and never will be, founded on the explicit consent of majorities. It always has been, and it always will be, exercised by organized minorities which have had, and will have the means, varying at times, to impose their supremacy on the multitude.'[45] The direct conclusion drawn by Mosca from all this is the one which has already been referred to above: 'positive political science' must 'demolish metaphysical thought' and reveal 'the absurdity of the democratic conception'.[46]

However, one should be very wary of drawing the conclusion that Mosca was anti-liberal as well as anti-socialist. There is no basis to such a notion, since his intention was to 'consider the labour movement' – which according to Gobetti, the most lucid of the young Italian liberals in the first years of the twentieth century, was becoming 'the natural heir to the liberating function previously carried out by the bourgeoisie' – solely in terms of his own enlightened and conservative, but strongly liberal reformism. In fact, referring to the distinction between 'utilitarian liberalism' and 'ethical liberalism' we may say that Mosca desired to reconcile the two essential inspirations behind liberal thought. His *comprehensive system* appears to be illuminated simultaneously by the values of individualistic utilitarianism, conservative reformism and an elevated sense of justice expressed in his considerable faith in the state.

It must be remembered that Mosca hoped that the bourgeois classes would achieve a stable organization and that an ideology of social co-operation guaranteed by the state would be developed, based on the hegemony of the middle bourgeoisie. In other words, he was putting forward a pale substitute for the class struggle, which would however involve wide sectors of the petty and middle bourgeoisie in the far-reaching changes that were taking place in Italian society during the first two decades of the 1900s. This is the area in which Mosca's most constructive achievement from a political point of view (the concept of 'juridical defence') was ineffectual. Its failure was not theoretical but political in as far as it was totally unable to grasp those aspects which characterized an epoch of great social mobilization, growing political and social maturity and radical modification to the traditional type of political struggle in contrast to the first decades following the creation of a unified Italian state. Here we once more come across the shift from an analytical scientific approach to deeply felt political considerations, and this points to the strengthening in Mosca of a hard core of ideological anti-socialism, the roots of which lie in his most steadfast conviction: the antithesis between liberalism and democracy.

In Mosca's concept of juridical defence an attempt is made in a liberal key to link politics and morality. In fact, this authentic Moschian doctrine of the state is founded on a very precise ethical-political element: the stated and defended value (well-known in political speculation: see Hobbes!) of *social order*, the protection of the individual and his property from riotous civil strife and anarchy, and the inescapable need for morality to be safeguarded in the practice of human, social and political relationships, and not only in each individual's conscience. This position arises theoretically from the antithesis – mentioned above – constantly present in Mosca's thinking and pervading his entire doctrine, and from his interpretation of liberalism and democracy, both conceived as authentic political formulas which sum up both ethical values and social practice. So to talk of Mosca's 'Machiavellianism' is inexact and misleading. It is true that Mosca was a realist and, like Machiavelli, insisted on sticking to the 'facts'; but is this enough to make a connection within a modern perspective between Mosca's system and the thinking of the Florentine writer? We believe that there is no foundation to this idea, since Mosca's work is a response to entirely different demands. His aim is to use a realistic approach in order to achieve an authentically liberal, political synthesis. His liberalism is, then, an ethical-political position, a world of clear secular values, a general doctrine of society and the political mechanism, a codified *moral sense* deriving from the requirements of public spirit. Consequently, his rejection of the Jacobin formula for democracy is theoretical as well as ethical; and his acceptance of the concrete historical-political experience of English liberalism represents the adherence to a morality and a politics which originate in real men whose adaption to the times, development and readiness to change draws on a variety of contributions while respecting basic differences. So it is Mosca's realism that is the truly 'Machiavellian' element picked up from the Florentine secretary's work.

Thus the formulation of ideas to be found in the *Elementi*, put forward at the end of the nineteenth century in Italy, assumes a fully ideological and symbolic significance as the scholar's personal response to the questions that had been posed since the century's beginning.

6

From the nineteenth to the twentieth century – political commitment and parliamentary experience

The years of direct political commitment occupy a clearly defined and by no means negligible part of Mosca's life. These seventeen years of fervent activity saw the scholar participate in the election campaigns of 1909 and 1913, sit in the Chamber of Deputies – on the Right – during the XXIII and XXIV legislatures, gain ministerial experience in the Government led by Antonio Salandra and, finally, become a Senator in 1919.

At the elections of 7–14 March 1909 Mosca succeeded Antonio Starrabba, Marquis of Di Rudinì, who had died in August 1908, as the representative for the Sicilian constituency of Caccamo in the Province of Palermo. This constituency had a population of 57,268 and was divided into 12 communes and 28 electoral divisions; the number of persons entitled to vote was 3391 and those who actually voted numbered 2249. Mosca's opponent was a clerical conservative, Prince Giuseppe Spadafora di Policastrello, almost the same age as Mosca and a councillor for the province of Palermo. The result was a victory for Mosca with 1260 votes against 964 for Spadafora.[1] In a profile of the newly elected deputies which appeared in *L'Illustrazione Italiana* the following was said about the new representative for Caccamo:

Everything one can say about the successful candidate in the Marquis of Di Rudinì's old constituency, Professor Gaetano Mosca, is contained in the following written for the *Giornale di Sicilia* by Cesare Lombroso: 'Although a convinced believer in socialism, I must express my best wishes to the successful candidate, Gaetano Mosca, despite his being a tenacious conservative. But few men combine as Mosca does such powerful thinking, broad culture and commendable honesty, together with great sensitivity. Men like this are too rare in Italian politics for us not to desire their victory, whatever side they may be on'.[2]

Lombroso's authoritative intervention is an example of human and intellectual solidarity which disregards partisan discrimination. This electoral success demonstrated that the scholar Mosca was able to win over the best part of the Marquis of Di Rudinì's support on an openly moderate-liberal platform; and this despite the fact that he lived in Turin and was out of touch with life in the constituency (he did, however, have a connection with the area: his wife's family originated from the large town of Montemaggiore Belsito). The electoral contest was a clear struggle between conservatives and moderates; rather than for the big landowner the voters opted for the intellectual: 'the lawyer, professor of constitutional law, political journalist' and 'contributor to the *Corriere della Sera*', as he was described in a biographical note at that time.[3]

At the following elections of 26 October to 2 November 1913, the first with universal suffrage, Mosca defeated his opponent, Spadafora, by an overwhelming majority. By this time the electorate had swollen to 17,883 of whom only 9217 cast their vote. The number of votes declared valid were 8881: 5944 for Mosca and 2761 for Spadafora.[4] It was a crushing victory and confirmed the effectiveness of Mosca's political and parliamentary activity during his first legislature[5] – his public appearances were as a *moderato ministeriale*: a conservative who for the most part supported Giolitti's reformist policies. Mosca's parliamentary activity during the XXIII legislature followed several clear lines which determined the manner in which he carried out his mandate. In the first place, he made some sweeping political interventions on the Italian colonies in Cyrenaica and Tripolitania (23 February 1912), reform of political elections (7 and 14 May 1912) and the Treaty of Lausanne with Turkey (3 December 1912). Secondly, Mosca was at his most insistent in debates concerning the state budget. He often intervened with detailed analyses and also indicated practical solutions to the different problems he raised and discussed. Lastly, there was the occasional, meticulous intervention in the form of questions and interpellations, especially – though not exclusively – with regard to matters which closely affected his constituency and Sicily.

Alongside his duties in Parliament Mosca continued his outside political activity by writing for the *Corriere* and, from 1911 to 1912, for the *Tribuna* as well, though he much preferred the Milanese daily.[6] The main themes to which the scholar directed his efforts as a deputy and as a political journalist were essentially those centered around the war with Libya and the workings of parliamentary institutions. A brief examination of these themes will serve as a link and critical comparison between his doctrinal and theoretical approach and his practical activity.

The first important subject with which the newly elected deputy put himself to the test was colonial policy. In 1912 he published the short work

Italia e Libia. Considerazioni politiche [*Political Considerations on Italy and Libya*] (Milano, Treves), which Gaetano Salvemini (1873–1957) judged 'excellent' because 'it summarizes in a few words and with remarkable clarity and seriouness what can be said with the greatest certainty about the new Italian colony, given the present state of our knowledge.'[7] The book consisted of three articles which had appeared in the *Tribuna* on 20, 21, 22 September 1911 and three from the *Corriere della Sera* of 2, 3 January and 20 February 1912; the unpublished essay '*Oggi e domani*' ['Today and Tomorrow'] (dated 12 April 1912) in which Mosca furnishes a synthesis of the most salient facts about the war and the problems posed by the conquest of Libya was added as a conclusion. However, although these are very important and interesting sources for an understanding of Mosca's more direct political and parliamentary involvement, we do not intend to dwell on the the various interventions relating to colonial matters.[8] What is worth underlining, however, is that behind Mosca's political activity spanning the nineteenth and twentieth century there lay a keen awareness of the social and ethical problems which were besetting Italy.

Against universal suffrage, 1912

In the second decade of the twentieth century Italy found itself in a new situation as a result of Giovanni Giolitti's policies. Even when their leading exponent was not directly in power (the second Giolitti Government lasted from 9 November 1903 to 16 March 1905 and the third from 27 May 1906 to 10 December 1909) these policies led to much zealous activity, widespread intiative and great general interest. The new situation also had its origin in a particularly intense social struggle in which the leadership of the Socialist Party gained increasing consent, and this introduced an element of intense political dialectic into the besieged citadel which was and is the liberal state.

Mosca's general horizon, however, extended no further than that of an enlightened reformism which he also illustrated and commented on in articles he wrote for the *Corriere della Sera*. Appearing between 1909 and 1913, they were nearly all dedicated to the problems of electoral reform, the excessive power of the trade unions, which was giving rise to a new 'functional feudalism', and colonial policy. The conviction which helped Mosca to navigate the political waters of the period is essentially contained in his assertion that one must examine 'the substance of social facts behind the legal form', since

the proclamation of individual rights was realized in a Constitution or Charter in which the separation of powers in the State was also ratified and more or less wide powers were granted to the elected Chambers. All of this would, however, have remained on the drawing-board if in those countries which adopted representative systems there had not existed forces capable of leadership; and by leadership I mean intellectually, morally and economically superior men who were independent of the bureaucracy, able to control and limit its powers, and collaborate in a useful manner for the public good. Without these leading forces outside of the bureaucracy, the Constitution or Charter would never have been conceded or, if conceded, it would have had no practical effect. This is because the separation of powers has no meaning unless it is accompanied by a variety of different political forces, and unless behind every organ of the State lies an important section of the class which is able to run society politically and from which the respective State organ draws vitality and sustenance.[9]

What must not be left out of consideration is the fact that according to Mosca

the modern representative State also contains the seeds of its own destruction and, not to beat about the bush, one of the most dreaded of these is the obsessive and limitless extending of the State's powers and those of its local appendages. Apart from the waste of resources to which it may and does give rise, as has been demonstrated many times, this immoderate expansion inevitably absorbs new economic and intellectual forces which are siphoned off by the bureaucracy from the non-bureaucratic classes. In this way a shift is produced in that social equilibrium which is an indispensable precondition for the balance between forces in the political sphere... In Latin America and Europe as well, there are plenty of examples of countries where the adoption of representative government has failed to do away completely with arbitrary acts on the part of the rulers, because society lacks the guiding force to control the action of civil servants and the military. At the very most, if an opposition is formed, it is almost exclusively recruited from among those who desire to become in turn employees of the State. And if we look at our own country, we immediately see that the regions where the Government, of whatever colour, is quite easily able to ensure itself of a good majority at every election are precisely those in which little private wealth has been accumulated and the intelligent and cultured have no other better career open to them than that of State employee.[10]

There is a growing tendency in Mosca to link his conception of representative institutions with a clear-cut rejection of those class interests which, as he puts it, lead to 'functional feudalism'. By this he means the type of 'social disorganization' which was typical in medieval Europe and which occurred 'whenever moral bonds were loosened and cast off, and with them the political bonds which held human society together'.[11] In particular, the scholar maintains that the new feudalism arises

when the workers' trade-unions, and especially those of public employees, demand obedience from and impose it on their members, even if this is the equivalent of open rebellion against the hierarchical social order and the law; when only yesterday the trade-unions negotiated on equal terms with the representatives of legitimate authority and today would like to crush them, it is clear that we are faced with a type of behaviour which, though its objectives are different, is very much like that of the old feudal barons in the choice of means.[12]

This way of understanding and tackling the problems of domestic politics is very far, on both a cultural and intellectual level, from that adopted by Giolitti. Although in the Chamber of Deputies Mosca sat among the myriad of groups making up the Liberal Party and by that very fact found himself on the government side of the assembly, several essential facts eluded his attention; in the first place, the dynamic nature of Giolittian policy, which was not at all opposed to socialism and emergent political Catholicism. On the contrary, Giolitti inclined towards a privileged political and parliamentary relationship with reformist socialism (by uncoupling it from its revolutionary wing) and towards using Catholic influence to bolster his policies at elections and in Parliament (in this case, by isolating the remaining advocates of the Catholic Church's political power over society and the state: a position known as clericalism). Mosca's position, on the other hand, reflected a static model of liberalism, even if his doctrinal and theoretical analysis was much more flexible and free of bias than his political actions. His form of liberalism was not related to 'democracy'. It was conservative in nature; in fact, from the outset of his parliamentary career he insisted on defining himself purely and simply a *conservative*.[13] And in the debate on electoral reform he adopted a consistent position which marked a complete separation and clear isolation not only from the Giolittian parliamentary majority, but also from the political positions expressed by Sidney Sonnino (1847–1922), the very leader of Italian conservatism. Together with Angelo Papadopoli (1843–1919), former patriot and conspirator against Austria, he declared his disagreement not only with the extension of the franchise, but also with the new element introduced by Giolitti's reform: the payment of salaries to deputies who until then had always carried out their duties without recompense.

Mosca's position is summarized very clearly in his speech to the Chamber on 7 May 1912. He starts off by stating the premise from which it is necessary to begin and which corresponds to his own conception of public life: 'In my opinion, ability in politics is firstly and above all the capacity to perceive the important questions of national interest. Today, unfortunately, this quality is not very widespread among the electorate, which does feel passionately about important national issues, but is also strongly influenced by local and class interests.'[14] The first obstacle to reform originates precisely at this point, from the 'millions and millions of illiterates' who are joining the electorate and certainly not improving 'its propensity... to understand the great questions of national life'.[15] Furthermore, Mosca used the occasion of the debate to develop his criticism according to the convictions derived from his doctrine of juridical defence. What he maintains is that parliamentary representation is of value if it does not register an imbalance 'between the predominant currents of ideas and interests in the Chamber',[16] for 'when all political forces in the country are fairly represented, we have a good system of election to the Chamber; not the best, because perfection can never be attained. When, on the other hand, there is some discrepancy between the legal country and the real country, then we have an electoral system which is defective and needs adjusting.'[17]

Even though his speech may appear contradictory, Mosca is consistent with the more scientific and systematic approach he had already defined in the *Elementi di scienza politica*. There is no doubt that, at a theoretical level, many of the positions worked out previously, especially in *Sulla teorica dei governi e sul governo parlamentare*, had undergone considerable modification. Indeed, the scholar acknowledges that the electoral law of 1882 (revised in 1895), which he had greatly criticized in the past, shows 'great political wisdom'. He now holds that it

established potentially universal suffrage. It permitted all those who were passionately interested in politics and public affairs to enter public life, to become part of the electorate with the minimum of effort. The fact that this law was an act of profound political wisdom, that it truly satisfied all the main interests in the country is demonstrated by the great calm with which the present electoral law has been received, by the general indifference in the country, which is also reflected in the Chamber. If there were really an imbalance between the political currents in the country and those represented in the Chamber, you can well believe that the country would be passionately for or against the bill we are in the process of debating. But since with the existing law all political parties have been able to make their presence felt and all those interested in public life can enter it – only the non-political remain outside – the people are unable to relate to the present reform.[18]

This judgement is not easy to reconcile with those expressed in his early work, which was aimed at demonstrating the contradiction between the 'real country' and the 'legal country', at showing the 'fictitious' nature of parliamentary representation understood as the representation of the country's moods, interests and aspirations. It can be seen, therefore, that Mosca was very willing to criticize and revise his work in the light of actual experience. He then goes on to assert that electoral reform will have no effect whatsoever on Italian political life, but that it contains a 'great threat' to the state by effectively lending considerable weight to the 'big associations of public employees'.[19]

The reasons more directly concerned with the workings of political institutions which explain Mosca's negative vote can be summed up in the view that

> as long as the majority remains the majority it must govern, and in order to govern smoothly it needs to be united and strong. The only duty of minorities, on the other hand, is to act as a check on the Government, to discuss in public all the Government's actions; and to achieve this, is it really necessary for the minority to be represented in proportion to the number of effective voters? Even if a minority has ten or twenty votes less, it can still fulfil its duty most adequately whereas a weak majority has difficulty in carrying out its task of giving strength and authority to the Government.[20]

This is Mosca's parliamentary position expressed in all its aspects (and also, it must be said, in all its abstractness). By this time the politically active popular forces in the country, which Giolittian reformism was attempting somehow or other to involve in the administering of the state, were the socialist workers and agricultural labourers and the Catholic peasant leagues. Through his unwillingness to carry out a detailed and realistic analysis of these forces Mosca proved himself to be the advocate of a state structure which, it is true, was solid and authoritative but no longer a viable proposition. Essentially, what he asserted in the Chamber was a political conception that could only be imposed abstractly on particular social groups and classes. It was the recurring *myth* of an idealized political class, which basically hinged on the country's educated middle class; in his parliamentary solitude Mosca appeared to be almost the epigone of this class.

In line with this stance in Parliament Mosca also declared his opposition to female suffrage during the debate on the new electoral law (1912). This is not the right place to go into the reasons put forward in support of his position. It is sufficient to say by way of conclusion in this regard that Mosca's political conservatism was of an excessively radical nature in the general debate on female and universal suffrage. In our opinion, this derived from the strong social considerations aroused by the subject. In reality, by dealing with the matter of electoral reform, the Italian political class of the period subjected itself to a true examination in public of its own values and convictions. An examination which, all in all, showed a greater maturity and boldness on the part of the parliamentary majority than in the case of students of political matters like Mosca. Nevertheless, the position taken up – immediately afterwards – by Giolitti and his majority in the face of the Libyan war and, above all, of the First World War unfortunately confirmed the purely tactical nature of this courageous capacity to consider the future of Italy in terms of widespread democratic participation. It also pointed to the collapse of previously professed values when human passions and the irrational were unleashed.

The great crisis in the Italian liberal political system, 1919–1922

The 1913 elections witnessed the simultaneous occurrence of two important events: the extension of the suffrage and the re-election of Mosca with the substantial majority referred to above. Thus began one of the longest legislatures in the history of the Kingdom of Italy, the XXIV (from 27 November 1913 to 28 September 1919), in the course of which the country went through the traumatic experience of a world war. The first phase of this trauma took the form of uncertainty about domestic and international policy, giving rise to agonizing conflict between neutralists and interventionists. This was followed by the harrowing experience of a very long and bloody armed conflict in which the country successfully passed through the test and showed that it had acquired a by no means negligible military capacity and a solid state structure.

During these years in which, given the exceptional circumstances, the XXIV legislature was extended *de iure* the two Russian Revolutions of February and, more importantly, November took place. The latter marked the definitive overthrow of the *ancien régime* within the immense Russian Empire and the birth of the first communist state. At the end of the First World War the world was no longer the same as before. The balance between the European powers, established at Vienna a hundred years previously and modified gradually but never upset, had been radically modified. The bourgeois world went through a very deep and intense crisis from the social and economic point of view as well as that of ideals and spiritual values. The new Soviet power and the reactionary states opposing it (represented by Italian Fascism, German Nazism and the authoritarian regimes proliferating in Europe and beyond) also bore witness to the participation of wide sectors of the population in the life of the state. This was in line with the new logic of incorporating the masses and with a new dimension of power aimed at concentrating and governing in harness political consent, economic activity, the ends of the state and those of its citizens. In Italy the first disturbing blow against Giolitti's carefully constructed system of balances was dealt immediately after the 1913 elections had confirmed the success of the Piedmontese statesman. It came in the form of the choices which the country was forced to make in its international policy at the outbreak of war in August 1914. Italy would enter the war on the side of France and England in May 1915.

This was the general political context within which the alternative to Giolitti materialized in the shape of the new Prime Minister, Antonio Salandra. Giolitti's reformist policies were increasingly opposed by the new leader's 'nationalist policy', the paradox being that Salandra was a creation of 'the long Giolittian regime';[21] through the pressure exerted to make the different liberal factions agree he had found himself on the side of the Chamber identified with the Giolittian majority. However, what changed when the Salandra Government took over (21 March 1914) was the underlying political inspiration. The strengthening of the Liberal Party through the adoption of Salandra's policies meant that the heirs of the Risorgimento Left (the radicals) had to be relegated to a marginal role and the agreement with the Catholics made more binding. Historians have underlined the fact that the conservative tone of the new Prime Minister represented a considerable moral and political change. In fact, Salandra's statement in the Chamber immediately after the elections that 'the flame, the idealist heart of Italian liberalism is patriotism...' also implied an advance to the nationalists. With regard to economic matters, Salandra had already expressed his very intransigent opinions. In the debate on the life insurance monopoly he acted as the true spokesman for the opposition and raised once more the fundamental questions. He praised in vibrant terms 'free enterprise', the 'unhindered ... accumulation of capital' in opposition to state interference in the economy, to 'State capitalism', the 'State as dispenser of credit', the 'paternalistic State' and to 'bureaucratic feudalism'. He did in fact acknowledge the relative benefits from the Deposit and Loan Fund [run by the state – translator's note], but 'only as an extreme limit which should not be crossed'.[22]

In this changed political framework Mosca found a clearer role and a political inspiration ideologically congenial to his own approach. He began his new term as a re-elected deputy and had his first direct experience in government as Under-Secretary for the Colonies during the periods 23 March to 5 November 1914 and 6 November 1914 to 18 June 1916. Mosca's political commitment was now expressed mainly at a ministerial level; his involvement was continuous and systematic (as Under-Secretary he chaired the Colonial Committee, among other things) and lasted for more than two years at an exceptional time when the First World War was making it extremely difficult for Italy to maintain its recent conquest of Libya. On the whole, therefore, Mosca's parliamentary activity as a deputy throughout the entire XXIV Legislature was quite limited. However, it is worth recalling, almost as a conclusion to his participation in the Chamber of Deputies (which he would leave after the war on being nominated Senator on 9 December 1919), the speech he made on the reform of political elections which introduced proportional representation with list-voting and the position he took up on the events in Fiume, the free city which had been occupied by the nationalist poet Gabriele D'Annunzio (1863–1938) and his voluntary troops.

The world had been profoundly changed by the First World War. Men had been affected psychologically and in their mode of behaviour by the 'great slaughter', the biggest and most devastating war which mankind had so far experienced. The 'post-war period' was a very hard time as well: a combination of disappointed hopes, great discomfort, a far-reaching social and economic crisis, the overturning of ideals and spiritual values and the birth of a new reality. This general situation is reflected in the speech Mosca made in the Chamber on 19 July 1919 concerning electoral reform. In addition to his firm conviction that the new reform is theoretically invalid,[23] he makes several judgements of a political and psychological kind which show a much keener political ability, a greater tactical awareness and a less schematic approach than in the past. His analysis of the war and its aftermath is very acutely based on moral motives, but also on accurate observation of reality. Mosca maintains that

the terrible moral crisis afflicting us is caused above all by the country's elation at victory and by the distress at seeing the beginnings of a new long post-war period in which the hardships suffered in the last years of the War will have to continue and, perhaps, even worsen for many people. It is natural that with people in such a state of mind the idea of political renewal should surface, something that will improve the situation and put new men in power; and the spokesmen for this aspiration come mainly from the new generation which experienced the trenches, especially those who, being more educated, aspire to the role of leadership.[24]

In this situation the deputy finds in young people 'a vague but strong desire for something new' and considers it necessary to provide a 'legal outlet' in order to avoid 'something irreparable being done'.[25] Using a significant metaphor, he compares electoral reform

to an injection of caffeine which combats the dangerous symptoms but does not suppress the main cause of a serious illness; it does not destroy the bacteria carrying pneumonia or influenza, but helps the patient to overcome a dangerous crisis. Therefore, I am voting in favour of electoral reform because it can help us to overcome a moral crisis which by a chance occurrence, in a moment of weakness in the State system or due to a slight error by the

Government might turn out to be fatal: that is to say, it could bring the country's development to a halt for an entire generation, for very many years to come.[26]

It is true that here his reasoning still follows a conservative logic, but its concreteness is of a much different kind than in the debate on electoral reform which took place in 1912.

It is also interesting to note that Mosca pronounces in favour of the 'preferential vote', maintaining that it is necessary for 'the voter to be able to discriminate'.[27] He adds that the struggle for the preferential vote (a new element arising out of the reform) does not worry him at all since 'elections are of necessity a struggle'. Therefore, compared to the situation in the past, the new electoral system brings into the clear light of day 'the fair and open struggle' between men with opposed political principles, which ensures a more dialectical relationship between individuals and between political positions. There is no trace in this speech of his earlier views regarding the illiterate (who were still numerous) and the lowering of the general standard of politics which would follow from the suffrage being extended. Mosca too believed that the extremely harsh experience of war had been a collective test of maturity for the whole Italian population. But in this respect he showed considerable skill at prediction, since as well as leading to a more mature awareness, the war had also unleashed forces, energies and unsuspected impulses which were all directed more towards the search for radical change than towards supporting the cautious reordering and development of social and political life according to a logic of stabilization.

Gaetano Mosca, Senator of the Kingdom of Italy – the polemic against syndicalism, 1921

Mosca's parliamentary question on the events at Fiume was his last act in the Chamber of Deputies, for at the end of 1919 he was made a member of the Senate where he played an active role until 1926. The nomination order was issued by the King, Vittorio Emanuele III, on 6 October 1919.

With the triumph of the Fascist regime in 1925–6 Mosca, though remaining a Senator until his death, abandoned political activity altogether. The preceding years from 1919 to 1926, on the other hand, were very dramatic and not only from a parliamentary point of view. The times were urging the radical revision of ideas and, as we have already indicated, it was precisely in this period that there took place the transition from the scientific system to the codified doctrine which characterized the writer's third and last period, beginning with the new edition of the *Elementi* (1923) and the republication of *Teorica* (1925).

What interested Mosca most in domestic politics during the 1920s was the central theme of the 'functional feudalism' represented by syndicalism. It was certainly not new to the scholar's thinking, but in this period he went into it at every opportunity both in the Chamber and in his journalism. In the *Tribuna* of 1 February 1920 an editorial appeared on the subject with the following introduction: 'Gaetano Mosca, an eminent student of politics', places the problem of syndicalism against a background of generally valid facts and 'fully highlights the significance and danger of recent events such as the strikes in the public services sector, the ends or consequences of which elude those who only see them in isolation, as they perhaps also elude those who organize them'.[28] Mosca's thesis is that the French Revolution of 1789 had shattered the remnants of feudalism (characterized essentially by the wide-ranging 'political, administrative and military' independence guaranteed to local bodies by the central authority). The state to which the Revolution gave birth, on the other hand, assumed a more centralized form, based subsequently on representative government. He maintains that the new way of organizing the state

provides a well-formed organism, but one more complicated than the feudal State. It relates to the latter like an animal higher up on the evolutionary ladder, which is unable to survive if deprived of one of its essential organs, relates to the polyp... In the modern State the separation of the administrative functions does not follow the local criterion, but rather a functional one according to the different nature of each activity. The result is that over the whole territory of the State one particular functional hierarchy supervises the military, another taxation, another justice and still others run the railways and postal-telegraph services. All these various hierarchies are linked to the central body called the Government, which co-ordinates and directs their activities.[29]

He concludes by referring to his efforts (over the last fifteen years) to draw the attention of public opinion 'to the grave danger of social and political disintegration' contained in syndicalism. He also specifies that this danger

threatens the so-called bourgeois State as much as the collectivist State, and the latter perhaps to an even greater extent. Indeed, so true is this that wherever collectivism has triumphed momentarily, it has had to repress at once with ruthless force any action against it by a single class.[30]

With regard to the speeches he made in the Senate, some of these are worth a great deal of attention from the parliamentary and domestic policy angle. It would, however, be useless to search among Mosca's parliamentary speeches for a reflection of the tense and dramatic situation existing in Italy immediately after the war. Indeed, Mosca took the floor of the Senate on 29 July 1921, during the debate on the vote of confidence in the new Government headed by Ivanoe Bonomi (1873–1951) – a left-wing democrat and formerly one of the most authoritative exponents in Italy of the revisionist socialism inspired by the German Eduard Bernstein (1850–1932) – in order to 'deplore' above all that in the statements from the new Government there was no mention of either international or colonial policy. In this intervention he also discusses and contests Bonomi's commitment to a programme of transforming the Supreme Labour Council into a 'National Labour Council'.[31] Mosca sees a grave 'peril' in this revival of the plan formulated by Arturo Labriola (1873–1959), ex-revolutionary syndicalist and former Minister of Labour in Giolitti's Government. He believes that the 'Council' would take on legislative functions and that its opinion would be binding for all proposed legislation regarding relations between capital and labour and also for decisions taken on economic policy. The plan meets with the scholar's complete opposition because, as he puts it,

we are facing a serious danger: that represented by the craft unions, to which I would like to draw the Senate's attention since, in my opinion, it is the most serious threat to present-day society. This is the case whatever form the State may take, given that the danger is the same for both the bourgeois and the socialist State. Indeed so true is this that Lenin, who has perpetrated all manner of mischief in Russia but is no fool, immediately divested the unions of the right to strike because the use of such freedom would have destroyed the State. And if the trade-unions are not curbed in our country as well, they will end by destroying the State – this is no exaggerated prediction of catastrophe.[32]

In Mosca's analysis the concept of organized minority recurs with regard to the different trade union groupings. He maintains that this kind of 'new Parliament' (for that is what it boils down to) would become a headquarters for these various minorities.

The concluding remarks to his intervention are dry and cutting. He declares his confidence in Bonomi's government, but would like it to be aware of the dangerous course opened up by Labriola's plan. According to Mosca, they must avoid letting themselves be conditioned 'by the trend of the times'. He ends as follows:

The present is the age of the trade-unions; they are said to represent a kind of historical fatality against which it is impossible ever to react. Honourable colleagues, I believe that historical fatality and the trend of the times are something which we ourselves to a large extent create. Historical fatality has taken over whenever we have been unable to block in time a movement containing the germs which are causing the present form of the State to decay, whenever we have been unable to prevent in time those germs of decay from organizing themselves and acquiring awareness of their own strength and of which instruments to wield.[33]

In the crisis of the liberal political system which had allowed him to combine and carry out with the same degree of commitment his university professorship, journalistic activity and parliamentary duties, Mosca now set about developing the organic, intellectual effort at conceptualization which falls entirely within the third period of his work, a period in which he organized his political thought into a definite and formal system.

Mosca and Mussolini, 1922–1926

It was during the three-year period 1922–26 that Mosca's positions as a political scientist, parliamentarian and statesman fully converged in the context of the dramatic conclusion to the liberal political experience in the face of Fascism. This convergence attained a consistency (both theoretical and practical) which on many other occasions was lacking.

First of all, Mosca the 'politician' should be considered taking into account the confused state of the ruling class: from the government of Ivanoe Bonomi (July 1921 to February 1922) to that of Luigi Facta (February to October 1922) it watched impotent as the armed blackshirts increasingly took the initiative and brought Benito Mussolini (1883– 1945) to power. Fascism formed the new practical–political element in Italy after the First World War. At the time the theoretical aspects of this new element were still vague and uncertain. In this respect, the Fascist Congress held at the Teatro Augusteo in Rome from 7 to 10 November 1921 was of great importance; on this occasion Mussolini clearly set out the theoretical–practical constituents of his National Fascist Party. Having declared his position concerning the choice between a monarchical or republican form of the state to be one of agnosticism, he continued:

In economic matters we are avowedly anti-socialist. I do not regret my socialist past; all ties with it have been severed. Nor do I feel nostalgic. The question is not how to achieve socialism, but how to get away from it. In economics we are also liberal, because we hold that the nation's economy cannot be entrusted to collective and bureaucratic bodies. We have had enough of that after the Russian experiment. I would hand back the railways and the postal-telegraph services to the private sector, since the present structures are unwieldy and vulnerable at every point. The ethical State is not the monopolistic, the bureaucratic State, but one which reduces its functions to the bare minimum necessary. We are against the economic State. Socialist doctrines have collapsed: the internationalist myths have declined and the class struggle is a fiction; it is impossible to divide up humanity. The proletariat and the bourgeoisie do not have a separate existence in history: they are both links in the same chain. We do not believe in these fairy-stories. Even where it has obtained power, the proletariat is imprisoned by capitalism. We are anti-socialist, but not necessarily anti-proletarian. There are those who say the masses must be won over. Some say history is made by heroes, others say by the masses. The truth lies in the middle. What could the masses achieve without their own mouthpiece, an expression of the people's spirit, and what would the poet do without the material to be moulded? We are not anti-proletarian, but we have no intention of making a fetish out of his Highness, the multitude. We desire to serve it, to educate it, but when it goes astray, to punish it. We must never promise more than we know we can deliver with mathematical certainty. What we want is to raise its intellectual and moral level so that it can take part in the history of the Nation. There is no possibility of improving the country's economy with an unruly proletariat suffering from malaria and pellagra. And we say to the masses that when the Nation's interests are at stake, all egoistic interests, whether of the proletariat or the bourgeoisie, must be left aside.[34]

Fascism's original theoretical radicalism found its immediate counterpart, however, in the abundant use of a shrewd tactical approach. In presenting his 'coalition' Government to both Chambers (16 November 1922) the Prime Minister, Benito Mussolini, boasted of his moderation. His Government was composed of Fascists, nationalists, right-wing liberals, Giolittians, 'popolari' (members of the Catholic-inspired Popular Party), military men and the neo-Hegelian philosopher Giovanni Gentile as Minister of Education. Mussolini's boast was expressed in these terms:

I could have had my own way entirely, but I refused to: with 300,000 young men armed to the teeth, ready for anything and almost mystically bound to my command, I could have punished all those who have defamed and attempted to besmirch Fascism. I could have turned that grey and indifferent lower Chamber into a bivouac for squads of soldiers.[35]

Mosca took the floor on 27 November 1922 in response to Mussolini's speech to the Senate, a speech full of flattery for the upper Chamber in which he declared the latter to be in his estimation 'one of the bulwarks of the nation', 'a force of the State, a reserve of the State, a body necessary for the just and wise administration of the State'.[36] Mosca's speech was short but to the point and highly significant. In addition, it was free from any ambiguity and we should look to its terse rhetoric for a precise political attitude. Mussolini had emphatically asserted that for the second time within the space of a decade,

the Italian people – the best part of it – has unseated a Cabinet and given itself a Government outside of, beyond and against any nominated by Parliament. The decade I am referring to is that from May 1915 to October 1922. I leave it to the melancholic zealots of super-constitutionalism to make a more or less lamenting discourse on the subject. I affirm that the revolution has its rights. And so that everyone knows it, I will add that I am here to defend or strengthen as far as possible the revolution of the 'blackshirts', and make it an intimate part of the Nation's history as a force for growth, progress and a balanced society.[37]

After reminding his listeners that power can be conquered – as in the case of the March on Rome – *only* in a situation where existing institutions are seriously weakened, Mosca examines the possible remedies for the crisis of the modern state; they are identified as the dictatorship of the proletariat according to the Soviet model, the return to absolutist government (bureaucratic absolutism), and syndicalism.

Mosca immediately rejects any return to absolutism. He is well aware that it would be very oppressive because of the new features it would assume, given that with 'the means at the disposal of the State' the government, supported by professional functionaries, would expand 'into all the civilian and military spheres of administration ... without any control over it'.[38]

The dictatorship of the proletariat, on the other hand, would represent nothing other than the replacement of the present ruling class by 'another more crude and violent political class'. The result would be 'not a crisis of government, but a real crisis of civilization, which would be turned back several centuries amidst unspeakable suffering'.[39]

His condemnation of syndicalism follows the usual lines and is motivated by the additional conviction that if socialism and communism are 'rooted in ideas, sentiments and doctrines, which are all difficult to change but can be modified, syndicalism, on the other hand, is rooted in the facts, in the economic structure of society'.[40] This represents for Mosca the biggest danger, because

if the system of individual voting in elections were replaced by class representation, the State would undergo a major and very dangerous transformation. Let us not delude ourselves; if we had our little class Parliament, even just for consultation, since the Honourable Mussolini teaches us that the validity of politial bodies lies not so much in the legal powers they possess as in the political forces behind them, that little Parliament could easily become the predominant governing body. Nor would the more learned trade-unions, like for example that of the university professors, be the predominant force in it, but rather those which fulfil the most indispensable roles in the economy. If a syndicalist Parliament came about, Agrippa's apologue would have to be rewritten: the hands, arms, feet and legs would no longer impose their will on the stomach, but on the brain.[41]

Mosca's critical analysis of these three solutions and the significant reference to the 'political forces' behind the 'legal powers', forces which furnish the latter with respect and substance, is a prelude to his positive suggestion that *'the restoration of representative government'* will impose itself 'out of pure necessity'.[42] In our opinion, this is the point at which a thorough symbiosis occurs between the contradictions and values of Mosca the thinker, who studied political doctrines and formulated one himself, and the experience of Mosca the parliamentarian, who witnessed in full the dramatic subversion of constitutional order. In sorrowful tones he makes the following declaration:

I who forty years ago wrote a young man's criticism of the parliamentary system, which I do not repudiate today however; I who perhaps have the honour of inventing the term, the political class, which the Honourable Mussolini does me the honour of using from time to time, but not exactly in the sense I intended; I who thus began my life as a writer am reduced in my old age to telling you to 'preserve for the time being what you can of the old structure, because the materials for the new one are not yet ready'.[43]

The confrontation with Mussolini is direct and precise – one could also say completely unrealistic – and worth looking at more closely, since it encapsulates what is not an isolated position, but the *theoretical* and *practical* illusion of a very sizeable section of liberal and conservative circles. They thought it was possible to find a *modus vivendi*, a way of collaborating with Mussolini which would serve as a prelude to his 'constitutionalization' through the very flexibility in the Kingdom's constitutional system. In fact, according to Mosca, victorious Fascism does not express the 'intellectual ... moral ... economic forces' such as to lead, for the time being, to a 'radical transformation' of the 'more or less rearranged' form of the representative system.[44] The 'restoration of representative government' must, therefore, 'rest on the shoulders' of the new Mussolini Cabinet and it is the duty of the whole Senate to help him in this difficult task. 'In order to restore parliamentary government', he states that

it is necessary to reorganize political parties, re-establish discipline in and out of Parliament and lastly to renew not the entire political class, but those four or five dozen individuals from among whom the rulers of the State used to be chosen and who, except in a few cases, did not possess the intellectual and moral qualities equal to their very high office. The Honourable Mussolini must replace them with others who are worthy of such a position by virtue of their energy and ability.[45]

Thus Mussolini's role was to be that of *dictator*, a dictator in the Roman tradition: the restorer of a revised and amended parliamentary regime.

There was undoubtedly much ingenuity in Mosca's position. However, what really concerns us here is not to acquit or condemn, but to comprehend the 'crux' of the problems with which the scholar was dealing. It was not only a matter of the crucial point on which a determined historical situation turns, but also of reflecting on the constitutional arrangements in the modern state, on the advantages and limits of representative government, on the defects of *social representation* (namely, the incapacity to represent the interests expressed by society at the decision-making level) and on the excessive *political representation* (namely, the overrating of the ideological interests represented by the political forces) in a political system which draws life and new blood from elections based on proportional representation. This position underwent no basic change in Mosca's subsequent parliamentary interventions on the question of electoral law in the period 1923–4. In fact, these interventions foreshadowed the speech in which he rejected the transformation of Fascism, between 1925 and 1926, into a new form of absolutism founded on militaristic organization and the dictatorship of a single party, and on the suppression of all freedoms.

Rejection of the Fascist regime

An explicit invitation to respect political freedom also found full expression in Mosca's famous speech to the Senate on the 'powers and prerogatives of the Head of Government', which he delivered on 19 December 1925. It is too well known to be analysed once again in this work. However, his vote against the bill which aimed to radically alter the constitutional set-up clearly drew its inspiration from the judgement made three years previously; it was now motivated by a more mature and exact awareness arising from the confirmed failure of the hypothesis according to which Mussolini could be integrated into the representative system. The situation at that particular time was well summed up in Mosca's words to the effect that the Senate was witnessing 'the funeral rites of a form of government'.[46] In a delicate situation which was open to radically new factors, Mosca regained his full sense of self-criticism and, at the same time, attempted to explain the contradiction between several of his analyses made in the past and his present political decisions. His intervention is expressed in autobiographical terms:

> I who have always been sharply critical of parliamentary government must now almost regret its downfall. I acknowledge that this system was in need of considerable change, but I do not think the time is right to transform it radically; and now that it is being renounced, it is only right to recall its merits.[47]

This represents a notable outburst of sincerity on Mosca's part and is appropriately followed up by the theme of his overall reflection:

Of course, the system of parliamentary representation should not and cannot be immutable; as social conditions change, political systems must also be changed. But should such change have been rapid and radical or slow and thought out? This is the very grave question tormenting me and which, as an old opponent of the parliamentary system, I believe should be resolved by following the most moderate and prudent course.[48]

Mosca's position was a difficult and painful one; and it was unconnected with matters incidental to his main preoccupations (as it will have been noted, in the entire analysis of Mosca's parliamentary activity from 1922 on hardly any reference is made to political parties, politicians or even daily political affairs). His aim was to discover a sense and purpose for politics beyond short-lived demands and surface forms. However, the ideological inspiration behind Mosca's attitude did not escape the critical attention of the supporters of Fascism, which by this time had become the new regime.

Besides his political studies and his doctrine, Mosca's experience as an active politician and a parliamentarian also urges upon us the need to rethink, in a manner which is neither episodic nor fragmentary, the state of the then existing institutions and political struggle, first separately and then in their relationship to one another. The positions of many liberal conservatives (such as Mosca and even Croce) cannot be viewed as contradictory on the basis that they did not accept the hierarchical and authoritative solutions imposed by Fascism, which would have been in line with their rejection of liberalism in its most up-to-date and progressive 'democratic' version. Instead, there was in the actions of these personalities (rather more than in their ideas, it must be said) a completely unresolved contradiction which was part of the very process that lead to national unity and of the political experience of the liberal state in Italy. This contradiction consisted in the gulf, which was never bridged, between a minority ruling political group, heterogeneous and economically well off, that monopolized the state and its functions up until the First World War, and the vast mass of the people overwhelmed by material want, basically uneducated, often hostile to any notion of 'government' – a synonym of oppression – and excluded from any real power. The inadequacy of institutions in the face of the great crisis of the 1920s lay precisely in their restricted social base; it was totally insufficient for repulsing the combined pressures of the popular and majority forces in Italian society that were rising against these very same institutions. Revolutionary socialists, communists, clerical reactionaries, Fascists and nationalists were putting pressure on the representative state, the heir of the minorities which had constructed the new unified state by essentially co-opting the ruling political class. In this perspective, the fact that Mosca had *Teorica* republished at the climax of the break with constitutional legality assumed the profound significance of a rigorous examination of his own conscience: an examination aimed at grasping in his early thought of forty years previously the real roots of a plant which, in time, had born the poisoned fruit revealed in the full light of day by the history of that period and the one which followed it.

7
Codification of the doctrine, 1923–1941

From the analysis carried out so far into the content, values, myths and ideology of Mosca's thought the fact clearly emerges that in its completed form as a scientific system this thought forms a true *political doctrine* in which the various elements are articulated within an organic structure. It constitutes a definitive theoretical result which was to serve as a basis for the pragmatic and contingent decisions made by Mosca in the first two fervent decades of the twentieth century. In terms of his political and scientific activity the reprinting of the *Elementi di scienza politica*, with a new up-to-date and dialectical section (1923), and of *Sulla teorica dei governi e sul governo parlamentare* represented – as we have seen – an organic and definitive reordering, a true 'codification' of Mosca's entire system of thought. The codification of his doctrine was thus a structured reply to the new political situation brought about by the First World War and the triumph of Fascism in Italy.

It is convenient at this point to examine the characteristics of the new edition of the *Elementi*. Particularly in the second part of his *magnum opus*, the scholar observes that his doctrine had so far met with 'little success' and he tries to explain the signs of decadence which he observed in public life in Europe generally and especially in Italy. Besides being an act of scientific daring or political pride in the face of the great crisis which was beginning to throw Italy into a state of confusion, the codification of his doctrine fulfilled a need which was deeply felt by Mosca. In fact, he clearly perceived that as a result of the First World War many of the concerns and ideas which had inspired his scientific activity were obsolete and strongly contested by the new times. In this third and final period of his thinking, Mosca aimed to identify the transient elements in the historical-political conjuncture and elaborate his doctrine on the basis of a closer examination of the principles and facts of politics understood as a permanent reality which is unfolded over long periods of time.

Ruling classes and civilization

The second edition of the *Elementi di scienza politica* reproposes the text of the first edition of 1896 with the addition of a second part consisting of 169 pages. It is not without significance that in the preface to this later edition Mosca explains that the second part of the book, besides being 'entirely new', was 'conceived and written in the last two or three years' in the full awareness that 'the variations occurring in the character and mentality of any man' have a precise limit as he grows older. This fact leads to ideas being crystallized 'in a definitive form'.[1]

The first chapter in the second part of the text is entitled 'Origins of the doctrine of the political class and the obstacles to its dissemination'. What is immediately striking on reading this chapter is Mosca's ability to regard his own research in historical terms. He asserts that the doctrine of the political class came into existence about a century ago and attributes its first appearance to Claude-Henri de Saint-Simon (1760–1825), establishing a long line of intellectual development which runs from this author to August Comte (1789–1857) and Hippolyte Taine (1828–93), from Ludwik Gumplowicz (1838–1909) to the first formulation contained in *Teorica*. Through his historical approach Mosca unifies an entire line of study and research which also encompasses the work done by his contemporaries Vilfredo Pareto and Robert Michels, among others.

This is a clearly stimulating procedure in terms of the history of ideas and leads to precise political no less than theoretical results. At the theoretical level the concept of the political class gives way to the more general and articulated *ruling class*. This modification is not just a matter of a mere choice of words, but corresponds to the profound change which European society (and especially Italy) had gone through in the decades between 1884 and 1922. This is confirmed by what is written in the opening to the new part of the *Elementi*: 'The doctrine that in all human societies which have reached a certain level of development and civilization, political control in the broadest sense of the term (administrative, military, religious, economic and moral leadership) is always exercised by a special class, or by an organized minority.'[2] In both his previous main works, *Teorica* and the first edition of the *Elementi*, the concept of political class had been applied rigidly: in the former as a synonym for 'government' and in the latter as a synonym for 'power'. Now it has become the somewhat more subtle concept of the ruling class,[3] that is, the efective aggregate of the forces which run society.

But this is not the only new feature which has been grafted onto the first version of the *Elementi*. Whereas previously Mosca had maintained a

Codification of the doctrine 87

constantly rigid distinction between concepts and had introduced, one after the other, the empirically acquired and rationally justified concepts of 'political class', 'political formula' and 'juridical defence' in order to synthesize his doctrine, in the new part of the book the scientific plan is radically altered. Mosca declares his awareness that simply to assert that in all forms of government real power resides in a ruling minority is not enough. Although such an assertion 'undermines the authority of the old guide-lines' – in other words, it throws into an irreversible crisis all the political formulas based on popular sovereignty, in particular the most radical formulations of 'popular government' in accordance with the conception of Rousseau – it is merely a 'generic truth' which offers no new formula and, above all, 'does not bring us at once to the heart of past or present political events'.[4] The aim of the new study, therefore, must no longer be 'a summary and generic affirmation'[5] of the doctrine of the ruling class as it has evolved over forty years of study; it must attempt to carry out that 'analytical study' which 'patiently seeks out the invariable traits possessed by various ruling classes and the variable traits with which the remote causes – always overlooked by contemporary observers – of their integration and dissolution are bound up'.[6]

In the method adopted the typical aspiration of Moschian positivism recurs: to follow in the social sciences as well that 'procedure which is much used in the natural sciences; in which a large part of the information that has now become an established part of human knowledge is due to propitious intuitions, some of which have been confirmed, others modified, but all elaborated and developed by successive experiments and experiences'.[7] Once again it is the growth of civilization and the different sciences which allows Mosca to write that 'if it should be objected that it is difficult, and we might add, virtually impossible to experiment in cases where social phenomena are involved, one might answer that history, statistics and economics have by now gathered enough experimental data to permit us to begin the investigation referred to'.[8] However, it must be underlined that a precise political end also recurs. In the Mosca of the *codified doctrine*, which in this work is fully worked out, we find this stated objective: to reach awareness of the cyclical reoccurrence in history of 'those great catastrophes which, from time to time, interrupt the course of civilization and thrust people that have won glorious places in history back into barbarism, be it a relative and temporary barbarism'.[9] So the task set for Mosca's doctrinal system is to reject any Utopian 'government by the best men' for the sole reason that in political life 'the word "best" . . . usually means the "best" man is the one who possesses the requisites that make him most suited to govern his fellow men'.[10] But, paradoxically, this conviction inverts the terms of Mosca's traditional mode of research: the secret behind the organization of the ruling class now no longer rests in a presupposed and axiomatic 'superiority' of life styles and behaviour, but rather in its relationship with the ruled, the governed, who are allowed to enter the ruling class if the juridical-institutional apparatus (namely, a real juridical defence) is functioning correctly. From this point of view, Mosca's political formula is basically the same as a 'sound balance between two fundamental natural tendencies ... conservatism ... and the urge to innovate'.[11] Mosca's deep conviction is expressed that civilizations can avoid catastrophic crises and really become 'immortal' provided 'they learn how to *transform themselves continually without falling apart*'.[12]

The codification of Mosca's doctrine as his response to the political crisis of the 1920s

Two elements which emerged in the writer's work during the 1920s corresponded to the great political and institutional crisis in Italy. The first of these, the new edition of the *Elementi*, has already been referred to as the work in which the writer completed the formulation of his concepts. It is to the second element that we must now turn our attention. It concerns the growing importance that Mosca attributed to history in his research into political doctrines. In the 1920s Mosca introduced into his work with increasing clarity and precision that distinction between political science and the history of political doctrines and institutions for which his book *Storia delle dottrine politiche*, published first in France (1936) and then in Italy (1937), would act as the academic and scientific 'manifesto'. Thus credit is due to the by that time elderly Mosca for having initiated a field of study which at present is producing an ever increasing number of important results.

In this work Mosca's realistic approach is closely linked to his inspiration from positivism, which he never disowned or failed to live up to. It is a paradox that at the moment when positivism was clearly defeated as a philosophical school and as an ideology of progress and was giving way to neo-Hegelian idealism and various irrational schools of thought, Mosca moved towards recuperating in his teaching and in the formulation of his doctrine several permanently valid features of Italian positivism. In Italy, in fact, positive philosophy took on its own peculiar characteristics and, especially from the second half of the nineteenth century, assumed the form of a clear 'reaction to spiritualism, to Catholic-inspired metaphysics' and, at the same time, of 'erudition in the field of history and the appeal to experience in that of philosophy'.[13] In

Codification of the doctrine 89

this respect, what the historian Pasquale Villari (1826–1917) asserted in his famous inaugural lecture for the academic year 1865–6 in Florence is still valid. In dealing with the theme 'Positive Philosophy and the Historical Method' he states that

> positive philosophy repudiates absolute knowledge of man; in fact, it repudiates all absolute knowledge without however denying the existence of what it does not know . . . It does not persist in studying abstract man . . . but real living man, who assumes a thousand different guises and is moved by a thousand different passions . . . philosophers . . . instead of uselessly making vain accusations of materialism and scepticism . . . should recognize in Machiavelli and Vico . . . the first seeds of this inevitable, new form of progress, which is leading us towards the truth and not materialism or doubt.[14]

The relevance of this lies in the fact that in his deepest convictions Mosca belonged to the culture of the last half of the nineteenth century. Neither, in our opinion, did the positivist influence surrounding the thinker conflict with his liberal-conservative approach. Politically speaking, positivism was not in fact necessarily democratic or inclined towards Darwinian-evolutionary socialism, as was the case in Italy. One need only consider the positivism of Charles Maurras (1868–1952) in France or the organization of Mexican society brought about by Porfirio Diaz (1830–1915). In the 1930s the Mosca of the codified doctrine made a clear political choice in favour of mixed governments. His conservatism resides in the conviction that only 'an education in gradual stages and long experience' can 'find practical ways of curbing the violent and evil instincts which often accompany the will to dominate. Such instincts have reappeared again and again during the great political crises which a long period of order and social peace had led superficial observers to believe were extinct'.[15] However, Mosca's method as displayed in his *Storia delle dottrine politiche* is wholly aimed at creating a real and conscious understanding of the men, the thinking and the workings of institutions by drawing on that side of historical research which furnishes 'totally reliable data': books, codes, inscriptions, monuments, etc., all elements which help us to know a civilization and its place 'in the history of mankind'.[16] Finally, in the considerations contained in the brief writings which make up his *Pensieri postumi* Mosca maintains that 'a civilization is an organism which has its youth, maturity and old age. No organism is immortal and the more complex ones are the most delicate and least resistant. If we think that our civilization is immortal, time will serve to disillusion us.'[17] Nevertheless, he follows up this naturalistic vision of society with a thought which seems to us to be of considerable interest:

90   *The doctrine of the political class*

the twentieth, and perhaps even the twenty-first, century will bring about such progress in the social sciences that a way will be found to change a society slowly without it going into a decline, thereby avoiding the often violent accompanying crises. Given that change is necessary and immobility impossible in human societies, true statesmen should act to ensure that slow but gradual change succeeds in avoiding dissolution, which is the same for social organisms as death is for individuals.[18]

In our opinion, this demonstrates that Mosca's positivist convictions were reaffirmed in extremely clear terms throughout this third period, and that his values and even his philosophy of knowledge cannot be separated from the results of his entire life's work; nor can one simply set them aside as Benedetto Croce did in his well-known review of the second edition of the *Elementi*, which first appeared in the journal *Critica* (1923) and then, from 1947, as the *Preface* to the several editions of Mosca's major work. It is therefore impossible to divorce the sense of history which inspired the later Mosca from his deeply felt conviction that 'exact knowledge of the past' is very useful, provided one 'knows how to discriminate between conditions in the past and those in the present'.[19] The interaction between history, political science and sociology clearly represents one of the most prominent features in Mosca's final formulation of his ideas and confirms what has been said up to this point with regard to the writer's renewed positivism.

Aims and results of Mosca's new political and historical research

Two things result from the need to locate the various stages in the formulation of Mosca's doctrine within their different historical contexts. It must be said at the outset, however, that the division into three periods referred to above (open system, scientific system, codified doctrine) meets different requirements.

In the early period, strongly empirical and centigent in approach, and hinging on *Teorica* and *Le costituzioni moderne*, it is above all the polemical criticism of the parliamentary system which recurs repeatedly. Mosca's objective is here extraordinarily ambitious: to establish the hypothesis of a new form of government which is better than both absolute government (at that time still very much alive in people's memories) and the new type of parliamentary government.[20] The link between the concepts of political class and political formula is already made specific at this point along lines which are not directed at 'changing political formulas or those central mechanisms of government which, modified or remodified, never profoundly alter the system of social organization'.[21] The theoretical-practical intention is already focused on what will later become – as we have seen – the juridical defence, that is, on asserting the inevitable existence of the political class and its accompanying formula. At the same time, there is the desire that the formation of this class occur 'on the basis of individual merit and technical ability' and that 'all its members keep a check on one another so as to avoid, as far as humanly possible, arbitrary or irresponsible actions on the part of an individual or a group'.[22] Radical polemics and conservatism are here fused into a doctrinal synthesis in which utopian elements are not lacking either.

In the period of the writer's maturity, which is centered on the first edition of the *Elementi*, the objectives of Mosca's research are formulated, above all, in terms of contesting the radical conception of democracy and, in fact, they develop into a form of genuine anti-socialism. This occurs in the name of the doctrine of the juridical defence conceived as the theoretical-practical antidote to the transformation of representative government into regimes in which 'besides being organs of discussion and public debate, assemblies come to concentrate all the prestige and power of legitimate authority in their own hands'.[23] In these cases the level of juridical defence is minimal because 'in spite of the curb provided by public discussion, the whole administrative and judicial machine falls prey to the irresponsible and anonymous tyranny of those who win the elections and speak in the name of the people'.[24] The extremely simple nature of the formula of democratic government and the simplification of social types according to socialist, egalitarian and collectivist thinking means – to Mosca's mind – that not only is the juridical defence needed for practical reasons, but that the new arbitrary 'metaphysics of democracy' which is the negation of 'positive political science' must also be rejected. He considers the latter to be the principal fruit of the final years of the nineteenth century.[25] The ultimate end of the doctrine, none the less, is here avowedly liberal since what is required is the use of all the instruments offered by a true juridical defence to prevent 'the degeneration that is common to all men whose acts are exempt from restraint and control';[26] acts which occur when 'the leaders of the governing class are the exclusive interpreters of the will of God or of the people and exercise sovereignty in the name of those abstractions in societies that are deeply imbued with religious beliefs or with democratic fanaticism'.[27]

In the period in which he codified his doctrine, from the second edition of the *Elementi* to the publication of the Italian edition of *Storia delle dottrine politiche* (1937), the most salient fact is Mosca's greater political flexibility, which leads him to a reassessment and defence of the parliamentary system. In a certain sense, a redefinition of the doctrine of the political class takes place in the light of a renewed historical sensitivity on his part and of the irreversible link asserted between political doctrines and political institutions: it is seen essentially as a method for achieving a form of politics which is rational and adapted to a high level of not only social, but also technical-scientific progress. This is the position which emerges in the new part of the *Elementi* that we have analysed and in the concluding chapter of *Storia delle dottrine politiche*.[28]

Besides a greater understanding of the links between the different elements making up the doctrine, the first thing to result from the proposed periodization is the fact that the doctrine takes on a notably different political and scientific significance when it is considered in each of the three periods indicated above. Thus it is possible to formulate a general interpretation, as well as an overall judgement, only *after* an analytical and critical reconstruction of these three periods. They correspond outwardly to a by no means negligible moment in the history of Italy from the first tormented decades following unification to the crisis of the liberal state and up to the creation of the Fascist state. Consequently, it is now clearer than ever that Mosca's doctrine must be located within its historical context rather than viewed as a generalized scheme.

The second result is that when we pass from the critical-philological reconstruction to the historical consideration of Mosca's thought, the fact emerges that the later Mosca, the Mosca of the codified doctrine, is more vitally involved in the contradictions of modern society and the political life which is its expression. What arises from this is that far from having exhausted its power to stimulate ideas and research, the doctrine of the political class can still demonstrate the truth of Piero Gobetti's observation that Mosca's theoretical formulation, as well as that of Pareto,

could have thrown light on the significance of the struggle in the social sphere if it had been more directly linked to the conditions of public life and to the historical conflict between the different classes. The concept of an elite which imposes its will by exploiting a complex of interests and general psychological states against the old rulers is strictly liberal in origin; liberal like the idea which discovers in social conflict the prevalence of independent elements and real energies and repudiates the inertia of those ideologies which are satisfied with believing in a set of metaphysical entities such as justice, natural law, the brotherhood of nations. The formative process of the elite is distinctly democratic: the people, or more exactly the various classes, display in the aristocracies that represent them the extent of their strength and originality... The parliamentary system, besides resisting this historical law in which dominant groups and minorities succeed one another, is nothing other than the most refined instrument for exploiting all the participant energies and for the prompt selection of the most suitable men.[29]

It must be said once again that in this latter version the doctrine of the political class includes the above-mentioned historicizing procedure as one of its constituent elements. We believe that this procedure renders particularly interesting not only the results of Mosca's work in terms of political science, but also his contribution towards creating a methodology for the history of political doctrines by linking it to the history of institutions.

The important aspect of the writer's political thought in this period is represented, therefore, by his wide-ranging reflection on a society which is changing and on the material factors underlying economic and social stability. As regards mixed regimes, Mosca specifies that 'for such a regime to last, a whole set of circumstances is needed which no legislator's foresight can suddenly create. The multiplicity and equilibrium of the ruling forces that only a very advanced civilization can produce are necessary.'[30] At this point, it would take too long to go into the theoretical and practical bases of this genuine social and political pluralism. Suffice it to say that it is likewise a new fruit of the last phase in the writer's research and an integral part of his increasingly firm awareness of history and institutions. It is this awareness which makes a work like *Storia delle dottrine politiche* with its complex and varied origin significant for the many possible stimuli towards a clearer understanding not only of its author, but also of a period of great and profound crisis in society.[31] In this respect, the marginal notes added to the third edition of the *Elementi* (1939) are worth noting, in particular where Mosca states:

We have already said that representative government is able to function properly wherever social conditions make it possible. The chief requirement is the existence of a middle class whose moral and intellectual level permits its members, or most of them, not to be in the direct pay of the rulers, as well as providing them with a political education such that they can effectively co-operate in the work of the bureaucracy. Where these conditions do not exist, representative government is merely an appearance, not a reality; and where they belong to the past and not to the present, this form of government goes into a steep decline.[32]

In the final codification of Mosca's doctrine the theme of power is related much more distinctly to the concrete reality of the ruling classes existing in society, and the desired form of government is undoubtedly that which is expressed through the representative system, since the latter only seems possible in societies which combine economic prosperity with a high degree of intellectual life and also of morality in the relationship between citizens and the State, especially when these qualities belong to the middle classes, which every country needs for the correct functioning of the State machine.[33]

So even in his final reflections Mosca was able to make a very interesting connection between facts concerning institutions, contained in his writings of the 1920s, and the element of doctrine peculiar to the history of political thought, outlined and defined in precise terms especially during the 1930s. Late in his life, Mosca now had the deep conviction that all research in the field of political science can 'help to change a nation's political future if it succeeds in changing the political thinking of its ruling classes, which has been – and it is to be hoped always will be – one of the determining factors in history'.[34] Thus Gaetano Mosca concluded his fervent life's work, and he left behind his *Storia delle dottrine politiche* to bear witness to his long and difficult study of society and power as they have developed historically. At the same time, to counter any too simplistic exaltation of empirical facts, he affirmed the fundamental importance of the formulation of concepts and doctrine in the affairs of men and institutions.

Dialectics in the doctrine of the political class – science, ideology and ethics

At a scientific level, the 1924 inaugural lecture at Rome University ('The ancient city-state and the modern representative state') represents a notable contribution towards a precise definition of Mosca's codified doctrine. It is much more than just a simple university lecture; it is also a lesson in politics, a statement of method and a research programme. And it is precisely at the level of the detailed historical examination of political doctrines in their relationship to institutions that Mosca developed his original approach to the new academic discipline in which he was a great scholar with a wide experience and culture. His work as a whole cannot be easily reduced in its definitive results to the rigid schemes of the great contemporary ideologies. It is important to repeat that, in Mosca, there is always a sense of political reflection which is not merely incidental and episodic. An example of this is the experience he gained in Parliament and in government which helped him in his approach to practical-political problems. The 'incidental fact' was always the object of deeper meditation, of a thorough-going analysis and led as a consequence to conclusions which were not at all ephemeral.

Codification of the doctrine

From our considerations so far of Mosca's work there undoubtedly emerges a certain difficulty in grasping the intrinsic theoretical-practical aims which Mosca set for his research. However, we find that his fundamental convictions were expressed in an especially lucid form in the last period of his work and life. This spanned a period in which the nineteenth century – an age touched to its very roots by several revolutions of great, and not only, political importance in which Romantic experience had become no less threadbare than that of positivism and the optimism of Progress was spent after that of 'Reason' – gave way to the totally new logic of mass industrial society expressed by the twentieth century in an increasingly clear-cut and explosive form. The wealth of references and reflections contained in Mosca's work during the crucial years of the 1920s and 1930s opened up the field to a whole series of new formulations which place the author at the centre, rather than at the margins, of the laborious and still incomplete political analysis of the new society. By acutely combining the empirical study of facts with his sense of history and political convictions, Mosca presents us with an analysis which is worthy of consideration with respect to the newly emerging mass society. In fact, the codification of his thought into a doctrine furnishes us with Mosca's interpretation of how to make the demands involved in preserving the representative political system – the excellent, even if debatable, mature fruit of the last century – coexist with the adjustments and institutional modifications required by societies like those of the present, which are no less frenetically dynamic at the economic and technological level than at the social level. Having thus summarized the complete formulation of the doctrine of the political class, we believe that our observations fully corroborate the methodological distinction made by Norberto Bobbio between the scientific value of a theory and the ideological use to which it is put. As has been seen, the entire Moschian system of thought contains its own intrinsic and salutary truth in the way it considers political phenomena as entirely the product of man and, therefore, verifiable on both a theoretical and empirical-historical level. In this perspective, a vigorous current of thought based on a 'scientific' approach, that is, of a predictive, rational and concrete nature and illuminated by political activity, began to develop from the penultimate decade of the nineteenth century; a current of thought which ran parallel to his own work and to which he contributed. It was further characterized by a highly irreverent attitude towards myths and ideologies, which made a notable contribution to the development of a critical spirit.

After having duly acknowledged the debt owed to Mosca's thought and the validity of its strongly interdisciplinary, methodological perspective in the field of political studies, it would be incorrect not to point out the more ideological limits to his entire work produced by the many values underlying the author's deeply felt aspirations. We hold that Mosca's conservatism is a reflection of a *political class* (not only was he born into it, he also took an active part in its affairs) which was unable to find the right theoretical-practical balance between the two terms which constantly dominated political life and which represent the two inextricably linked themes of modern politics: *power* and *freedom*. For Mosca, freedom is above all the juridical defence, a system of checks and balances. It is mediation. It is a negative limit which never manages to become a driving element from which passions and ideas emanate, which is not able to involve more and more strata of society in a real dialectic of social change and modification of a given historical reality. Power is the instrument for maintaining *order* (the supreme value in Mosca's eyes). But it is an order which is rigidly set within a bourgeois social and cultural framework and the other social classes are excluded from co-operating, except in a very partial or individual way. It is a form of power which is basically inert and at the service of a social order enclosed within the bounds of a genuine bourgeois class concept of politics in no way connected with the vital modern dialectical relationship between different socio-economic interests.

These are the ideological and theoretical limits which also condition in a negative sense the more strictly political moments of the writer's general commitment and which, nevertheless, are corrected by Mosca's 'sense of history' in the last stage of his thought and work. It is probable that this unmistakable contradiction between scientific results and ideological limits in the formulation of Mosca's ideas possesses an underlying consistency in his fundamentally moral outlook. It must not be forgotten that from the time of *Teorica* he had carried out research into the social and political mechanisms which discipline man's moral sense. During the course of this exposition of Mosca's ideas we have emphasized that the ethical motives ever present in his political thought are neither commonplace nor trivial, but have their own precise dimension which was capable of notably conditioning the entire development and formulation of his thinking. At this point we believe we must point out that in the last period of his research the all-absorbing goal of Mosca's theoretical-historical elaboration was precisely the development and strengthening of this moral sense. In our opinion, this new essential fact should be linked, above all, to Mosca's pessimistic conviction – referred to on several occasions – which contests all optimistic visions of the relationship between the individual and society. As he himself wrote, this pessimistic conviction implies 'that the moral element is always the main factor which, more than any other, contributes to the achievement or failure to achieve those goals that every individual sets himself in life'.³⁵

8
Legitimacy and power during the European crisis of the 1930s

As has already been mentioned above, the position which Mosca adopted in the very last years of his life reflected the deeply felt need to rethink his overall intellectual and personal experience and reorganize it into a definitive system of thought. This position formed an important aspect of the crisis affecting Europe in the 1930s, of which the correspondence between Mosca and Guglielmo Ferrero provides a very interesting testimony. This reference to Ferrero is not just made in passing, but because this writer has enjoyed an international reputation especially for his critique of the mass character of political power in the modern world. Beyond the friendship the two writers felt for one another, they were linked by an intellectual and ethical empathy dating back to the period in which Ferrero formulated his well-known theses on legitimacy and Mosca undertook the codification of his doctrine. These were the years in which Fascism and Nazism triumphed by illegal and violent means, and by destroying the most elementary human rights. Thus the dramatic historical conjuncture through which Europe was passing in the 1930s formed the dramatic context in which their relationship developed not simply as one between academics, but in a truly dialectical spirit. These thoughts came to mind on rereading the heartfelt words dedicated to Gaetano Mosca by the 28-year-old Ferrero in 1899 and collected under the title of *Lo Stato e la libertà secondo uno scrittore italiano*.[1] A good method of evaluating Ferrero's political thought and its originality is to begin by comparing the two men. After an intellectual and human experience which was not without its painful conflicts, Ferrero the man and his work have been rediscovered by the initiative of scholars who deserve credit for having made known both aspects by adopting a fundamentally correct approach.[2]

The parallel between Gaetano Mosca and Guglielmo Ferrero presents itself almost automatically. Both of them witnessed and passed judgement on the history of this century; none the less they represent two radically different approaches to political analysis. Their different methods are the obvious reason for the great difference in the two almost parallel revivals which the two writers have experienced and are still experiencing. In Mosca, the prevalent factor is the close interweaving of juridical culture, historical analyis of a often comparative kind, and the courageous use of personal empirical experience (all elements which ensured that his approach was not limited to politics). Ferrero's writings, on the other hand, even in the eyes of his most generous critics, come across as a mixture of an antiquated and flowery journalistic prose and historical interests arising from an extreme sensitivity to the mere 'daily happenings' in politics, though it must be admitted that his perception of such events was more lucid than in academic studies by other writers.

We shall now attempt to single out some lines along which a critical analysis and, in a certain sense, comparison of the two writers may be carried out. It has been generally asserted that the part of Ferrero's work which is still currently valid and significant is his Napoleonic and post-Napoleonic trilogy, published for the first time between 1936 and 1942 and only appearing in Italy in 1947 and 1948.[3] As this trilogy was first published outside Italy – the first two volumes in Paris in 1936 and 1940 and the third in New York in 1942 – at a time when the democratic and anti-Fascist Ferrero had been exiled by victorious Fascism and was meditating systematically on politics and history in the quiet of Geneva University, it tells us something about this prominent moment in the writer's political thinking, also in terms of his emotional reaction. It must be stated at once that we are dealing with a formulation of ideas which, in our opinion, has particularly suffered from the corroding effect of time and the confusion existing in that period. With regard to *Ricostruzione*, undoubtedly the key work in the trilogy, Henry Kissinger was right to criticize in his *A World Restored*, published 15 years later, what Ferrero had written on the Congress of Vienna. Kissinger reproached the Italian writer both for his 'moralizing' and for the way in which he based his reconstruction of the political-historical moment solely on the indications contained in the memoirs of Charles Maurice Talleyrand-Périgord (1754–1838).[4]

The role of ideology in Mosca and Ferrero

A careful reading of the whole of Ferrero's trilogy shows clearly that the importance attached by him to the 'principle of legitimacy' has often been misunderstood and distorted beyond any reasonable limit. It forms the main plank in the final formulation of his ideas, as well as being the concept which stands out the most. In fact, although the central position of the concept of legitimacy in his thinking is given full expression in the trilogy, its significance can already be seen in his correspondence with Mosca; it was the constant note, the *idée fixe* of Ferrero not only during the 1930s but also in the preceding decade.

In 1934, after reading Mosca's analysis of the historical development of political thought in the still draft form of the didactic text *Lezioni di storia delle dottrine e delle istituzioni politiche* [*Lessons in the History of Political Doctrines and Institutions*], Ferrero raised two objections with his friend while at the same time expressing his appreciation of his latest effort. On the one hand, Ferrero holds that Mosca attributes too high an importance to doctrines 'as the cause behind events', whereas 'doctrines are often... the intruders of history'; on the other, he maintains that the concept of 'political formula' should be strengthened and turned into a true 'principle of legitimacy'. It is worth reconsidering what Ferrero actually wrote in this respect:

As a people grows more civilized, possession of the instruments of power is in itself insufficient; their acquisition must have been carried out while observing certain rules and principles which confer the universally recognized right to govern. Outside of such principles government has no legitimacy; it is the usurping of power. While you seem to consider the political formula as a kind of diversion or game, in my view the principle of legitimacy is a most serious and essential matter. It is the very essence of civilization. A civilized people which degenerates from legitimate government to government based on usurpation becomes weak-minded. And, unfortunately, two thirds of the governments in the world today came into being through the illegitimate seizure of power. In the last twenty years the world has been plunged into barbarism precisely because many legitimate governments have fallen, giving way to a series of usurpatory acts. How long will this last? That is the big question.[5]

The tenor of Mosca's reply is very significant, and it must be remembered that as early as 1896 he had formulated the conception, essential for the understanding of his political thinking, which is contained in the specific doctrine of the juridical defence.[6] Mosca does not enter into the merits of what his friend had written about the formula, thereby avoiding the need to discuss the concept of legitimacy in the emotive terms used by Ferrero. Naturally it would have been impossible for the realist Mosca to agree, firmly attached as he was to the idea that an organized minority (that is, the political class) always exists which is able at all times to impose its will on the unorganized majority. He points out to Ferrero that the root of political wrongs lies in the biggest anomaly existing in the modern world: the contradiction between political equality and economic inequality. According to Mosca, it is only 'in periods and countries of general prosperity' that this contradiction remains innocuous, but it becomes intolerable and fatal in a generalized crisis such as afflicted the world in the 1930s.[7] Here there emerges in Mosca a conception of considerable importance in the formulation of the doctrine of the political class; a conception which would be laid out in a concise and definitive form in the very last paragraph of *Storia delle dottrine politiche*. It concerns the importance attached to *mixed regimes* for the running of modern political systems: a type of regime

in which neither the autocratic nor the liberal system is totally predominant, and the tendency for an aristocracy to form is mitigated by a slow but continual renewal of the political class. In this way the latter manages to absorb those elements of healthy power that slowly emerge among the ruled classes. But for such a regime to endure, a set of circumstances is required which no legislator, however wise, can suddenly bring about. What is needed is the multiplicity and balance of ruling forces that is found only in a very advanced society: power based on religion must be separate from political power; the management of the economy must not be solely in the hands of those who rule the State; the possession of arms must not be monopolized by one section of society separate and distinct from all the rest; and a good level of education and technical preparation should be a requisite for admittance into the ruling class.[8]

The balance of ruling forces and the principle of legitimacy

Mosca's realism secures him against any emotional impulse and allows him to single out a substantial social pluralism and a corresponding balance of ruling forces as the constant factors in the political order of modern societies. In comparison, Ferrero's principle of legitimacy appears very weak and not at all convincing. The weak link in Ferrero's thinking is the abstract notion of legitimacy, which he admitted to having taken word for word from Talleyrand;[9] consequently from a culture – that of the Restoration – which operated on two converging planes but was far removed from the reality and demands of the 1920s and 1930s. The post-Napoleonic period of the European and international balance of power was characterized by *realpolitik* and the aspiration to reconstruct an organic political order founded above all on the co-operation between dynastic loyalty and religious observance (thus *legitimism*, in the sense of an ideology rather than as a synonym for legitimacy). In short, behind the concern for stability expressed by the principle of legitimacy conceived in this way, one senses far more the anti-revolutionary thinking of a Carl Ludwig von Haller (1768–1854) or a Joseph De Maistre (1753–1821) than a capacity to understand the radical change introduced into world history by the French Revolution and Napoleon.

At this stage, however, it is legitimate to also ask what this kind of culture and its values have to do with the political culture of the democratic and secular Ferrero. He had been among the first to sign – in 1925 – Benedetto Croce's counter-manifesto against Fascism in which support was expressed with unshakeable determination for 'our old belief: the belief which for two and a half centuries has been the spirit of resurgent Italy, of modern Italy'.[10] And what sense does it have – beyond any analysis of the relevant social, political and cultural forces – to maintain as Ferrero does that

from the end of the eighteenth century philosophy, literature, science and politics have created for Europeans and Americans a world which would be splendid to live in, if it were not an imaginary one full of fictitious hells and paradises. Lost in this imaginary world we have gradually misplaced a sense of the great reality of life. We no longer know precisely what war, peace, revolution, order, justice, law, power and legitimacy are.[11]

In our opinion, far from being the most topical and original this is the Achilles' heel in the formulation of Ferrero's ideas. He projects a feeling of existential bewilderment onto his intellectual endeavour, but forgets that the 'confusion' of the modern world – the new world born from the new culture of English liberal empiricism, French encyclopaedism, the political revolutions (from the American to the French), the secularization and industrialization of society and the change in the very concept of the state – was a favourite theme at all the reactionary turning-points which abound in the history of Europe between the First and Second World Wars. We are aware that this critical approach will probably seem radical in comparison to the hagiography which makes him out to be the forerunner of the principle of legitimacy. But it is equally justifiable to ask: what kind of legitimacy? If – adopting a clear and basic English definition – legitimacy is 'the rightful rule or exercise of power, based on some principle (e.g. consent) jointly accepted by the ruler and the ruled',[12] then it is indispensable to discover the basic values behind the principle of legitimacy invoked in each case. To put it frankly, these values are presented in Ferrero's work in a still inadequate form despite the avowed intention to provide a definition and analysis expressed, for example, in his work entitled *Potere*. However, the weakness in the elaboration of his ideas derives in particular from his unwillingness to take modern philosophy into account; a position which clearly emerges in the conclusion to *Potere*, especially in the following assertion: 'After Descartes, Western philosophy has become more and more detached from the solid realism of Greek philosophy, the Bible, Thomism and the common sense of the average man: it has in part attempted, in one way or another, to negate the existence of the world'.[13] It has therefore seemed appropriate to locate the weak spot in Ferrero's work in its theoretical limitations, which make it both obsolete and impractical as a doctrine for the present age.

In the heart of the European crisis

It has already been shown that Ferrero adopted at one and the same time at least two different approaches to politics. Not only are they different, they also contradict one another. Nevertheless, though inadequate when taken separately, their dialectical interweaving may well give rise to several original lines of interpretation.

In a first phase Ferrero's approach was that mentioned above, characterized by a state of bewilderment or even desperation in which he was totally unable to grasp the profound significance of the crisis in Europe. In no way was it a *crisis of legitimacy* (which government has ever enjoyed an obedience comparable to that asked for and obtained from the German people by Adolf Hitler's Third Reich or from the Russian people by Josef V. Stalin?). In fact, the deep significance of the crisis lay in the gulf and opposition between economic and social interests; in the conscious rejection of social, cultural, political and institutional pluralism as conceived by Gaetano Mosca; in the inability of the political classes to govern a society which had become a 'mass society', intensely stratified into different forms and of a totally new kind compared to any past model, through the continual process of transformation under way in the modern world.

The second approach, already indicated above, is very lucid in its consideration of the 'everyday quality' of politics, though also suffering from contradictions when it has to broaden its fragmentary ideas into a more general discourse. However, it does appear to have stimulated more profound thinking. For example, the short work *La democrazia in Italia* provides a valuable consideration of the period in which it was published and of the subjects it deals with. But it is almost a paradox that what interests us here is the fact that Ferrero manages to set aside the abstract examination of 'quantitative' civilization, contrasted with 'qualitative' civilization, and to grasp the deeper and more real theme of social life: the danger and harm from the abuse of state power.[14] This is what Mosca achieved so well in his speech to the Senate of 19 December 1925 in which he announced his decision not to vote in favour of the 'utterly Fascist' laws for transforming the liberal state.

104   *The doctrine of the political class*

By following up this line of argument, it becomes clear that a key to the interpretation of Ferrero's overall political thinking may be found in his brief contribution to the survey *Dove va il mondo?* (1923). In it he makes the following assertion:

There is no doubt that a strong leaning to the Right exists in the world today. But in what does it consist? In the desire, widespread among all the upper classes in Europe, to create dictatorial governments in which they are able to govern as they please without being hindered by legal constraints or having to answer to a controlling body. I also think that many States are destined to experience such dictatorial governments devoid of the seal of legitimacy.[15]

This is an obvious example of the contradiction indicated above between Ferrero's acumen in examining the prevailing tendencies of the day and the completely abstract manner in which he challenges the 'seal of legitimacy' of emerging dictatorial governments. In Russia in 1917, in Italy in the 1920s and in Germany and Spain in the 1930s legitimacy could not be denied to the new regimes solely on the assumption that the only principle of legitimacy to have survived the First World War was 'the will of the people expressed through universal suffrage'.[16] Indeed, it was a fact that the new regimes were established with a wide degree of popular support. We are aware that to evoke the subject of the legitimacy of the mass totalitarian regimes in this century leads to a series of worrying questions and problems which have not been tackled adequately; and the solutions offered have been even less adequate. None the less, Ferrero goes on to say something quite illuminating in this respect:

All peoples who do not wish to be subject to a regime like the one Bolshevism has given to Russia will have to be governed by democratic institutions; they must make the effort to lift these institutions out of the repugnant stupidity into which they have fallen in almost every other country and make them fit to govern properly. I see no other alternative.[17]

This clearly illustrates, in our opinion, that in the first years of the 1920s Ferrero saw the danger as coming essentially from the Left, in the form of Bolshevism (which, incidentally, may have been true, even if in Italy the March on Rome went against the general trend) and held that the only way of avoiding it was through a renewal of democratic beliefs and institutions. Thus Ferrero was another who seemed unaware of the menacingly novel aspects contained in the new demagogic regimes – clearly dictatorial but with mass support – which were advancing in Europe (and first of all in Italy). When this reality became a personal matter, as shown by the interesting diary for the years 1926–7 of his son

Leo,[18] besides experiencing exile, Ferrero began to rethink the principle of legitimacy in the ways referred to critically above. However, it is precisely from this connection and from this contradiction that there emerges one of the most interesting aspects for investigation – still of interest today – in Ferrero's political thought.

The work of this writer should now be read and understood, in particular, as one moment in the wide range – relatively virgin ground for its implications and provocative ideas – of anti-Fascist political thinking in Italy between the two world wars. Carlo Mongardini is probably right when he picks out from among Ferrero's intuitions the capacity to go beyond the 'theory of elites' in its nineteenth-century version and use it to create a first link between his conception of the principle of legitimacy (understood as the ethical principle behind a political regime) and the practice of representative democracy. To expect from Ferrero a fully systematic and theoretical response (as is the case with Mosca) is, in truth, to ask too much. This is especially so when one takes into account the weaknesses exposed in the two cornerstones of his thinking in the crucial period 1920–40: his ideas about mass society and the concept of legitimacy. It must also be said that, unlike that of Mosca, Ferrero's entire work does not come near to elaborating, even in terms of institutions, the political concepts he put forward; consequently, it is pervaded to a greater extent by the author's moods, sensations, reactions and anxieties, which does not make for rational exposition and well-reasoned argument.

The crisis in Europe at the end of the 1930s had world-wide implications and it sent a huge wave of anti-Fascist, anti-Nazi and Jewish emigration with great intellectual qualities towards North America. This fact helped to foster, outside of Europe, a series of readings and interpretations of all these themes which would converge, in different forms and often indirect ways, in the first syntheses of elitism, the theoretical component of a new and realistic conception of political democracy, the development of which is traced in Part II.

PART II
Elitism, Neo-elitism and Democracy

9
The 'Italian school of elitists' – between myth and reality

Despite the passage of time and the change in political, social and cultural conditions Gaetano Mosca's doctrine has, on the one hand, still proved to be worth a separate analysis and assessment (covered in the first part of this book); on the other hand, it has also been developed further in an indiscriminate combination with contributions from other writers, even to the extent of forming part of a new and more composite political theory. The latter postulates and identifies as the characteristic feature of modern democracy the permanent existence of political groups which essentially have the same values and ends, and which compete with one another for the conquest and management of power.

From the point of view of historical and conceptual development, the following questions arise: how was this theoretical proposition gradually formulated, what significance does it have and what are its future prospects? In fact starting from a still generic and eclectic 'theory of political elites', the conceptual development in this area of research and formulation of ideas has given birth to so-called *elitism*. The latter deserves special attention because it presents, at one and the same time, scientific data explaining the intimate nature of power and diverging ideological objectives. At this point we need to clarify a point of terminology. Throughout the first part of this book the term 'doctrine' was used to emphasize the prescriptive as well as scientific-descriptive character of Mosca's research. In this second part, the term 'theory' is frequently used with its original Greek meaning (θεωρία) in mind and signifies, for the most part, a general intellectual vision of politics without specific prescriptive and ideological connotations.

From Mosca's political class to Pareto's elite

As has already been pointed out on several occasions, what is specific to the formulation of Mosca's doctrine is the importance he attaches to the purely political element, no longer conceived theoretically and formally but in realistic terms derived from the dynamic of social forces. This is the level on which the doctrine of the political class is measured against and compared with the other formulations that, taken as a whole and in their various combinations, make up the so-called 'Italian school of elitists'.

When in 1902, with the publication of *Systèmes socialistes* [*Socialist Systems*], Vilfredo Pareto put forward the term and concept 'elite' (written in the singular but with a plural meaning) his intention was not to limit the formulation of his doctrine – similar to but by no means identical with Mosca's – to the sphere of politics and the state, as Mosca had done. On the contrary, from *Systèmes socialistes* to *Trattato di sociologia generale* (1916) – the English edition of this last work appeared under the title, *The Mind and Society. A Treatise on General Sociology*[1] – Pareto's work moved in the direction of elaborating the concept of elite in essentially social terms. It is therefore quite evident that over and above any superficial similarity, the two conceptions of Mosca and Pareto are profoundly different. Mosca's conception is centered – as we have seen – within a context of culture and values firmly tied to law, institutions and politics; that of Pareto, in contrast, is set within the economic and sociological framework formed by the author's distinctive scientific approach. It must be remembered, moreover, that Mosca's doctrine is not the result of abstract speculation but of careful reflection on history, politics and the way institutions work in Italy. Pareto's doctrine, on the other hand, can be defined as a more general vision of social development which is largely derived from considering in an international perspective the economic dynamic of the modern, industrialized world.

Despite these differences, there is a powerfully determining (almost obsessive) factor common to both writers: the refusal to accept the logic and philosophy of socialism in its radical and Marxist version. Mosca's attitude in this respect is well-known and has already been dealt with; that of Pareto is analogous and we will mention it briefly. For both Mosca and Pareto, Marxist analysis and socialist praxis have the defect of being too abstract, though they are of some practical use; and both writers refer to a fixed and constant fact, intrinsic to and essential for politics: the fact of ruling groups which have always existed and always been protagonists in history. This is as far as the analogy between the two theories stretches. The material fact of the *political class* as understood by Mosca, though supported and justified by the *political formula*, was insufficient for Pareto's purposes. This lead him to undertake a penetrating investigation into ideologies and their utopian implications, which run counter to the spirit of science. At a conceptual level, Mosca's approach is reversed by Pareto since he indicates – as has been correctly observed by one of his major interpreters, Giovanni Busino, who succeeded Pareto in the Chair of Sociology at Lausanne University – that 'the aim of studying Utopias, as well as ideologies, is to show the mechanism by which elites are created'.[2] In other words, Pareto's political elite arises from a skilful exploitation of the 'sentiments, ideals and illogical motives of individuals', from the genuine skill of groups wishing to play an important and dominant role and obtain a consensus by organizing 'the ideas and sentiments of individuals through collective representation'. This is achieved by getting the governed social groups to interiorize 'an ultimate objective' which accords with their own needs and satisfies their hopes and desires.[3] Consequently, ideology with all its mystifying and intoxicating potency acts as the precondition around which elites are formed into cohesive bodies. And out of the clash between ideologies emerges the opposition between dominant elites and rival elites ('counter-elites') and the continual circulation of elites, which induced Pareto to write the famous passage in *Trattato di sociologia generale* in which he asserts that 'aristocracies do not last. Whatever the reasons may be, it is undeniable that after a while they disappear. History is a cemetery full of aristocracies ... The decline of certain aristocracies is not only due to a numerical factor but also to a qualitative one in the sense that their strength diminishes.'

Since the subject of this present work is not the thought of Pareto, we shall dispense with any further and deeper analysis of the Paretian concept of political elite. It is sufficient to have pointed out the similarities and differences in the work of the two writers in order to understand how the exceptional fortune enjoyed by the Paretian term 'élite' has, with the passage of time, come to signify a point at which distinct theoretical formulations converge, including that of Mosca which preceded it chronologically. In a critical perspective, it should also be pointed out that both these theories already displayed at the beginning of the twentieth century a certain inadequacy in the new area of the empirical and theoretical investigation of political parties and mass movements. Hence the arrival on the scene of a new theory, that of Robert Michels, the youngest among the 'classic elitists'.

There is no doubt that the different theories of Mosca and Pareto exerted an influence on one another. The argument which broke out between the two men in 1907 as to the precedence of the 'doctrine of the political class' over the 'theory of the elite' is symptomatic in this respect. Mosca's view was that the real fact of the minority nature of power had become a 'widespread and popular' belief, and Pareto agreed with him on this point.[4] But the importance of Mosca's elaboration, the point where he diverges from the 'common sense' leading to this very belief, lies in the way it is explicitly and consciously formulated into theory. These are the terms in which the great liberal economist Luigi Einaudi, who had been a colleague of Mosca's at Turin University and thus knew him very well, established the undoubted fact that Mosca's doctrine preceded that of Pareto. This occurred during a debate in the 1930s sparked off by several Italian Fascist writers who had transformed the results of the research undertaken by Mosca and, above all, Pareto into an ideology justifying 'dominant aristocracies' of which the dictatorial regimes in Europe at that time were supposed to be an expression. In reality, Mosca's intuition is founded on the clearly and explicitly expounded concepts of political class and political formula, which form the 'cornerstones' of a theory which looks to history and everyday life for verification.[5] So we find in Mosca a new conception of politics which is totally removed from the dynamic of nineteenth-century society.

When considering some of Pareto's original conceptual formulations of a more typically political rather than sociological kind, it is difficult and also misleading not to take into account the work of Mosca. Indeed, Pareto himself admitted to having read the first edition of the *Elementi di scienza politica* some time around the turn of the century.[6] Ideas circulated between them and they exchanged letters and opinions; this should always be kept in mind even though both authors were loathe to point it out in their works. There is no doubt either that the Paretian notion of the elite had, in turn, an influence at the conceptual level on the second edition of the *Elementi*. As we have already seen, in this edition the concept of ruling class replaces for the most part the more limiting nineteenth-century one of political class. This new conception of the ruling class is manifestly derived by Mosca from the diversified and stratified reality of social, cultural, economic and political elites, a vision clearly Paretian in origin.

It must be added for the sake of completeness, however, that Mosca and Pareto not only differed in the approach adopted for their respective research but also, so to speak, in tone and personal inclination. In this respect, what Giuseppe Prezzolini (1882–1982) – who at the beginning of the century had seen in Mosca 'a great and original mind for those times' – had to say to the author of this book in a long letter of 1977 is still valid:

Pareto had a warmer, more open and far-reaching mind, and he was a more political and livelier writer than Mosca; he wrote in French and was immediately translated into English; he was a brilliant writer with a knowledge of ancient Greece – he was not solely versed in Latin like Mosca – he had travelled, and lived for a long time in the international atmosphere of Geneva. He was a man of independent means whereas Mosca, in order to get on in life, had to seek a parliamentary nomination.

Prezzolini's judgement is very clear-cut and almost blunt in its comparison of these two intellectuals whom, in his view, 'Italy was unable to recognize, honour or make use of'; and their ideas, propagated and widely known in a period spanning the nineteenth and twentieth century, assumed an influence and value independent of the cultural contexts and systems of thought in which they had originally been set. Since it is quite obviously arbitrary to speak of a syncretic 'Mosca–Paretian elitist theory', we shall adopt the term 'paradigm' instead. Used by George Lowell Field and John Higley, two US academics, it expresses a less rigorous conceptual unity in favour of a more interesting and verifiable hypothesis for study and research.[7]

The influence of the first research into political parties: Ostrogorskij and Michels

The present state of research leads us reasonably to suppose that the Russian political writer Moisej I. Ostrogorskij (1854–1917/19) never read any of Mosca's works, which are not quoted, even indirectly, in his most extensive and systematic work *La Démocratie et l'organisation des Partis Politiques*. Nevertheless, we owe to this genial and still little studied author the elaboration of a very interesting political analysis.[8] It is based on the concept of ruling class which appears in the very first pages of his main work and on the concept of *leadership*, the latter understood literally as the expression of a 'natural elite' which is formed in the political struggle in spite of and against existing formal institutions. Ostrogorskij's examination of the experience of political parties, both in Great Britain and the United States of America, displays a wide-ranging reflection on the formation, growth and circulation of ruling groups, and already in the context of his own age he posed the problem as to how this 'natural elite' is formed within the political struggle. He believes that it is destined for leadership and represents a fundamental and crucial aspect of democracy. This Russian writer was widely referred to from the very first edition of *Zur Soziologie des Parteiwesens in der Modernen Demokratie* (1911) (the English edition of this work appeared under the title *Political Parties*) by Robert Michels who took up and extended the theme of leadership, linking it in various ways to the theories of both Mosca and Pareto.

The figure of Ostrogorskij has been included for the sake of historical and philological completeness and because of his unmistakable role as a pioneer in this field, which deserves recognition. In his view, the problem to be resolved is that of political parties within the liberal-democratic system, in which he had great faith since he considered the creation of the 'free democratic city' the supreme achievement of human dignity. The problem to be faced according to Michels, on the other hand, is that of democracy inside the mass political party; he accurately perceived that permanently organized minorities, such as political parties, were destined to manage consent and political participation. Thus the party becomes the operational structure in which the real possibilities for developing democratic life are or are not created. So we may say that Michels and his book of 1911 rounded off and closed an area of research which, in conceptual and historical terms, had originated with the publication of Gaetano Mosca's *Sulla teorica dei governi e sul governo parlamentare* in 1884. In fact, Mosca's central conviction concerns the permanent existence of an organized minority which imposes its will on the disorganized majority and legitimizes its own power by using as an ideological instrument the set of values and beliefs held in common by society. This conviction became, in time, an axiom which could be equally applied to the inner workings of modern society, unified on an international scale by industrialization (Pareto), of liberal-democratic political systems (Ostrogorskij) and, lastly, of the socialist and working-class party, the prototype for all modern organized parties (Michels).

All of these different theoretical and historical contributions have, taken together, led to a transformation of the Moschian doctrine, just as reciprocal influence has modified all the different formulations which make up what we may now define as the 'elitist paradigm' in the modern sense of the term.

The link between Michels and Mosca is much more explicit and linear than that between Pareto and Mosca. It should be remembered that it was Michels himself who always referred to Mosca as one of his mentors. However, Michels's thinking was strongly influenced by German and French as well as Italian culture, and a very subtle and significant mingling of intellectual, scientific and cultural stimuli can be seen in his work of 1911. A student of both the thought of Karl Marx and the practice of socialist militancy, he was a friend and collaborator of Max Weber (1864–1920). He succeeded in his most important and original writing in ingeniously combining a vast range of ideas and this allowed him to identify the transformation of the Moschian 'organized minority', still expressed by a world of election committees and restricted electoral assemblies, into the oligarchy which he saw as inherent in the extensive and popular organization of a class party based on social struggle like that of the German Social Democratic Party.

The specifically Italian quality of the 'Mosca–Paretian paradigm' and its progressive internationalization

The next theme to be dealt with follows on more or less automatically from those considered above. First of all, we must clarify to what extent the theoretical formulations of Mosca, Pareto and, to a lesser degree, Michels form a specific part of Italy's political and ideological history or whether it is more exact to view their range and significance in an international light. All three writers had an Italian background, though the way they were shaped by it differed in each case. At this point, therefore, we need to outline some aspects of Italian history. Even a superficial knowledge of it suggests at once something obvious and almost banal: the fact of the different societies which succeeded one another on the Italian mainland and the large Mediterranean islands of Sicily and Sardinia (and including for a long period Corsica) during more than three millennia constitute a far more deeply rooted reality than the unified Italian state set up only in the second half of the last century. Italian society with its different geographical and historical elements is the product of a continuity in human terms which developed over a particularly long historical period, involving an impressive co-mingling of peoples, cultures and civilizations. The hegemony of Rome over the peninsula (and over a large part of the then known civilized world) represented the focal point for a first synthesis of the civil life of society which was growing up in ancient Italy. The long period of transition reaching from the decline of Rome in the fifth century AD to the modern age, that is, the beginning of the sixteenth century, and then on through to the present requires an appropriate interpretation: one which describes how modern Italy, seen both at the level of society and the state as an independent and unified, cultural and political organism, arose from the reality of the Roman world, manifestly imperial and universal but also respectful of the individual local peculiarities which abounded in ancient Italy.

Italy's problem throughout history was the relationship between a territory which was highly fragmented politically and in terms of numerous, widely diverging historical experiences and the painful, drawn-out process in which the consciousness of a common identity and a common political destiny gradually matured. The characteristic elements in this historical process were linguistic similarities, religious feeling and the cultural development fostered by intellectuals (clerical and lay), who through their communication with one another already represented the overcoming of narrow local perspectives and foreshadowed a society established on a national scale. In this context, the very concept itself of

Italy was a problematical fact in the passage from fragmentation to unity through a historical experience which, whenever common to all parts of the country, was determined by the great universalistic realities (Papacy and Empire) or by foreign domination; and whenever local history predominated, it was the history of Venice, Florence, Milan, Naples, etc. This was the situation up until the events which lead to the setting up of a unified state in the nineteenth century. The Italian state was created by the proclamation of the Kingdom of Italy on 17 March 1861, which united a large portion of the national territory, and by the successive annexations between 1866 and 1919. Thus the conclusion to the heroic age of the Risorgimento, though it may not have surprised and fired the Italians themselves with enthusiasm, nevertheless opened up the way to a process of social and political integration which has had particularly devasting effects and has still not been achieved in full.[9]

We believe that if one views Mosca's thought and work in this perspective, they take on a significance which is more exemplary and political than in the case of Pareto and Michels. It has already been seen that besides its scientific ends, Mosca also gave his work a precise ideological character. In this way his political ideology was translated into a true doctrine of institutional integration in which the formation of a new political class, educated, economically independent and morally sound, was seen as the highest possible expression of juridical defence within the still fragile structure of the state in recently unified Italy. Due to the failure of the parliamentary institutions of his time to meet the requisites of such a doctrine, Mosca developed his severe criticism of the parliamentary system (above all in *Teorica* during his early period), which has given rise to many misunderstandings about his views. What we have in mind are those interpretations, mentioned above, which read him in an authoritarian and even Fascist or semi-Fascist light. The general orientation which is expressed in Mosca's thought is clearly both too pragmatic and too Utopian, but it has the merit of making men and the social classes which bring them together into the real protagonists of every political regime.

Since no more than a summary is being attempted at this point, we are unable to examine in more detail a theme through which Mosca's thought is intrinsically linked to the entire area of liberal doctrine. Mosca did not only conceive and experience liberalism through the limited perspective of Italian political-parliamentary affairs in the first decades after unification. He was also compelled, above all from the 1920s, to get to grips with the broader questions, both ideological and practical, that were being posed by the advent of Fascism and Nazism. This is the moment in which Mosca's entire theoretical construction revealed an incapacity to grasp the new reality in which the ground was being prepared for the rise of a mass society. In the period from 1925–6, when Fascism became a dictatorship with its own particular features (demagogic, military and with mass support) up until his death Mosca continued to analyse many questions of a doctrinal and institutional nature. We feel we must underline, however, the fact that he did not manage to make a specific and significant contribution to the subject of political parties. Nor was this gap filled by *Church Sects and Parties* published in *Social Forces* in 1935; this piece was a version in English of chapter VII from the first part of the *Elementi* penned by Hannah D. Kahn who had translated the entire work into English under the title *The Ruling Class*.[10]

The problem must be seen, therefore, in terms of the incapacity of a shrewd political analyst like Mosca to understand, even after Michels's research and ideas on the subject became common knowledge, the two central facts regarding the formation of ruling groups in a modern mass society: the political party and the organized trade-union. These two facts were overwhelmingly present in the Fascist State based on a corporative structure, that is, on the organic representation of the various interests acting in society through the division of labour, and on an institutionalized one-party system. Such a limit gives Mosca's work a dated quality by circumscribing it essentially to the liberal era preceding the First World War, the misery and splendour of which he fully grasped; for the era of Fascism which succeeded it we are left with nothing more than an ethical and methodological approach.

There is, however, a second and somewhat more relevant aspect which concerns the entire Italian school of elitists: the internationalization of the Mosca–Paretian paradigm. As we have seen, Mosca's doctrine was worked out, generally speaking, along the same lines as those of Pareto and Michels; and so at a high level of synthesis and abstraction it may be stated that though these writers did not form a school in the strict sense, they carried out a common and organic series of studies and research which are of fundamental importance for anyone wishing to understand politics.

Even though in a less direct and continuous manner than Mosca, Pareto and Michels produced a set of doctrinal formulations which are clearly different from one another and from those of Mosca. None the less, they are all linked together by a profound and inexorable connection with contemporary Italian politics and through the personal experiences of the three writers. Pareto's entire life bears witness to this: from his first steps as a young man in Genoa (1873) to his unsuccessful candidature for the Chamber of Deputies in 1882; from the polemic on free trade in the 1890s to his nomination as Senator just before his death

(1923). The same is true of Michels, although he was Italian by choice and not by birth. Having always been interested in Italy, and noticeably in the socialist and working-class movement – to which he dedicated two extensive critical studies in 1910 and 1921 – Michels was particularly steeped in the political, cultural and scientific climate of his adoptive country from the time of his entry into Italian academic circles in 1907 to his active participation in the Fascist movement.[11] Therefore, although they profoundly differed in their theories and practical-political attitudes, it is no surprise that Mosca, Pareto and Michels are considered as the founding fathers of the Italian school of elitists. It has been observed that this expression 'is a way of simplifying matters, but it has its reasons',[12] which are rooted in the particular social and political significance of Italian history and the role of these three figures in it.

Thus the trio of 'classic elitists', defined – perhaps too narrowly – by Walter G. Runciman as the 'minor forefathers of political sociology', represent both a type of political thinking rooted in reality and a mythical school of science and ideology. This, at least, is how the classic founders of the Italian school of elitists have been perceived by the intellectual political tradition. An example of this is what James H. Meisel writes in the new 1962 edition of his famous work *The Myth of the Ruling Class*:

A spectre is haunting the Century of the Common Man – the spectre of the Elite. The two powers of the world have entered into an unholy alliance to exorcize this spectre: Eastern Communists and Western Democrats are of one mind about this matter ... It is high time that the new school proclaim its aims and meet this nursery tale of the Spectre with a Manifesto of the Elite itself.[13]

This is an invitation which is still topical and worth considering; but it must not be forgotten that this 'Manifesto' is made up of several distinct sections and when referring to them, it must be taken into account that subsequent to the classical formulations, *political elitism* has assumed different meanings and values which deeply reflect their particular cultural and ideological contexts. While we wait for the necessary exhaustive and systematic research to be undertaken, what is said in the following chapters is at least valid as a general hypothesis of interpretation and for the fact that it puts forward concrete examples. Special attention has been paid to the interweaving of the theories worked out by the classic Italian writers with the eclectic formulations of elitism in the 1940s within the English-speaking tradition of political studies, as well as with those produced more recently, using an empirical and highly scientific method, by a genuine neo-elitism which has lately come to the fore against very different social and cultural backgrounds. We are well aware of the complexity of this subject and of its enormous bibliography.

However, an approach seems useful which though aware of its incomplete nature, investigates some essential aspects of the question and begins to compare very different intellectual traditions, in some cases in dialectical opposition to one another.

10
The development of elitism in the English-speaking intellectual political tradition

Although Karl Mannheim (1893–1947) clearly deals with the theme of elites in his classic works of the 1920s and 1930s, there is no specific mention in the bibliography – unless we are mistaken – of Mosca's doctrine. On the other hand, there are references to the work of Pareto – in the German (Leiden, 1935) and subsequent English (1941) editions of *Man and Society in an Age of Reconstruction* – and that of Michels is mentioned on a few occasions. Neither Pareto nor Michels receive any mention at all in *La rebélion de las masas*, the fundamental work written by José Ortega y Gasset (1883–1955) and published in 1930, whereas they both occupy a prominent position in James Burnham's *The Machiavellians. Defenders of Freedom*, which appeared in 1943.[1]

According to James H. Meisel, Mosca's thinking first became known in the USA in the 1930s following the appearance in English translations by Arthur Livingston of the above-mentioned adapted version of Pareto's *Trattato di sociologia generale* (1935) and the second edition of the *Elementi di scienza politica* (1939). In Meisel's view, Mosca's thought was introduced into the English-speaking world above all in the wake of Pareto, but their ideas were received in a confused and undifferentiated manner.[2] The influential role played by the 'Chicago School' must not be forgotten in this regard. Formed in the years immediately following the First World War around the figure of Charles Edward Merriam (1874–1970) (author of the important work *Political Power* (1934)), it was composed of academics such as David Truman, Herman Finer, Renzo Sereno and, above all, Harold Lasswell[3] to whom Joseph La Palombara has paid homage in the first volume of the 'Gaetano Mosca International Archive' (appearing in both an Italian and an international series – the latter in English). They were all well acquainted with Mosca's work and were responsible for making the Italian scholar known to American intellectual political circles.[4] A further consideration to be borne in mind, which has been given full prominence by Juan J. Linz, the most authoritative scholar of Michels, is that in 1927 Michels taught a summer course at the Political Institute in Williamstown, Massachusetts as part of the activities of Chicago University. Finally, the undoubted influence exerted by Giuseppe Prezzolini and Gaetano Salvemini in the USA should also be taken into account. Very different from one another, they were both interested in the question of elites.

A new democratic conception based on elites – Schumpeter and Burnham

These chronological and environmental factors also explain the important fact that the problem of *elitism* was taken up by Joseph A. Schumpeter in his major work, *Capitalism, Socialism and Democracy* (1942). Although the Austro-American economist does not mention Mosca and Michels and refers only rarely to Pareto, nevertheless chapters XX to XXIII can be – despite the use of expressions like 'leader' and 'leadership' rather than the unknown elites or political class – viewed as the clear result of a compatibility between democratic theory and elitism derived eclectically from the classic Italian school. In fact, Schumpeter reverses the tendency by introducing the idea of the elite into democratic theory as one of its indispensable components.[5]

With regard to the results of Schumpeter's work, the acute and relevant judgement of the Canadian political scientist Crawford Brough Macpherson has already been referred to in the Introduction. Among other things, he was one of the first English-speaking academics to deal critically with Pareto and Mosca, whom he studied between 1937 and 1941.[6] Macpherson believes that Schumpeter's merit lay in the fact that he put forward in a completed, though somewhat reduced, form a 'model' – in the broad sense – of a political system, that is, 'a theoretical construction intended to exhibit and explain the real relations, underlying the appearances, between or within the phenomena under study'.[7] A model that was able to interpret and bring up-to-date the liberal-democratic theory which existed in the 1940s and 1950s. Attributing its paternity to Schumpeter, what Macpherson calls the 'pluralist elitist equilibrium model' depicts in essence the functioning of a democratic system as a constant dialectic of competition between ruling groups (elites). They put themselves forward to the electorate (Mosca would have said they *impose themselves*), which grants them power according to rules of procedure for ensuring that the ruled have a real and constant opportunity to participate in the selection of their rulers. This is not the place for a critical evaluation of this 'model'; besides, it has already been done in a radical fashion by Macpherson himself from both an ideological and ethical perspective.[8] Such is the spirit in which the Canadian academic rebukes Western societies for maintaining this type of democratic organization which, in reality, gives preference to 'affluence' over 'community'.[9] It is here essential to point out that this conception of political democracy sustained by an entire apparatus of Keynesian economic theory, state interventionism and bureaucratic specialization is still by far the most dominant in the everyday political experience of those countries that continue to be governed by democratic-parliamentary regimes.

In the case of Schumpeter, therefore, what we undoubtedly have is a reformulation and application of the political elitism of the classic Italian exponents, based on the realistic and scientific core of the 'Mosca–Paretian paradigm' without taking over fully and explicitly its cultural and ethical values or ideological ends. Despite the fact that he was not a political scientist but an economist, devoting himself from 1911 onwards to the theory of economic growth, Schumpeter clearly came under the scientific influence of Pareto at the very beginning of the 1940s. At that time he was investigating what he defined as the 'human nature of politics' and increasingly tended towards an extra-rational and even irrational approach.[10] The compatibility and integration which he proposed in conceptual and concrete terms between democratic theory (revised and brought into line with the needs of contemporary commercial-industrial society) and the reality of political elitism constituted an original result given that the two bodies of doctrine had remained theoretically separate in the formulations of the classic elitists.

Schumpeter gives chapter XXII of his book the significant title 'Another Doctrine of Democracy', and in it we find an approach and several concepts, formulated in a surprisingly similar manner to that of the classic exponents of political elitism. An example, which could have been penned by Mosca himself, is the following assertion:

Not only do the voters not decide anything, they do not even choose with an open mind the Members of Parliament from among the eligible population. In all normal cases, the initiative is taken by the person who puts himself forward as a candidate for Parliament and for leadership at the local level, which may lead to his election as an MP. The electors are limited to accepting this candidate in preference to others or to rejecting him.[11]

It would be very difficult not to see the close similarity which exists on a conceptual plane between this type of approach and Mosca's doctrine as presented in chapter IV of this present work, which deals with the Italian writer's early thoughts concerning the question of elections. However, Schumpeter's elitism does not attempt to tackle in particular the difficulties of ideology, but rather moves in the direction of a thoroughly critical and realistic revision of classical theories of democracy. He does this by applying in an original way his knowledge of economics, and he depicts the democratic system as a world of procedures and guarantees able to ensure the circulation of ruling political groups through public competition which is open, but clearly dominated by those who are decisive and determined to impose their own victory. Schumpeter's great skill in re-elaborating the ideas developed with regard to this subject in various countries and disciplines has ensured that, over a period of time, the political theory of this Austro-American economist has gradually gained an almost totally independent status. A significant example of this is to be found in the very recent book *The Battle of Democracy. Conflicts, Consensus and the Individual*[12] by Keith Graham, lecturer at Bristol University. In the extensive chapter dedicated to elite theory this author takes *Capitalism, Socialism and Democracy* as the starting point for his analysis of the entire theoretical current, leaving out of consideration all the classic forerunners. This interpretation is given a more complete form, within a historical and theoretical perspective, in an analysis by Robert A. Alford and Roger Friedland of the University of California (Santa Cruz and Santa Barbara) contained in *Powers of Theory. Capitalism, the State and Democracy*.[13]

But the work which above all codifies the eclectic nature of elitism, referring extensively and explicitly to its classic exponents, is James Burnham's *The Machiavellians*. This work is divided into seven parts, three of them dedicated to Mosca (III), Michels (V) and Pareto (VI) respectively. The ideas of this American writer, with Marxian and Trotskyite leanings, have often been misunderstood. In his pretentious book on the history of economic thought the Frenchman Henri Denis even goes so far as to accuse Burnham of holding 'substantially Fascist ideas'.[14] There is, in fact, no real justification for such a superficial judgement. By the beginning of the 1940s Burnham's research was no longer influenced by the logic of Marxist political praxis according to Lev Trotsky (1879–1940), and it brought forth the concept of 'the managerial revolution', which was to enjoy great success as a tool for analysing contemporary society. The theses contained in both *The Managerial Revolution* (1941) and, above all, in the conclusion to *The Machiavellians* (1943) are built up on a solid foundation derived from an intelligent and perceptive combination of the theories of Mosca and Pareto, as well as those of Marx and Trotsky. The view of political elitism highlighted by

Burnham originates in the deeply held conviction according to which the need to safeguard freedom is strongly associated with the growing specialization and bureaucratization of industrialized societies in the twentieth century (the so-called dominion of the managers in the capitalist system and of the *apparatchiki* in Soviet communism over the owners of capital and the holders of political rights respectively).

For Burnham, then, political elitism points to a clear-cut current of thinking which includes all those he defines as 'modern Machiavellians' who

do not waste time discussing the merits and shortcomings of the myth of democracy seen in terms of 'self-government'. Instead, they take a deep interest in the reality of democracy defined in terms of freedom. They realize that the degree of freedom in a society is of the greatest importance for the whole social structure and for the individuals who live therein.[15]

The conclusion at which this author's research arrives is the need to form a scientific elite which, besides having a greater capacity to renew itself, will govern in such a way as to ensure rationality and freedom.[16] What Burnham adds to the parallel theory formulated by Schumpeter is a note of disenchantment and pessimism.

A legitimate question which arises at this point is whether the notions of Schumpeter and Burnham fall within the logic of what two scholars in Australia, Geoff Stokes and Bill Brugger, have recently termed 'the technocratic challenge to democratic theory'.[17] The answer is affirmative if this kind of analysis is done without taking into account the overall political and cultural context which we have outlined, as well as the different intellectual traditions encompassed by it; but it is manifestly negative if the theoretical and practical results are considered. In fact, what must be considered are two quite different things which, however, are connected at a deeper level: the competition between elites as a feature of democracy in present industrialized societies and the need to provide the more and more permanently established ruling political groups with a solid ethical and scientific training, in order to safeguard the highest degree of freedom as a measure of civilization and progress, belong to a modern conception of democracy. This is true even though such ideas may be expressed in a conservative tone, as is especially the case in the writings of Burnham after the Second World War. None the less, it is wrong to see these works as written solely from a position of hostility towards both ideological communism and the reality of Soviet imperialism, which is how they are interpreted by two other Australian academics, Herman Wintrop and David W. Lovell.[18]

It must be added that many of the values, convictions and passions which had inspired the classic theorists were present in the eclectic notion of elitism formulated in North America during the 1940s; however, the new factors which would serve to advance the understanding of politics must have been quite evident. Important in this respect is Thomas B. Bottomore's observation that 'the elite theorists themselves have had an important influence in producing the new definitions of democracy, such as that of Schumpeter, which are then held up as being compatible with the notion of elite'.[19] So the indirect benefit deriving from the influence of elitist notions is the universal acquisition of a more realistic conception of the democratic political system, less mystical and emotive than the traditional one.

Scientific reformulations of elitism and the development of neo-elitism

With a more fully scientific treatment in mind, it is to an organic and systematic work like *Power and Society* by the Americans Harold D. Lasswell and Abraham Kaplan (published in 1950 but written during the previous decade) that we must turn in order to find Mosca, Pareto and Michels brought together and expressly designated as the 'Italian school of elitists', a term often used in the research and debates subsequent to the work of Schumpeter and Burnham.[20] According to Norberto Bobbio, the take-off point for elitism in the USA dates from the appearance of the above-mentioned book by Burnham, but above all from that of the later *The Power Elite* (1956) by Charles Wright Mills. Bobbio also believes that in both cases these works originated outside academic circles. This is an interpretation which looks rather more to the works than the backgrounds of Burnham and Mills. For the former there is as yet no up-to-date and critical biography, whereas an excellent work has been written about the latter: Irving Louis Horowitz's *C. Wright Mills. An American Utopian*.[21] Working on a good deal of heterogeneous material and developing organically some of the ideas contained therein, Lasswell and Kaplan express their scientific rigour with less immediacy but greater penetration, and they have been decisive in forcing the American academic establishment and, consequently, the whole of English-speaking political science to attempt to deal with the question.[22]

This is how political elitism grew to become an important factor in the world of politics, even if C. W. Mills's book, half pamphlet half prophecy, is a polemical and brilliant but somewhat unreliable analysis of the power structure in the United States. Though less striking and emotionally involving, but more scientific, the well-known study on the myth of the ruling class by James H. Meisel deserves attention precisely because of its philological rigour and the thorough knowledge displayed by the author of Mosca's works (and also of Pareto's). A German-Jewish emigrant to the USA and collaborator for two years of Thomas Mann (1875–1955), he correctly placed these works in their proper contexts and circulated them in Anglo-American academic circles from whence they spread out through the entire world including Italy where, as will be seen, these reformulations of the ideas originally produced by its own classic political writers were received as something truly original.

Modified and reproposed in an eclectic form, elitism has been of value in introducing into the scientific endeavours of the post-war period – especially in the years of American hegemony in the empirical-sociological field – a way of reflecting on certain themes that in Italy and Europe had for the most part been lacking or only very timidly asserted by non-Marxist democrats. These themes were the minority foundation of power, the instrumental mystification of ideologies and the authoritarian nature of organized state and non-state structures. Mosca and Pareto form the point of reference in this area of study, the true origins and inspiration of which have been revealed by the scientific work of writers like James H. Meisel and Thomas B. Bottomore. In making their analyses, they have applied rigorous critical analysis in order to ascertain the political values incorporated in this field of research as well as its scientific significance.

The influence of Michels has been less important and of a different kind; his positions were already quite distinct within the trio of writers. It is not without significance, however, that in the introduction to the paperback edition of Michels's *Political Parties* (New York, 1962) an authoritative political sociologist like Seymour Martin Lipset uses concepts taken from the analysis of Michels, though combined with others of different origin, to put forward the suggestive hypothesis of an 'elitist theory of democracy'.

Despite its being essentially pieced together 'in the laboratory', the result of an abstract (and at times arbitrary) generalization, this image of a theoretical elaboration common to an 'Italian school of elitists' has exerted an influence on the method and approach adopted, by no means negligible in terms of results, and on the directions taken by political and social research in the period following the Second World War.

There then arose a new position which we shall define as *neo-elitism* so as to distinguish it from that of the classic exponents and from the first eclectic and synthetic reformulations (*elitism*) carried out by various writers like Schumpeter and Burnham. In the history of political ideas, events often take place that stand in a surprising relation to one another, which is only discovered when books are read not just for their content but also in the light of the time and place of composition. While in the American scientific and cultural world of the 1950s the above-mentioned stimulating research by Lasswell, Kaplan, Mills and Meisel was being undertaken, the first edition came out in Italy of a very important book by Giovanni Sartori, which has been considered for some time a true classic. The work to which we are referring is *Democrazia e definizioni* (published in 1957 and brought out soon after in English under the title *Democratic Theory* (1962)). In our opinion, it is one of the most important contributions on the subject of political democracy to have been written in the post-war period.[23] Whereas the works of Mills, Meisel, Bottomore and Peter Bachrach (the author of *Theory of Democratic Elitism* (1967)) are bold and original attempts, made in countries with a long-standing and established democratic tradition, to approach the awkward subject of elitism in its relationship of compatibility or non-compatibility with the ideals and myths of democracy, the research carried out by the Italian Sartori – just over ten years after the end of the War brought a return to freedom following 20 years of dictatorship – poses the difficult problem of penetrating to the heart of the effective reality of *democracy*.

Eleven years after the first edition of his book appeared, Sartori wrote the explanation for the headword Democracy in the *International Encyclopedia of the Social Sciences*; here he very effectively maintains that the term is 'difficult to define' and that 'the more "democracy" has taken on a universally recognized positive connotation, the more its conceptual content has evaporated away and it is now the vaguest label of this kind'.[24] In going on to make a basic comparison between the prototype of democracy as it existed in the fourth century BC and modern democracy, Sartori also asserts that paradoxically, 'whereas for the Greeks literal democracy was a *possible* form of government, for us literal democracy is an *impossible* form of government'.[25] This latter statement preludes to a link-up with the above-mentioned thesis of Schumpeter that if in a democracy the role of the people 'is to produce a government', this is accomplished by means of a *highly procedural factor*, which means that 'the democratic method is that institutional system for reaching political decisions in which some individuals obtain the power to make decisions through a competitive struggle for the popular vote'.[26] Taking the theoretical formulations developed in the US and the English-speaking intellectual tradition of that period as linked at a conceptual level, this is equivalent to no longer affirming exclusively the pure compatibility between a modern theory of ruling groups and democracy understood as an institutional system expressing and controlled by the people's will. What it does, above all, is to single out the new fundamental problem for the existence of a democratic regime, a problem formed by the extremely close physiological bond that exists between popular participation in the life of institutions and the ways of forming and selecting ruling groups. But all this means also moving increasingly closer, at least in theory, to that model of 'participatory democracy' outlined in a problematical form by Macpherson as a current addition to the 'pluralist elitist model of equilibrium' derived from Schumpeter.[27] Sartori's analysis is, therefore, clearly a part of the unusual return journey from Italy to the USA and back made by the doctrine of the political class. This aspect will be dealt with explicitly in the next chapter, devoted to an examination of the positions adopted by the intellectual political tradition in Italy with respect to these themes in the period after the Second World War.

Neo-elitism as an instrument for understanding the contemporary world in political terms

It is now easy to see why the debate centered on political elites is being renewed in the United States and, more generally, in the English-speaking world from a new and stimulating perspective, one that has opened up a vast and fertile field of research and also led to very suggestive theoretical ideas. Take, for example, a book like *The Theory of Democratic Elitism* by the American Peter Bachrach which, although several pages are given over to a not particularly profound reading of Mosca's work (and also that of Pareto), does express a very relevant truth of a methodological kind that we have been putting across in the course of our exposition. According to Bachrach, before Mosca's doctrine 'could be integrated' successfully into the context of the modern theory of democracy, it was necessary for the latter to be subjected to 'a radical revision, one which would transform it from a theory based on ideals which are a part of the dignity and value of human beings into a political method independent of particular ideals or fundamental values'.[28] Thus once again we have a precise connection between Mosca and Schumpeter, the usefulness of which is seen by Bachrach to lie in an effective confirmation of Mosca's doctrine; this in so far as Schumpeter's reconstruction of 'the democratic order' is founded on exactly the same conclusion reached by Mosca: the need for 'open elites' to govern 'a stable political system'.[29]

In our view, this integration of elitism and the reformulations of the concept of democracy in the period from the end of the 1950s to the end of the 1960s represents a clear and definitive contribution to the general questions which have here only been touched on. Much more so than the polemical skirmishing of Robert A. Dahl and Paul M. Sweezy in response to Mills's provocative theses on the structure of the elite, written in the singular and conceived as a permanent unified power structure with the ability to fuse together the three functional elites dominant in American society (the economic, political and military). This kind of conceptual integration may be looked on as a blueprint for a more articulated analysis which still needs to be carried out, at least in part.

There is no doubt that R. A. Dahl's most complete work, *Polyarchy: Participation and Opposition*,[30] makes a much more sophisticated contribution to the subject, also at the level of empirical research. Dahl places his interpretation of democracy as a competition between a plurality of elites in a context of ideas which are rightly traced back to, among others, the work of Mosca, known through and quoted from Meisel's book *The Myth of the Ruling Class*.[31] By way of these successive approaches and new ideas the outline of a doctrine is taking shape which is not at all negligible or banal. In the fifteen years from the publication of *The Power Elite* to *Polyarchy* the core of a truly new interpretation has, we believe, been consolidated: an interpretation of democracy in modern society, with both a doctrinal and an empirical side, in which there is no denying the influence of the classic Italian writers who make up the mythical, but at the same time real and sometimes intellectually provocative 'Italian school of elitists'. Other active ingredients in this interpretation are the recent contributions from Italian writers, like Sartori, who have done some admirable theoretical work on this subject.

In a recent study on the development of political theory in the USA John G. Gunnell, Professor of Political Science at the University of New York (Albany), has defined the chronological period under consideration as spanning the moment he calls the 'behavioural revolution: 1950–59' and the subsequent one in which many efforts at research and analysis were recuperated and brought together ('recouping and regrouping: 1960–69').[32] Both of these moments, though characterized by different methods and contents, display a very strong theoretical tendency towards political formulations of a liberal-pluralist kind. It should also be said that, according to this very discerning scholar, American culture in this entire period produced a greatly developed capacity for speculation and an equally high level of scientific endeavour before the 'dispersion' which marked the 1970s.

Finally, this debate on the question of political elites and on the connection between elitism and the classical, in some cases rigidified, conceptions of democracy has produced one result acutely perceived by Geraint Parry of Manchester University in his acute study on elites (1969). According to Parry, 'the elitists have forced political philosophers to re-examine the status of many values associated with democracy, such as equality and freedom; as a consequence, they have made it necessary for democratic theory to be revised and impossible for even the opponents of elitism to ignore its conclusions'.[33]

The general social and ideological movement which, from the end of the 1960s to the 1970s, shook the liberal-democratic part of the world based on a capitalist economy has had the effect of relegating and throwing a bad light on any thinking or research relative to a minority or elitist conception of power. However, the mystical and idealistic egalitarian programme cannot deny for long the reality which it swept aside and which is now reasserting itself. This is a social and political reality of domination, of minority and corporate power – sometimes even of an occult nature as shown by the recent scandal in Italy concerning the Freemasons' lodge known as 'P2', still shrouded in mystery – the like of which the world has never seen before. Hence the need for a renewal of the type of research which is open-minded, realistic and free from ideological or party-political exploitation so that the intimate nature of power in the world in which we live can be properly investigated; and also the revived interest in the conceptual and critical instruments which contemporary neo-elitism has been fashioning.

11
Gaetano Mosca and the intellectual political tradition in Italy after the Second World War, 1945–1985

We shall now take a close look at some aspects of post-war Italian studies on the thought of Gaetano Mosca which form an integral part of the more general theoretical question of political elitism. One must take into account, first of all, that the results from the new theoretical reformulations developed in the English-speaking world, principally in North America – as outlined in the preceding chapter – were gradually deposited on top of the earlier, mainly academic, Italian interest in Mosca's thinking. In short, elitism in its eclectic version and also with its academic and scientific results was superimposed on the original doctrines of Mosca and Pareto. In some cases the outcome was novel and enlightening, but in others misleading because of the wide gaps in detailed historical examination and in a critical knowledge of the themes and original texts. None the less, there have been some interesting achievements at the level of the elaboration of concepts.

As a general preamble for the non-Italian reader, we wish to point out straight away that throughout the entire post-war period the intellectual political tradition in Italy has taken shape and developed under the banner of a diffused political commitment closely bound up with political parties. This is in no way meant to imply that the entire intellectual political tradition has been instrumentalized for partisan ends. However, the process has been very widespread both because of the existence of two universalizing ideological movements strongly organized socially and politically, the Catholic Church and the Communist Party, and because of the inherent weakness of all other positions. In *Politica e cultura* (1955), a fundamental work by an academic belonging to the liberal-socialist area, Norberto Bobbio makes a clear distinction between the idea of a 'militant philosophy' and that of a 'philosophy in the service of a party'.[1]

He highlights in exemplary fashion both the reasons which lead to political commitment as a civil duty and practical activity, and the motives which work in favour of culture as an independent and critical form of awareness directed towards defending, at all times and in all cases, the 'freedom of illuminating reason' against the tactical and instrumental demands of daily political practice. Bobbio's attempt to distinguish the levels on which intellectuals operate (attitude and theoretical-critical elaboration) reflects the drama of an entire culture in extremely large sections of which ideological and party-political bias prevailed over the requirements of disinterested knowledge. In reality, behind such variously motivated instrumentalization there were (and still are) the precise interests and privileges of vast cultural circles related organically (to use a term from Antonio Gramsci's vocabulary) to the different political forces from which they draw their inspiration.

Organized through the network of its myriad social structures and represented politically by *Democrazia Cristiana* – the majority party in all governments since 1946 – the Catholic area has constituted in Italy more than just a collection of values. It is also a complex of powerful employees' associations, professional groups, district organizations, etc., whose aim is to achieve a fuller integration into the innermost realms of the state and of the new economic, industrial and financial structures, the so-called *parastato* (state-controlled sector); created and run by politicians, it accounts for more than 50 per cent of the country's entire system of production. Thus, sustained by the enormous power it holds and administers, Catholic culture has been able to make up for its own deficiences in theory and in bringing its conceptions up-to-date by simultaneously championing the classical liberal-democratic ideas negated by Stalinist communism and the ideologically vague, but effective forms of solidarity which unite the Catholic and populist inspirations behind the state in the country's economic and social life. In the absence of real alternatives, this confused mixture of doctrine and praxis has worked on a practical level by providing the dominant political framework for about four decades of democracy.

The communist area (which up to the mid 1950s also included the political-cultural domain covered by the Italian Socialist Party) has represented and still represents – at least in part – a living experiment in a 'parallel society', very similar to the situation in which the Catholics found themselves in the period from national unification to 1946. After the Christian Democrats, the second largest force in Parliament is formed by the Communist Party whose influence ranges from trade unions to co-operatives, from the power held at local level – mostly as the majority party – over wide areas of the country to its many-sided cultural organization. As a result, it is said to be the only theoretical and practical alternative. However, international events and the adaption of Italian communism to the domestic situation have led it to adopt a quite moderate line increasingly directed towards expressing loyalty to parliamentary institutions. Having got over the Cold War and Stalinism, Italian communism has formulated its own doctrine which justifies and extols coexistence and competition with the other political forces on the basis of the almost universally accepted liberal-democratic Constitution of 1948. Despite such a position being hard to justify for a political organization programmatically tied to Marxism–Leninism, it has established the Italian Communist Party as one of the factors acting for political and social stability in the country; in addition, it has allowed it to have a growing share in real power (at the political-parliamentary level) and in the new dimension of the massive economic and social influence exerted by the public sector.

We have had to insert these brief parenthetical remarks because these essential facts cannot be left out of account when discussing the intellectual political tradition in post-war Italy; and because it must also be pointed out that there has always existed a lively and very authoritative area of intellectual activity between the two worlds of the Catholics and the communists: an area almost totally deprived of any real decisional power which has, none the less, had a great influence on cultural life, at least to the extent of the deep and radical changes brought about by the big youth and mass movements from 1968 onwards. What we have here is no more than 'an area of influence', since the attempt to give shape to the idea of setting up a 'third force' to unify all modern, lay and progressive sectors of society has failed on several occasions. There has, then, always existed between the Catholic and communist spheres a limited political space occupied by various political parties (Socialist, Social-Democratic, Liberal, Republican). Though separated by many differences, they take as their reference point liberal or non-Marxist socialist thinking, or the liberal-socialist proposal. Since the late 1950s the Italian Socialist Party has increasingly distanced itself from the Italian Communist Party. In such a context this 'area of influence', though made up of a small minority, has permitted the Socialist Party – representing only just over 10 per cent of the electorate, but exercising a very strong cultural influence – to play an essentially innovative role both in the intellectual debate inside the country and within the coalition governments formed, from the beginning of the 1960s, by the Christian Democrats in alliance with all the smaller parties belonging to this 'area'. These are the so-called Centre-Left governments (now referred to as 'governi di pentapartito', that is, five-party coalition governments composed of Catholics, Socialists, Social-Democrats, Liberals and Republicans). Responsible for quite a number of errors and serious delays, they have nevertheless had the effect of modifying the links between power and influence in civil society and in the state. Unfortunately, this process of substantial democratization of the Italian state, never particularly receptive towards popular demands (see Part I), and of large-scale modernization of society and the economy has not followed a linear course; instead, it has been the uneven consequence of factors external to political programmes. To be viewed in these terms, first of all, is the great change which swept through Italy from the end of the 1950s to the beginning of the 1970s as a result of a radical restructuring of the economy and massive internal migration. This was followed by a situation of authentic civil war created by the terrorist activity of the late 1960s and almost all of the 1970s. The profound changes in psychology, habits and social organization, the unpreparedness in the face of armed terrorist extremism have led, in fact, to a redistribution of political power and a considerable slackening in the cultural debate and the formulation of political ideas. The Catholics and Communists have exhausted and overcome their dialectical antithesis by means of the 'historical compromise', which in the dramatic climate of extreme right-wing and, above all, left-wing subversion led to the formation for a brief period of governments of 'national solidarity' supported by the Communists, the largest opposition party. The conquest of real power by the Italian Socialist Party, from the beginning of the 1980s, at the level of Parliament, the state and the public sector of the economy (symbolized by the nomination and renomination of a socialist as Prime Minister in recent years) has had as its negative counterpart a complete drying up in the production of ideas and political propositions within this 'area', which, as we have already noted, represents the liveliest element with the most initiative in non-Catholic and non-Communist circles.

This, then, is the historical background against which the intellectual political tradition in Italy has, in the last forty years, also had to come to grips with the development of elitism dealt with in the second part of this book. In the brief analysis below we will follow, above all, a Moschian inspiration in line with the methodology adopted throughout this entire study. Of course, other detailed examinations are most welcome which refer both to Pareto (already widely covered) and to Michels (much more neglected in this field of studies). The analysis has been divided into three parts corresponding to the following three periods: the rediscovery of the liberal meaning of Mosca's thought in the years immediately following the Second World War; the return to Italy of elitism from the

Anglo-American world; and the placing of these themes within the context of the current crisis in Italian intellectual political circles.

The rediscovery of the liberal meaning of Gaetano Mosca's thought

Between 1946 and 1952 several studies in this field were published by Mario Delle Piane of the University of Siena. Valuable as a systematic body of work, their essential significance lies in the image they present of a liberal Mosca notwithstanding his minority theory of power and polemical criticism of the parliamentary system. A similar intention may be found in the work of two other academics, Bruno Brunello and Pietro Piovani who, to a greater degree than Delle Piane, try to situate Mosca's work within the development of Italian political philosophy from the nineteenth to the twentieth century. This kind of research poses the need for a historical understanding of Mosca's doctrine, and it may also be seen as linked to a renewed Italian interest in the history of political doctrines; an interest demonstrated by the republication in 1951 of the bibliographical essay dedicated to Italian studies in the history of political thought by Rodolfo De Mattei who teaches this subject at Rome University. It had first been published in a shorter version under a different title in 1938. In this essay Mosca is mentioned specifically by his old disciple and university assistant for his important methodological approach combining the history of political thought and that of institutions.[2] Various other writings, all by academics, have appeared on this subject, including Norberto Bobbio's well-known essay 'Liberalism Old and New'. In our opinion, the latter has fixed a first conceptual reference point in this rediscovery of Mosca, which is still at the stage of generalities; it has also the opened up a new and more general range of interests.[3]

Remaining within this period, it must not be forgotten that Antonio Gramsci's *Prison Notebooks* were published for the first time at the end of the 1940s. In this work repeated reference is made to Mosca, at times in a very polemical tone – as we have already seen. In 1949 the book *Dittatura, classe politica e classe dirigente* appeared as part of the collected works of the liberal-socialist writer Guido Dorso (1892–1947). Combining programmatically Mosca's theoretical elaboration with that of Pareto, it is an interesting attempt to reconcile the permanent fact of the minority foundation of power with the need to ensure circulation and renewal in the power structure itself. The rediscovery of the progressive-liberal thought of Piero Gobetti and the availability of many of his writings from 1945 was also a factor in the revived interest in Mosca, loved and esteemed by the young liberal writer as one of his mentors, not only in academic matters but also in life and morality.

At a time when Italy had only just emerged from the dramatic experience of Fascist dictatorship and military defeat and was struggling to establish a new civil and political existence within the framework of truly democratic institutions, this rereading of Mosca – and Pareto – was undertaken with a clear purpose in mind. The various contributions mentioned above are all specifically democratic, non-Communist and non-Catholic in inspiration. The motive behind this examination of the classic writers' thinking (in particular Mosca whose death was at that time still a quite recent event) was evidently the desire to understand, from a philosophical and theoretical point of view, in what the liberal intellectual tradition of the country consisted. Consequently, the past was interrogated for inspiration and to throw light on the present. In fact, a central topic of political reflection in post-war Italy has been the history of Italy after unification, studied in order to grasp the problems and contradictions by which it was beset until the clean break represented by Fascist dictatorship. What, then, is extremely interesting about this phase is precisely the search for an underlying compatibility and continuity between the doctrines of the writers variously inspired by liberalism and the ideals of a restored but still fragile Italian democracy. The reader is already familiar with this approach since it characterizes the first part of this book, which draws widely on these problems, sources and the writers absorbed by them, and substantially shares the same ideas and scientific concerns.

The return of the 'theory of elites' from the Anglo-American world to Italy

The second period opened with both the production of ideas within Italian political studies and the external stimulus from American sociology, particularly the publication in the mid 1950s of Charles Wright Mills's *The Power Elite*. Even though this work, translated into Italian in 1959, contains very few direct references to Mosca (one in the text and two in the notes), it belonged to a climate of renewed interest in the theme of power and its real forms. This explains its success and the influence it exerted on Italian culture at the end of the 1950s, a time in which research methods and horizons were rapidly changing and developing. However, we shall dwell no further on this aspect of the problem which confirmed the opening up of a part of the Italian academic world to influences from outside. In 1957 the above-mentioned major study by Giovanni Sartori, *Democrazia e definizioni*, was published. Moreover, new academic studies were carried out and the work and personality of Mosca were mentioned, in more general terms, in newspapers and periodicals on the occasion of the first centenary of his birth in 1958.[4]

But it was above all the vast international presentation and discussion of ideas at the IV World Congress of Sociology, held in Stresa in September 1959, that represented a vigorous rebirth in Italian academic circles of sociology and political science, both of which had been banished by the idealism of Croce and Gentile dominant between the two world wars. In the 1961 Introduction to the volume *Le élites politiche* [*Political Elites*] (which summarizes the reports and results of the seminar on this topic at the Stresa Congress) Renato Treves underlined the substantial, if not overwhelming, influence of Mills's work on the entire Seminar. Pointing out the importance attributed internationally to the Italian elitists, Treves (Professor in the Philosophy of Law at Milan University and one of the most important figures behind the renewal of sociological studies in Italy, above all in the field of the sociology of law) did not fail to stress the backwardness and underdevelopment which had existed in Italian political studies up to that time. He attributed the cause both to twenty years of Fascism and, especially, to 'the fact that in our country, unlike in other countries, political science has still not been established and affirmed as an independent and uniform science'.[5] The emphasis placed by him on the close link between political science and sociology thus lent an overall significance to that important scientific and academic event, in which the particularly important Italian presence represented by Norberto Bobbio, Alessandro Passerin d'Entrèves, Giovanni Sartori and Treves himself tied in perfectly with the contributions from authoritative foreign scholars like James H. Meisel, Thomas B. Bottomore, Joseph La Palombara, Juan J. Linz, Alain Touraine, George E. Catlin.

Two things emerged, in our opinion, in this second period: the affirmation of the sociological and political-theoretical depth to Mosca's work and the dropping of the idea that the minority foundation of power is incompatible with democratic ideals. It was not by chance that the paper presented by Norberto Bobbio at the Stresa Congress was entitled 'The Theory of the Political Class in Italian Democratic Writers'. In this perspective, it also seems useful to recall the introduction to the anthology *Le riviste di Piero Gobetti* by the intellectual and authoritative left wing socialist politician Lelio Basso (1903–78); in it Mosca is quoted several times without ideological bias as one of the primary sources of Gobettian thinking.

Various other contributions of both a scientific and didactic kind, all a result of this new climate of research, played a positive role in spreading these theoretical-political questions also among university students. This was followed in 1966 by Bobbio's repeated proposal to interpret Mosca directly through his own writings; it took the form of a successful anthology entitled *La classe politica*, which consolidated and encouraged study in this area as well as providing new, including philological, tools for research.[6] Finally, the systematic collection and publication by Bobbio in 1969 of the *Saggi sulla scienza politica in Italia* [*Essays on Political Science in Italy*] (referred to several times herein) restored Moschian thinking to its conceptual originality and intellectual autonomy; an equally rigorous and wide-ranging study is also dedicated in this book to Pareto. So the most solid achievement of the overall research into these themes during the decade 1959–69 lay in the awareness that Mosca's doctrine is different from Pareto's, even if both writers responded to the suggestive influence and questions generated by the liberal intellectual tradition. In addition, there was a growing realization that in a different context and in a different geographical area a new synthesis in the interpretation of politics, which draws in various ways on the different contributions of the classic Italian writers, was forming under the name of the 'theory of elites'.

This period also witnessed the circulation in an Italian edition of *Elites and Society*, a fundamental work by Thomas B. Bottomore which was published in 1964 and translated in 1967. Compared to similar Italian and non-Italian studies, the great merit of this study lies in the way it examines the concepts of 'elite' and 'ruling class': it takes into account the original theoretical formulations and distinctions of Mosca, Pareto and Schumpeter and, above all, centres its own analysis at the point where the political tendencies of this century intersect. In this analysis the thought of Karl Marx, on the one hand and that of the liberal elitists Mosca and Pareto, on the other, are used as instruments to analyse the state of society, which had changed radically since the First World War. Despite the antithesis between them, both conceptions have in fact a strongly realistic side and have helped to lead political knowledge away from the mystifying circle of pure, abstract ideology. However, Bottomore's extremely accurate reading of the classic authors allows him to evaluate critically the conclusions reached by C. Wright Mills relative to the existence in the USA of a homogenous and unified power elite; he underlines the fundamental difference between the concept and reality of the ruling class and the ideology that accepts and theorizes the existence of a universally dominant homogeneous and unified elite. Unlike in the theory formulated by Mills, Bottomore refers above all to that 'recent and excellent analysis of Mosca's work' to be found in James H. Meisel's *The Myth of the Ruling Class*. And he very perceptively shifts the centre of interest from the level of abstract theory and ideology, on which equality is set in opposition to elites, to the practical need to study, as he himself has done, 'the circulation of elites, the relations between elites and classes, and the ways in which new elites and new classes are formed'.[7] The egalitarianism intrinsic to the thought of Marx (a conception carried to the extreme with the theory of the 'withering away of the state' and the setting up of a communist society) is thus opposed by a different ideological conception on the firm basis of the permanent historical division between rulers and ruled. A conception which tends to ennoble the omnipresent ruling group by attributing to it intellectual excellence and moral superiority, whatever the social origins of its individual members.[8] Isaiah Berlin has written that Marx possessed a great ability 'to put forward clear and uniform solutions, in empirical terms accessible to all, of the problems which afflicted men most and to draw several practical conclusions from this, without having recourse to manifestly artificial deductions'.[9] What we find, then, in the different formulations derived from the notions of ruling group and competing elites is a capacity, similar to Marx's thinking but less passionate, for simplifying and revealing reality. The value of Bottomore's work lies in his realistic and dialectical presentation of the the opposition between Marxian socialism and 'elitist' liberalism. In doing so, this scholar deserves our gratitude for having shed light on the equally unrealistic and essentially Utopian ideological basis to both these political conceptions. Behind Marxian egalitarianism lies the iron-hard reality of proletarian dictatorship. Behind the historical and sociological separation between rulers and ruled of the classic elitists, on the other hand, there is the theoretical projection of a non-egalitarian attitude towards society: social discrimination used to be enacted in terms of blood ties and historical privilege; in the present and future this is and may be expressed through merit and ability at best and through money, demagogy and unscrupulousness at worst.

At the start of the 1960s Bottomore showed himself to be a very skilful interpreter of the massive new changes affecting contemporary society, increasingly unified and subject to a process of osmosis between separate countries. This phenomenon also applies to Italy, even though Italian intellectuals, mostly ensnared by political and party ideology, are unable to thoroughly grasp the importance of the English scholar's interpretation despite the fact that it has been translated and is often quoted. In the Italy of the 1960s there were too many outdated communists and old-style liberal conservatives for Bottomore's interpretation of the new social and political reality to be appreciated in full. Perhaps the only defect is that he did not push to its limits the specific examination of the concepts of 'political class' or 'political elites'. There is no doubt that Bottomore's book is a pointer to a line of research which, drawing inspiration from other sectors of Italian intellectual circles receptive to ideas from beyond Italy's borders, has now become well established in academic circles. Once again, nevertheless, these scientific matters go hand in hand with the requirements of the political situation in Italy. The first years of the 1960s witnessed a feeling of euphoria derived from empirical research into social reality, from sociology and political science, and from the political reformism of the first coalition governments composed of the Catholics, Socialists and what are known as the lay parties (Liberals, Republicans, Social Democrats). But, in contrast, the decade of the 1960s also saw the first savage acts of terrorist extremism and an ensuing deterioration in public life and even in normal social coexistence.

The 'Mosca–Paretian paradigm' and the contemporary crisis in the Italian intellectual political tradition

When looking at Mosca's thinking in its various phases, we already mentioned the danger that any division into periods risks being arbitrary. In the field of political and social studies, however, it is difficult not to come under the influence of contemporary events. Whereas in the immediate post-war period, after twenty years of dictatorship and the glorification of a gregarious and hierarchical political order, it had been vital to put the spotlight on Mosca's liberal sentiments, fifteen years on from the end of the War the situation was different. At the start of the most intense process of social and economic transformation ever experienced in Italy, reflection on society and power essentially moved towards reappropriating Mosca's theoretical elaboration or, more exactly, the eclectic synthesis of elitist doctrine that was being brought about through the circulation of ideas and the integration of different intellectual traditions. That this synthesis had a basis in reality was undeniable, and on the whole, it met the need for a concrete approach which was now being demanded of political analysis. So it is difficult not to subscribe to Norberto Bobbio's judgement that: *'The theory of the political class has yet to be proved wrong; it is still today one of the cornerstones of political science, almost a commonplace, and the burden of proof is on those who reject it, not those who accept it* [author's italics].'[10]

Thus opened the third and rather more complex period. A period which, though the 'Mosca–Paretian paradigm' has been studied with new attention and much detailed examination, has nevertheless appeared ideologically circumscribed and virtually impeded by the crisis which exploded in the Italian intellectual political tradition at the beginning of the 1970s and still continues today. In fact, the wide circulation of the paradigm among academics and specialists has not been matched by an adequate general diffusion and appreciation of this remarkable tool for interpreting political reality.

Scientifically and academically, this third period has given rise to diverse and even contradictory results. On the one hand, sociologists, political scientists, and philosophers of law and politics are now investigating the thought of the classic authors on a general and abstract level. But at the same time, and perhaps slightly eclipsed by the former, books and essays of a clearly historiographical style are appearing which apply a more distinct methodology in the attempt to understand the classic writers and their ideas. They aim to consider men and ideas within the framework of a biographical and intellectual, political and moral reconstruction covering sixty years of Italian history. Contributions like that by Eugenio Ripepe (Professor in the General Theory of Law at Pisa University) on *Le origini della teoria della classe politica* have tended to bring Mosca back within the bounds of the theoretical research into politics and law by examining the antecedents and premises to Mosca's formulation of his ideas and the context in which they matured and developed.[11]

The general need for this kind of approach has also been the motive behind the various contributions from 1968 on by the author of this present study (an outline of the research undertaken is given in the Introduction), by Carlo Mongardini and by Giorgio Sola. A debt is owed to Mongardini (Professor of Sociology at Rome University) for, among other things, the recovery of Mosca's personal papers and archive, while Giorgio Sola (Professor of Political Science at Genoa University) published, in 1982, the first critical editions of *Sulla teorica dei governi* and the *Elementi di scienza politica*. The common thread in all this scientific work is the demand that the rich background referred to should not be left out of consideration but, at the same time, that the first requirement for a scholar and his work is to show an understanding of history and an awareness of philology. Ripepe's 1974 study of the Italian elitists is also part of this trend. In it Mosca, Pareto, Michels, Gobetti, Dorso and Filippo Burzio (1891–1948) are subjected to a dialectical examination which defines with precision their individual contributions and underlines the refraction of ideas and reciprocal links between them.[12] Furthermore, we consider as part of this trend several works of particular interest which fulfil a more general need to bring attention to these themes. It is of considerable importance, for example, that in an authoritative work signficant for its originality and great success like the multi-volume *Storia d'Italia*[13] there should appear a contribution of great intellectual weight from Alberto Asor Rosa (a communist scholar highly esteemed in academic circles) on the culture of unified Italy in which the work of Mosca is highlighted by 67 references within an attempt at interpretation of great cultural value.[14]

Many other names could be mentioned in this regard, including Jerzy Szacki who makes some important references to Mosca in volume III of the Einaudi *Enciclopedia* (1978), which anticipate the splendid elucidation by Giovanni Busino of the term 'elite' in the same work. Similarly, credit is due to Luciano Gallino for having made sure that the term 'political class' was given a separate heading in his valuable *Dizionario di sociologia* (1978).[15] Continuing the research begun by N. Bobbio, a young collaborator of his, Michelangelo Bovero, has made a systematic attempt to define and make known the various theories on elites.[16]

This survey would be incomplete if no mention were made of the important research being conducted by Giovanni Busino and published in the international review *Cahiers Vilfredo Pareto* (based in Switzerland since 1963). It represents a very successful example of how organic research of an interdisciplinary and international character can be carried out while still respecting single political and social theories, distinct historical and sociological methods and, lastly, different national contexts. The *Cahiers Vilfredo Pareto* and the publication since 1964 of Pareto's *Opere Complete* [*Complete Works*][17] under the editorship of Busino, offer an enormous source of material pertaining to the questions dealt with in this book. Busino's scientific activity has now provided us with an organic body of research and texts on elitism in general, as well as on Pareto. In terms of continuity, length and depth it offers a top-class contribution to scholarship and knowledge. Even though more modest and of more recent origin, a similar endeavour – especially with a view to Mosca's thought – is behind the volumes of the 'Archivio Internazionale Gaetano Mosca per lo studio della classe politica' to which we have referred on several occasions. As has already been stated in the Introduction, a wide-ranging group of scholars from Italy and other countries has been analysing and documenting little known or even completely unknown aspects of Mosca's biography; questions concerning method and texts; and problems of understanding and interpreting the Moschian doctrine in and outside of Italy. In our opinion, this analysis and documentation will permit an evaluation of Mosca's thought and work on the basis of a more mature and detailed understanding.

If it is true, therefore, that the scientific results from the studies of the individual classic writers are clearly of interest, the same cannot be said with regard to the subsequent transition, identified in the previous chapter, from eclectic and academic elitism to what we have called neo-elitism. The intellectual political tradition in Italy today has so far produced nothing of this kind.

The greater diffusion of this complex, elaborated theory of elitism has received an obvious set-back from the drying up of political creativity. Throughout the 1970s Italy suffered badly from the grave tension existing in the country; it had a discouraging effect and diverted much intellectual energy away from debate and the formulation of ideas. Consequently, whereas a substantial amount of specialist study and research was being undertaken, the ideological debate and the very vitality of society were bogged down by a confusing and highly tense daily existence. This situation was to a large extent produced by the schematic simplifications which replaced the creative questioning and research of the preceding period. The ideas and analyses arising out of elitism, with all its various nuances and different converging notions, have had to contend dramatically with the considerable weakness in Italian political thinking in the last part of the twentieth century. The concepts and doctrine derived from the teachings of Mosca, Pareto and Michels already furnished at a very early stage the analytical tools for dealing more competently with the great unresolved questions of our times: the crises of political representation, of real participation in decision making and of the failure to select elites. The considerable scale of prejudice and hypocrisy has manifestly played a negative role in terms of the formulation of doctrine. During the more or less quarter of a century since 1945, Italian intellectual life has consumed its civic passion in political commitment, for the most part inside parties, and in the no lesser committed but minority activity of research and scholarship. Despite the many contradictions, the possibilities for a process of osmosis between the two areas have existed throughout this entire period. Since the second half of the 1970s there has been a change, and for the majority of intellectuals in this latest phase it has meant renouncing ethical-political commitment or any form of commitment in favour of intellectual activities which are less serious, but more fashionable and marketable.

In present-day Italy the ethos of a true 'participatory democracy', which still seemed possible not so many years ago but now belongs to a distant almost mythical past, has apparently been superseded by the rule of *partitocrazia* ('partocracy'), a term which signifies the predominance or excessive power of the party system which takes the place of representative institutions in the running of national political life. However, the complex experience we have been describing cannot be left out of account by the intellectually courageous minority of scholars in this and other fields of study who are trying to achieve the difficult balance between ethical-political values and the new powers of a society like Italy, both industrial with pockets of underdevelopment and post-industrial at the same time. For many years to come, this experience will form a framework for anyone who intends to avoid being trite and examine in detail the phenomenon of politics. Inhibited from putting forward proposals for more than ten years, political speculation in Italy has unfortunately lost contact with the country's deeper reality and the passion for being a protagonist in social life. After the great wave of pragmatism, realism and optimism of the 1950s and 1960s the Italian intellectual community is today fragmented and basically incapable of contributing to the interpretation and rationalization of the political reality which expresses the world we live and work in and which encapsulates the light and shade of forty years of massive social transformation. In this situation of crisis it is no wonder, therefore, that we are still waiting for the themes brought to light by the classic exponents of the 'Italian school of elitists' to be extensively resumed and developed further in line with the profoundly democratic demand that the formation and circulation of elites (both inevitable processes) take place openly in the full view of the majority and not in the dark corridors of power.

12
Towards a critical conclusion

Having thus delineated several of the essential lines along which elitist theory has been developed and transformed since its founders laid down their ideas in a definitive form, we are now in a position to pinpoint some further aspects for future research and reflection.

The content of the theory formulated by Mosca and Pareto has been very accurately traced by Bottomore back to a true 'political doctrine', which in its original form 'was opposed to, or critical of, modern democracy and still more opposed to modern socialism'.[1] Against the background of the fall of many liberal-representative systems in Europe in the 1920s and 1930s, the evolution of the concept of democracy has forced people to think very deeply about the very essence of democracy. After the first syntheses of elitist theory achieved by Schumpeter and Burnham, a new version of the democratic doctrine, stimulated by – among other things – the critical contribution of the classical theory of elites, gradually asserted itself between the 1940s and 1960s. In this way a truly new theoretical tendency came into being which lacks organic coherence but is of considerable interest: neo-elitism. It combines the essentially electoral participation of the governed with the need for ruling minority groups to be formed and maintained as effective centres of power and decision making.

However, as Giovanni Busino has rightly observed, 'rigour and lucidity have still not reached the point where they can free us from the perplexity and deception of ideologies'.[2] In other words, the emotive aspect of democratic ideology has too often prevailed over the procedural and electoral aspect. Consequently, in this area of research intellectual daring is needed more than ever.

Elitism versus Welfare-statism: Lowell Field and Higley

A convincing proof of this is the already-mentioned work by G. Lowell Field and John Higley published in 1980; in our opinion, *Elitism* marks a radical turning-point in this area of theory.[3] It starts from the idea that as a critical and conceptual tool elitism was practically left in obscurity throughout the whole 50-year period 1925–75 and concludes that it has been undergoing a vigorous revival since the mid-1970s. This is a very debatable thesis, all the more so given that the synthetic approach of these authors leaves no room for the distinctions and annotations which, in our opinion, are required in order to widen out the framework for research. Several of these have been mentioned in the preceding chapters. John Higley, Professor of Political Science in the University of Texas at Austin, is an American academic who worked at the Australian National University of Canberra for more than a decade. His interest in the work of the classic Italian elitists matured gradually during his formative years in the mid-1960s, above all under the influence of G. Lowell Field, Emeritus Professor at the University of Connecticut whose field of research is Italian politics and institutions during the Fascist era.[4] This is the same university where Higley took his degree and made the acquaintance of Joseph Lopreato, a scholar interested in the classic elitists and also now teaching at the University in Austin.[5]

The framework for research worked out by Field and Higley concedes very little to an examination of the historical-doctrinal perspective, unlike the approach adopted in this study. Instead, it is very much tied to the contingent political events of contemporary society and in particular those of the 1970s, a period in which 'Welfare-statism', the result of a fusion between liberal and socialist principles, was entering into a crisis. It is still too soon to formulate a definitive judgement on the interesting theses put forward by Field and Higley, in which a central element is the following conviction: 'Most really important and helpful actions can originate only with persons who are strategically placed and influential, that is, with elites'.[6] Only through a wider discussion of their theses will it be possible to find out whether the generic and creative (though at times confused) notion of neo-elitism in the last few decades has now given way to a different formulation, one which is inherently coherent and able to provide an organic and original political doctrine. There already exist several theoretical premises, but these are still at an intial stage and present many gaps. For example, in *Elitism* the theme of the political party is hardly touched on and yet it is fundamental for the complete definition of a *doctrine of elitism*. On the other hand, a very useful aspect is the interest shown in the internal consistency (or lack of it) of elites, analysed according to the categories of *consensual unification, imperfectly unified elites* and even *disunified elites*.[7]

In its dialectical and antagonistic relationship to Welfare-statism, neo-elitism represents a discovery which belongs, for the most part, to the political experience of the Anglo-American world. What we have in this case is a very deep crisis which has affected most of the political–social and economic ideas deriving from both the New Deal of Franklin D. Roosevelt (1882–1945) and from British labourism after the Second World War. The crisis is not only one of ideas; it is above all due to the obsolescence of a particular mode of social reorganization. Although it has been innovatory and very positive, this model has nevertheless proved to be inadequate in facing up to and mastering the great technological changes that have characterized the last half of the twentieth century. The neo-elitist interpretation of the two US writers is profoundly linked to these theoretical–political experiences, even if the features of the crisis in the classic models of the Welfare State vary according to the country. None the less, Field and Higley's critique is very radical and its target is precisely the American and English models of the Welfare State.

With regard to the reformulation of neo-elitist concepts, there certainly exist other interpretations which should not be neglected; it is impossible, however, to give an exhaustive account of them. Several specific contributions to research into and detailed study of the themes treated herein have been made at various times in the period stretching from immediately after the Second World War to the present time.

An attempt to go beyond the theory of Schumpeter: Otto Stammer

We have in mind, above all, an important essay by the German political sociologist Otto Stammer (1900–78), first published in 1951 in 'Schmollers Jahrbuch für Gesetzgebung, Verwaltung and Volkswirtschaft' and later in book form.[8] In this work the relationship and compatibility between elites and democracy is examined with great insight. For Stammer too, the starting point is the classic study by Joseph Schumpeter and reference is made to a range of relevant standard and new works written in German. Moreover, Stammer makes some interesting observations on Schumpeter's theoretical approach, which he considers to be a correct one. None the less, he also maintains that 'his definition of democracy . . . [is] inadequate in as far as . . . it fails to fully grasp the problem of the masses and that of *elites*'.[9] This critical judgement is very pertinent because it comes from a man like Stammer who experienced at first hand the collapse of the liberal-democratic system in the Weimar Republic (1933). This event resulted from the failure to establish a close link between the masses, individual groups in society and the running of the state; as a consequence of this failure new elites of a non-democratic (or more exactly anti-democratic) kind were able to infiltrate the unstable institutions and whip up enthusiasm among the people for new objectives which undermined the representative system. In this way, these new elites succeeded in turning the support of the masses away from parliamentary democracy and in bringing down the existing political system.

At this point it must be said that Stammer's conclusions are very provocative and worth looking at not only from a historical but, above all, from a theoretical viewpoint. They concern 'the essence of the democratic system' which is, in his view, very different in mass industrial society compared to past historical models. He states that

political leadership in a democracy is not only a matter for individuals especially skilled in the art of politics. On the contrary, such individuals, who under certain circumstances are a bonus for the system, depend on elites for the running of the State and the running of the parties and similar political policy-making bodies which are the primary determining factors in a democracy. In fact, these individuals can only be effective from within such elites.[10]

As can been seen, this is a particularly mature analysis and regards not only the doctrines formulated by the classic authors, but also pays special attention to the concrete dynamic relations that are always found to exist between social groups, political parties and institutions. These are natural relations, but they also have an undoubted pathological side since, according to this German sociologist, the elites which make up the ruling groups 'are never effective in a democracy if privileged factions are formed inside them, if they turn into oligarchies as in the theory of Mosca and Michels'.[11] This amounts to a renewal and affirmation as an element of doctrine of Mosca and Pareto's classic theme according to which ruling groups formed with the participation of the whole of society are an important and truly dialectical factor, in as much as 'elites, as instruments of State power, do not solely transmit political opinions and decisions to the people. On the contrary, they also take part in a genuine two-way process of formulating political objectives which runs from the top to the bottom and vice versa'.[12]

In drawing up a balance-sheet of what is known about Mosca in the German-speaking world, Arnold Zingerle, Professor of Sociology at Bochum University (West Germany), has written that '... it is rather limited, fragmentary and uneven compared to the reception enjoyed by many other foreign writers, now authorities in political science and sociology, especially after the Second World War'.[13] This opinion is probably well-founded as far as concerns the amount of research done on Mosca, but it should be further qualified in the light of several indications given by Zingerle himself in this same essay and also of the recent renewal in Germany of interest in political theory both from the doctrinal and historical angle.[14]

The German intellectual political tradition adheres strongly to the now widespread methodological demand – given the indisputable and permanent existence of minority groups which hold power – according to which it is currently essential to move towards a non-ideological understanding of the nature of these groups so as to form a realistic picture of democratic politics in contemporary society. This is a highly topical theoretical position which from the lectures at the *Hochschule für Politik in Berlin* (1962) to the German contributions at the recent international congresses on 'democracy' in Gallarate (1980) and Rome (1981) points to a keen interest in this area on the part of accomplished scholars in the German-speaking world.[15]

Furthermore, it is evident that the well-known thesis on the 'fiction of representation' in the democratic political system formulated by Hans Kelsen (1881–1973) forms part of the general cultural background of German political writers. As early as 1945 this expert in juridical studies made the following unequivocal assertion:

If political writers persist in defining the parliament of modern democracy a 'representative' body ... they are not putting forward a scientific theory but upholding a political ideology. The function of this ideology is to conceal the real situation, to maintain the illusion that the people are the legislator despite the fact that, in reality, the function of the people – or in more exact terms the electorate – is limited to producing the legislative body.[16]

This thesis brings us back to the need for a more fundamental approach in examining these problems. In such an approach the juridical aspects, which especially in US studies are partly sacrificed to a wider interest in sociology and political science, return to the centre of attention bringing with them many theoretical and practical questions. While these link up with the core of Mosca's teaching and that of the other classic authors, they also pose the unavoidable problem of understanding the elites which are the component elements of a parliament.

A critical interpretation of corporate elitism:
José L. Orozco

A further stimulus to research comes from the work, strongly philosophical in approach, of José Luis Orozco, Professor of Political Science at the Universidad Nacional Autónoma in Mexico City. At the Seminar held in La Trinidad-Tlaxcala he presented an interesting and documented report on 'Darwinism and Corporate Elitism'.[17] This contribution is related to various other writings by this discerning Mexican scholar who has studied in great detail the way in which positivism and Darwinism have been read and received by the intellectual political tradition in the USA and Mexico. Orozco began to take an interest in Mosca's work in 1969 after much meditation on the classic political writers of bourgeois thought at its height during the main phases of rationalist enlightenment, positivism and pragmatism.[18] According to this writer, 'unlike the organic-naturalist project of Darwinism and English-speaking pragmatism, and unlike the vitalist-spiritualist project of German or French irrationalism the elitist project of Gaetano Mosca does not abandon belief in reason and in the history of enlightenment and positivism'.[19]

A logical and lay humanist, Mosca comes across in Orozco's view as 'an authentic free thinker of liberalism'. Although there is a desire on the part of some to include the Italian thinker in the Machiavellian tradition (according to Burnham's definition), in reality he

is part of an ethical, constitutionalist dimension: his system of values is opposed to fashionable spiritualism and pragmatism which can be readily used to support the normative supremacy of intangible commands and energies, which include the arbitrary nature of force – race, evolution, the fostering of the spirit, the will to power, manifest destiny, scientific administration or the purely mechanical physiology of behaviourism.[20]

Orozco's analysis is well constructed and has a sounder basis for tackling Mosca's theories in his thorough knowledge of the work of both Benedetto Croce and Giovanni Gentile.[21] What he sees in the formulation of the doctrine of the political class is essentially a singular manifestation of the fact that the bourgeoisie abandoned the attempt to preserve its character of political universality; by this he means 'the assertion according to which liberalism proclaims itself (as in Rousseau's *volonté générale* or Sieyès's *tiers état*) the possessor of an integral and egalitarian social universality, the guardian over the general will of all citizens which embraces and stands above all classes and egoistic interests.[22] The 'real and scientific' division introduced by Mosca between 'rulers' and 'ruled' breaks up a highly ideological vision of society but also what is basically a mystification; it therefore has a positive and liberating function.

It is interesting to consider that this Mexican scholar, the author – among other things – of a long polemical essay on political science in the USA and an accurate and very extensive critical anthology of political thinking in the USA between 1890 and 1980, sees in a certain doctrinaire elitism in that country the latest expression of a Darwinian-evolutionist tradition connected to the great influence of Herbert Spencer on the intellectual political tradition in England and English-speaking America. This is a position which points to the 'voluntarist and magnetic' elitism of 'representatives' according to Ralph Waldo Emerson (1808–82)[23] and the theory of corporate elitism put forward by Arthur F. Bentley (1870–1957) as early as 1908 in his book *The Process of Government*[24] as fundamental categories in North American political pluralism some time before the provocative and suggestive 'theory of elites' of Italian origin came onto the scene in the 1930s. This is a theme which Orozco has considered in great detail and it is worth evaluating carefully to see what significance it may have for the difficult assessment of the connections between the theory of democracy and the 'theory of elites' in the North American intellectual political tradition.

In a geopolitical area which, in addition to the USA, encompasses Canada and Mexico – countries in which the questions dealt with here are highly topical, also (but not only) as a reflection of US influence – the extension of the category of elitism from the political or social field to that of the big corporations and their organizations deserves special and detailed attention in terms of the substantial innovations it may bring forth at the level of historical and theoretical research. We should also add that the very fruitful method of combining theory and historical and sociological research has resulted in two weighty studies by US field researchers Peter H. Smith and Roderic Ai Camp (both present at the La Trinidad-Tlaxcala Seminar): one on the recruitment of political elites in Mexico in the period 1900–71 and the other dealing with the formation of political leaders in post-revolutionary Mexico.[25] These contributions, together with several other well documented ones presented at this 'Gaetano Mosca International Seminar', provide an indication of how a vital reformulation and synthesis of several of the many scientific and doctrinal contributions already mentioned is proceeding in a very concrete manner in this until now undeservedly neglected area. New categories of interpretation for discussion and the results of organic empirical research into the groups which dominate Mexican society are contributing positively towards the creation of a further version of elitism which is both a political interpretaton of society and a more direct and firmly based understanding of it.

Marxism and ethical elitism: Aleksandar Sekulovič

Apart from his ideological anti-socialism which has been fully discussed in the first part of this book, in Mosca's thought the theoretical relationship between his ideas and Marxism is not examined in any depth. Nevertheless, his often simplifying realism at the social level leads to many points of agreement with the rival doctrine. In fact, a rereading '*en marxiste*' of Mosca's entire theory would appear to be worth the effort. It is very interesting to note, however, that in a communist country which has produced a writer with the interpretive power of Milovan Gilas (the Yugoslav who examined the Russian communist system through the social category of the 'new class' formed by the communist political bureaucracy of proletarian extraction) a book recently appeared which is entirely dedicated to Mosca. It is the work of Aleksandar Sekulovič, a communist leader, long-serving diplomat in Rome, and political essayist.

Published in Belgrade at the end of 1982, *Teorija političke klase* is the first work dedicated to the political thought of Gaetano Mosca to appear in Eastern Europe.[26] The reason for this is not that in this part of the world, and especially in Yugoslavia, books on the theorists in this field are scarce; there already exists a wide literature on Weber, Pareto, and the modern elitism of Schumpeter, Mills and others. The main works by all these authors have been translated and are well-known in Yugoslavia. The political thought of Mosca, on the other hand, is very little known and misunderstood in Slavic cultural circles. Indeed, Yugoslav scholars have not been very favourably disposed towards Mosca, accused of having contributed through his doctrine to the theoretical justification of Fascism. Sekulovič states that this prejudice has been the main motive for his interest in the Italian writer's political thinking. Taking as his premise the unfounded nature of this accusation, Sekulovič, who had previously made a study of totalitarian regimes (and was winner in 1970 of a competition on Stalinism in *Gledista*, the famous Belgrade review), makes it a point of scientific integrity to inform the Yugoslav reader about the true thought of Gaetano Mosca by providing a faithful summary of his main ideas. Given the intellectual background in Yugoslavia, this book had to be of the mainly informative kind even though its stated aim was a different one: to refute erroneous interpretations of the Italian theorist. This informational aspect is implicit in the way the book was written. First and foremost, Sekulovič considers that the first duty of a scholar is to look at the facts, to start from living social reality and he asserts that Mosca can still serve today as a reference point for all those working in the field of political science. According to Sekulovič, Mosca's realism and positivism are also the source of his ethical-political ideals. He writes:

> For Mosca, the best society is the one in which the gap between theory and praxis, between norm and reality is the smallest. In his view, even though the power structure may be imperfect, that society in which this gap is smaller is more 'in order', from an ethical point of view, than a society in which this gap is wide.[27]

Agreeing with those who have defined Mosca as a 'destroyer of myths' and emphasizing his intellectual honesty, Sekulovič reaches the conclusion that the Italian writer was not a social reformer in search of the perfect society, but rather a scientist who explained and interpreted society as it existed and the reasons for its inadequacies, and suggested ways of improving it.[28]

Of particular interest is Sekulovič's attempt to show that the doctrine of the political class is neither conservative nor reactionary, since anyone who records an objectively existing fact cannot be labelled a conservative. In this respect, he recalls the fact that C. W. Mills has been considered, also in Yugoslavia, one of the most progressive sociologists of modern times for his criticism of the political class in the USA. But Mosca too made a critical study of the Italian political class of his time and so radical was it that he could be called 'the Mills of his age'.[29]

In illustrating the Moschian concept of political formula, Sekulovič dwells – perhaps too cautiously – on the relationship between elitism and Marxism. He concludes that Mosca's interpretation of Marxism is too simplistic, as is his vision of socialism as a totalitarian system. However, he underlines the fact that the subsequent historical experience of real socialism has made topical once again Mosca's warnings of the 'risks' inherent in socialist doctrines and the states based on them.[30]

The Yugoslav writer believes that the key to Mosca's political thinking lies, above all, in his philosophical conception of nature and human society. Unlike the great social and religious doctrines, which all have a common denominator in the cast-iron belief in 'the goodness of human nature', Mosca sees men as they are: 'a mixture of good and bad'.[31] Therefore, since men are not perfect, it is impossible for their main achievement, human society, to be perfect. This means that Mosca is a scholar interested in the *possible*, one for whom the very aspiring after the impossible, after a perfect and ideal State is to be considered negative and sterile. The best is that which appears possible, realizable. That which is not possible at a particular moment or at any time, even if ideally speaking it is the best, is dangerous or better still 'conservative'. This is why Mosca maintains that since democracy cannot be achieved, it is a conservative tendency. The main function of the idea of 'perfection' is to deceive men, to distract and enervate them so that by chasing after an illusion, they miss the opportunity to do what is required in real life.[32]

Having reconstructed Mosca's political and ethical vision, Sekulovič considers the scientific importance of Mosca's thought and its role in the development of modern political science. He has no doubts that Mosca is the founder of modern elitism who saw democracy not as government by the people, but as government by a minority under the control of the people.[33] So the chief problem for this new elitism based on ethics – as presented in the thinking of the Italian writer – is not the creation of a people's government, but rather of a responsible and morally sound minority whose actions are directed towards the common good. To this end, which humanity has yet to attain, Gaetano Mosca has made a substantial contribution and in his final conclusion Sekulovič says: 'Gaetano Mosca's political theory is not aimed at justifying public authority and those who hold it, but at discovering the means to ensure that it acts as far as possible in the interest of the majority'.[34]

Like the whole approach of this interesting book (still untranslated), this is a conclusion which leads us far from the questions we have been dealing with. These are all common to the differentiated but similar political and cultural contexts to be found in liberal-democratic countries (or those with political regimes of a very special kind, like the presidential system based on an institutional party in post-revolutionary Mexico). It is not difficult to sense the ideological uneasiness rather than the hum of empirical verification behind the ethical elitism outlined by Sekulovič. In fact, the 'new class' of Gilas is all too familiar to those who live in countries under a communist regime (even in those with strong national characteristics and more tolerance, as is the case of Yugoslavia). The elitist nature of this class has been clearly underlined by Gilas who wrote the following almost thirty years ago: 'This new class, the bureaucracy, or more exactly the political bureaucracy has all the characteristics of those which preceded it and some orginal ones of its own'.[35] Delving into the origins of the phenomenon, Gilas maintains that 'the initiators of the new class' must be traced back 'to that group of professional revolutionaries' who formed the 'essential core' of the Bolshevik Party. Thus, with Stalin as prompter

the new ruling class gradually developed from this very restricted group of revolutionaries who for many years were its main driving force. Trotsky pointed out that the germ of the future Stalinist bureaucrat is to be found in the old professional revolutionaries. What he did not see was the beginnings of a new class of property owners and exploiters.[36]

The ideological and bureaucratic elitism which can be deduced systematically from the history of communist parties represents, therefore, an institutionalized reality of no little importance. This is because it demonstrates that underneath the radical differences in the political, economic and social system there exists the basic truth of elitism *tout court*, which is an essential and integral part of communist political doctrine.[37] The effective existence of nomenclatures in communist regimes is a concrete fact which undermines the theoretical reliability of many criticisms directed against the classic Italian exponents of elitism from a Marxist or similar such perspective. The research undertaken by Sekulovič points to a very different way of approaching such themes.

Elitism and the intellectual political tradition in the French-speaking world

As has already been noted, the French intellectual political tradition is in general not very receptive to the issues raised by elitism. It is probably the case that in France the very concept of elite evokes an area of politics which the storming of the Bastille and the Great Revolution are unconsciously felt to have liquidated for ever. Consequently, only a few dozen lines are reserved for Mosca, Pareto and Michels in *Histoire des idées politiques* by Marcel Prélot, which is none the less a work with a broad theoretical and juridical basis;[38] neither are they treated any better by Jean Touchard in his textbook with the same title.[39] Although their book *Les conceptions politiques du XXe siècle* is over one thousand pages long, François Châtelet and Evelyn Pisier-Kouchner mention Michels and Ostrogorskij merely in passing and refer solely to the partial 1971 and 1979 editions in France of the classic texts;[40] and no change in attitude is apparent in the Italian edition of the collective work *Storia delle ideologie* edited by F. Châtelet and Gérard Mairet.[41]

We could go into this aspect in more detail, but that would imply attempting a broader-based judgement and a more articulated analysis – neither desirable nor appropriate at this point – of how the study of political science and the history of political doctrines has progressed in France since the Second World War. Besides, an intelligent interpretation in terms of a priori judgements and political-ideological prejudices has already been provided by Francis Vecchini, an acute French scholar who has correctly viewed Mosca's work in the context of

Italian political history.[42] In fairness it must be remembered, however, that between the two world wars Mosca's work was received with open arms; this reception is the object of a documented investigation by Robertino Ghiringhelli, a scientific collaborator of ours at Milan University.[43] However, the collaboration between Mosca and Gaston Bouthoul which led to the above-mentioned first edition of *Histoire des doctrines politiques depuis l'antiquité jusqu'à nos jours* (1936) and the two subsequent reissues in France (1955 and 1965) belongs to a different period in French and European culture. In this period much interest was shown in, among other things, the ideas of Pareto (a substantial part of his work was first published directly in French) and Michels (many of whose various writings were also published in French in their first versions). Though not forgetting the above-mentioned commendable work of Giovanni Busino at Lausanne University (in a French-speaking area dominated by French culture), the present state of things in this scientific and cultural field is less impressive.

There are, however, other striking examples which cannot be ignored. One of these is the scholar Georges Burdeau who has dedicated a lifetime's study to political science and written the *Traité de science politique*, a monumental political-juridical study in 13 large volumes. In this work an entire section of several pages is devoted to the political class.[44] But Mosca's name only appears in a footnote as part of the full title of the book by James H. Meisel! The scientific and historical aspect of the question, the theoretical genesis of the concept and the successive (also ideological) stages in the development of a world-wide political culture are not even given a summary treatment.

None the less, the political class is conceived by Burdeau according to parameters which are inherently and rigidly Moschian; they are even more radical and much less problematical than those used by the Italian writer himself in his codified doctrine of the 1920s and 1930s. For example, Burdeau says the following:

This class cannot be confused with any other. Its members may come from very different social backgrounds; they are associated with distinct classes, in the current use of the term. But this social, economic or occupational labelling is overcome by participating in political life. The same occurs in the political class as in a religion which brings together the faithful who are completely different from one another on the temporal plane.[45]

Despite the fact that it refers to several North-American works on the subject, Burdeau's treatment of the political class is much more strongly rooted in its author's specifically and technically juridical culture. In addition, it echoes a varied and heterogeneous range of French works from the classic analyses of pressure groups by Jean Meynaud to studies on the participation of functionaries in the making of political decisions, and including political-ideological works of a neo-Marxist type like the one by Nicos Poulantzas. In the latter several interesting pages are devoted to the theories of elites, the ideas of Mosca and Michels being viewed through the prism of American works in political sociology.[46]

The essential data referred to here permit one to assess the manner in which – inside an intellectual tradition not particularly open to this kind of theoretical approach – some of the intuitions which form the basis of elitism in its modern version have to a certain extent been assimilated. But rather than a merging of elements like that accomplished within the English-speaking intellectual tradition, in this case the process should be thought of as a more complex one in which ideas and stimuli are picked up from different cultures and combined in various ways within the French intellectual political tradition, using a method of dissection and recuperation that is not always easy to identify; neither is its significance easy to define. In Burdeau's work, in fact, elitism does not appear as a separate theme in itself which is considered according to the formulation now adopted in Anglo-American, Italian, German and Mexican intellectual political circles. Nevertheless, it is clearly asserted in its original and rigorous political-institutional form which is represented by the Moschian conception of the political class. By moving in this direction, the French intellectual political tradition is certainly regaining, over and above the summary references and gaping omissions, at least a part of the significance of Mosca's doctrine. Unfortunately, it is an exceedingly retarded process of recovery.

Burdeau's entire research was undertaken according to a political inspiration based on old-style liberalism, and he pays special attention to describing the juridical-constitutional mechanisms suitable for putting into effect a 'certain idea of law' which, common to rulers and ruled alike, renders acceptable the existence of both power and political obligation.[47] This approach is used by Burdeau in an even more direct and almost popular form in his two books *La démocratie* and *Le libéralisme*.[48] In these volumes, however, a certain unease on the part of the author is noticeable when he comes to conclude his analysis with a synthesis of the crucial themes examined. If for this scholar democracy is defined at the outset as 'a philosophy, a way of life, a relationship and, almost incidentally, a form of government',[49] during the course of the book it becomes the object of an interesting study which, none the less, also feels the need to arrive at fixed conclusions. But this turns out to be impossible because, as the writer asserts at the end of the book, 'democracy is not an idea with an immutable content' since 'its characteristics are those attributed to it by the dreams of men'.[50] In moving from democracy to liberalism, Burdeau's analysis then concludes with the fideistic affirmation that the 'truth of liberalism lies not in theory; it lies in man'.[51] What this basically amounts to is the putting forward of a set of ethical-juridical convictions much closer to the most dated aspects of Mosca's teaching and his liberal ideology, with all its previously mentioned limits, than to the neo-elitist formulations examined in the preceding sections.

This tendency in French culture is clearly given a change of direction by the work of Raymond Aron (1905–84), which mainly encompasses the field of sociology and political science and is too well-known to be gone into again here. If anything, what must be recalled is the fact that in *La lutte de classes* he works out an interesting conception of elitism, which is traced back, at least in part, to its origins in Mosca and Pareto.[52] The same is true of *Démocratie et totalitarisme*, especially with regard to chapter VII dealing with the 'oligarchical nature of constitutional-pluralist regimes';[53] nor should one neglect Aron's full treatment of Pareto in his book on the stages in the development of sociological thinking.[54] However, precisely because it forms an original and composite political thought drawing on many sources, Aron's work deserves a study all to itself. We have no doubt that such a study would provide not a few interesting indications and suggestions pertinent to the themes we have been discussing.

We also believe that a similar organic work of interpretation is needed for the several works written by Maurice Duverger on political parties, the interpretation of politics and political systems.[55] What we can give at present are pointers to the direction such work should take in the future. This is something which has still to be taken up within the French (and also French-speaking) intellectual political tradition, and any further delay will cause it to lag behind. As well as the specifically French case, one must also take into account the great influence exerted by France on the intellectual political tradition in French-speaking areas or on scholars who are linked by an umbilical cord to the French tradition. Some examples may serve to clarify this aspect. Several indications, slightly extravagant within the terms of their discourse, are to be found in serious works dealing with other themes. We refer to the excellent research carried out by Zeev Sternhell, a writer who has studied in France, teaches at the Hebrew University in Jersualem and is the author of an interesting work on the revolutionary Right and the French origins of Fascism in which there are, however, several totally inexact references to Mosca and Pareto.[56] And we especially have in mind the studies by the French–Canadian Léon Dion on 'pressure groups' in the USA; they

Towards a critical conclusion

make a very useful contribution towards an understanding of the basic structural realities (the elites active in the social, economic and political spheres) which support and animate our theoretical discussion of neo-elitism.[57] This is also true of the various studies of French bureaucratic elites by Ezra N. Suleiman, a scholar in the USA with a Franco-American background.[58] There is in both these writers, but especially in Suleiman, the theoretical-historical awareness that neo-elitism forms an important basis for empirical research.

Within this brief survey, a role of some importance must be attributed to the comparative research which has been carried out for many years by Mattei Dogan of the CNRS, both individually and jointly, at the *Centre de recherche sur les élites*. Dogan's work in France (and also in the USA) now constitutes a fixed reference point for all scholars in this field notwithstanding the differences between the ways in which empirical research is done in the various disciplines: sociology, political science, history of political thought and history of ideas. Dogan's scientific and cultural commitment is of great interest for the link which this academic provides between Europe and the United States; he also has a direct connection with, among others, Italian academic culture.[59]

Lastly, there are the very stimulating tendencies in this cultural area which, alongside excellent reinterpretations of sociological works like the book by Guy Perrin on Pareto (a work which came out of Lausanne University),[60] could provide the basis for a systematic rereading of the *Traité de sociologie* edited by Georges Gurvitch (1894–1965).[61] Present-day French and French-speaking sociological culture is begining to show an interest in the themes we have treated herein. This is shown by studies and research like those – mentioned above – of M. Maffesoli and J. Zylberberg (1984 and 1985) in Paris and Quebec, and also by the V Congress of the French Association of Historians of Political Ideas (AFHIP) held at Aix-en-Provence in the autumn of 1986. At the congress a historical-theoretical paper on the theme of elitism was given, for the first time ever at an official French gathering, by the author of this book.

Between past and future

In conclusion, we wish to underline the fact that though limited to a few essential examples, these (conceptual and methodological) re-elaborations of neo-elitism have above all opened up a very stimulating panorama of ideas and proposals aimed at increasing our knowledge of the constantly changing face of politics in present-day society. This interest in widening the horizons of research beyond the bounds of what has already been established and codified is nowadays more or less common to all the new formulations of political theory to which we have referred; formulations which have not remained unaffected by the overall influence of elitism in its various forms. For the themes with which we have been dealing definitive conclusions are clearly still some way off; at most, there is the prospect of some 'partial conclusions' from the attempt to fix – as we have tried to do – more precise philological and historical reference points and to highlight an intricate interweaving of interests and research which point to a highly articulated state of ideas and openings towards the future. Anachronistic denunciations and erroneous ideological interpretations of elitism having been rejected as synonymous with anti-democratic conceptions of power, it would be opportune for those studying politics in various countries to now make a co-ordinated effort, simultaneously comparative and international, theoretical and empirical, to test critically and scientifically the complex research work which we have been describing and interpreting. This is the way to make further progress towards formalizing new political syntheses which are able to unify the ethos and values of popular participation, institutionalized in precise legal forms, and the deeply entrenched fact of the formation of elites. There is no doubt that the – to our mind – most complete and convincing modern formulation of elitism, that of Schumpeter, has provided the basis for three subsequent conclusions (both theoretical and practical) of considerable interest. These concern:

1 the conviction that political power is basically always exercised by a minority over a majority, even under a system based on freedom and with institutionalized mass participation;
2 the belief that political power has its origin in a complex and permanent socio-economic, ideological and cultural dynamic between organized minorities engaged in a constant struggle with one another for non-violent supremacy, and for alternation in the conquest and use of power;
3 the equating of democracy with a political regime strongly rooted in the customs, history and different interests acting within society; a regime which is able to guarantee competition between the various minorities according to formal procedures that ensure at all times freedom, the participation of the ruled masses in institutional life and the circulation of ruling groups.

Schumpeter put forward elitism in an exemplary manner as a true political doctrine which has the capacity to go beyond the limits of the classical 'theory of elites'. Schumpeter's elitism consists of a combination of the classic democratic representative regime, a clearly defined system of freedoms and the greatest possible circulation of elites. However the doctrinal spark, that is, the prescriptive element in Schumpeter's elitism provided, historically speaking, the conceptual tools for neo-elitism: a conception of politics which now, in turn, constitutes a true socio-political theory with a critical background of great value. The existence of this theory leads to the consideration that there has been a profound change in both the basic concepts of elitism, especially regarding the original Italian formulation, and also the concepts which make up the practical and intellectual patrimony of the liberal-democratic tradition. It is at this point that the doctrinal aspect, liberal-democratic in nature, of Schumpeter's synthesis can be measured against the rapid changes which have been taking place since the Second World War, against the generalization and ubiquitous spread of modern mass society.

These changes show the ideological and doctrinal effects of the widespread influence and popularity of socialism, in the broadest sense of the term, and the implementation of policies inspired by it. Welfare-statism, which Field and Higley discuss, is as a doctrine and practice particularly significant in this respect. Thus neo-elitism finds itself situated in a context which is quite different from that of the pre-war and war years, and it is helping to further extend our understanding of the central phenomenon of modern politics: the form power has assumed in technologically advanced (or advancing), post-industrial and post-colonial societies. In this perspective, the theoretical aspect – more descriptive than applicable – is distinctly predominant. A powerful contribution has been given to the formulation of this theory by the continual circulation of ideas between Europe and the USA and by Anglo-American sociology and political science having taken up this theme during their boom period, especially in the 1950s and 1960s. This is a clear symptom of post-war reality with its internationalization of separate intellectual traditions, which is a characteristic of the new mass society everywhere notwithstanding the fundamental dichotomy between the capitalist and welfare-statist West and the welfare-statist East with its state-run economies.

For years neo-elitism has been centered on this re-examined and reformulated theoretical system in an attempt to further our knowledge of the reality of power in society and in the organization of political institutions. However, except in a few rare cases which have not advanced beyond the initial stage, the theoretical aspect of neo-elitism has not been translated, at least up until the late 1970s, into a tendency to formulate ideas of a prescriptive and operative kind. Speaking in Moschian terms, one could say that the idealization of all political formulas has resulted in the obfuscation of the true minority nature of power; but what neo-elitism needs is facts. Numerous empirical studies have been carried out on well-defined political, social, cultural, etc., groups, that is, the elites actively present in various geographical regions and social environments, and they clearly indicate the increasing tendency of neo-elitism to integrate the theoretical aspects mentioned above with the empirical requirement of understanding scientifically the dynamic of groups and individuals in societies which have changed radically in terms of their composition and values, as is the case with all contemporary societies. These are considerations which relate specifically to that part of the world which is known as the West, but the large amount of research into political, economic and military ruling groups in many developing countries should also be borne in mind. However, the integration of theory with empirical investigation has not always occurred in the full awareness of all the implications involved. Lastly, it must be pointed out that, above all in the last few years, the jointly theoretical and practical aspect of neo-elitism has increasingly tended, in our opinion, to lead to the adoption of a doctrinal-political position, which is justifiable given the worsening of the grave crisis in all political thinking in both West and East.

Neo-elitism is a theory worked out on a strongly empirical and realistic basis, as its entire history demonstrates. Through its tendency to reconcile, also at the psychological and conceptual level, the minority foundation of power with the values of liberal and pluralist democracy in its new mass dimension, it has stimulated in terms of deeds and ideas a reconsideration of the existence, formation, organization and aims of different elites. None the less, neo-elitism contains an unresolved question which is not simply theoretical but ideological, in the broad and non mystified sense. Given that for centuries, from the systems constructed by religions to those of revolutionary groups aiming for power, men have payed the greatest attention to the formulation of codes and behaviour, rules and styles of living, and justificatory ideals so as to form homogeneous and selective groups that dedicate their passions, activities and lives to common objectives, what are the moral values and practical ends which today inspire the new elites?

In the preceding sections we have attempted to depict, in a manifestly incomplete but sufficiently significant fashion, the shape which is being assumed by several embryonal political doctrines; such doctrines are underpinned conceptually by neo-elitism which has prepared the ground for their present formulation. The new elitist paradigm of Higley and Field; the critical identification and description of corporate elitism by Orozco; the ethical elitism of Sekulovič, which is almost a countermelody of hope to the rigidly authoritarian practice of the political bureaucracies dominant in Eastern Europe and the communist world; and the articulated and complex comparative research in a democratic-pluralist key by Dogan mark out a panorama which is no longer just theoretical, yet still not fully doctrinal (that is, both descriptive and prescriptive at the same time).

If, then, we are still waiting for an unambiguous political doctrine, there is nevertheless no lack of intellectual inducement to move on from the now somewhat static position into which theoretical and practical neo-elitism has rigidified to the formulating of elitist political doctrines that are feasible within the context of the substantially participatory and mass form of democracy in contemporary societies. It is evident that present-day neo-elitism has failed to link up actively and definitively with both the fixed values which have always existed and inspired political action, and with the various social and economic interests that form the no less important programmatic aspect of such values. The explanatory truths brought forth by neo-elitism have so far been of a chiefly speculative kind, often strongly opposed by ideological passion and prejudice. Consequently, the neo-elitist analysis is by itself insufficient and must become an integral part of the highly ideological, idealized and, by now, enormously mystified spheres of values and interests which are the frames of reference for vast numbers of the governed. The integration of neo-elitism into the traditional liberal-democratic and pluralist current in the West represents, in our opinion, a specific intellectual accomplishment of the last twenty years. We believe that it is also of value for all the humanist-socialist, labourite and social-democratic movements in Europe and North America. There is no doubt that the pre-eminent theme of political elites is errupting into realities and domains which are inspired by other different values. One need only think of the enormous issues raised by this question both in countries with Communist regimes and in so-called third-world countries under authoritarian political leaderships, mostly of a military kind.

In a historical perspective, however, this amounts to a genuine return to the origins of a current of thought which in spite of all its proclaimed objectivistic intentions, has essentially grasped the subjective side to the phenomenon of power: the unavoidable requirement that the small number of individuals called upon to rule over the mass of other men see the necessity for moral propriety and proper training. Indeed, never before in history as now towards the end of the twentieth century, has the problem of the need for responsible, efficient, honest, learned and far-sighted leadership been posed in all societies irrespective of the type of state and political regime. Never before has this problem assumed such an immense and urgent importance as it has today. To rethink the origin and development of elitism, in all its versions and variations, thus provides a real challenge which forms a line of continuity stretching from the history of the last century and reaching dramatically into the heart of the present and, above all, the near future.

Abbreviations

These abbreviations indicate the editions of Gaetano Mosca's works referred to in the Notes.

CM	G. Mosca, *Le costituzioni moderne* [*Modern Constitutions*] (1887), now in G. Mosca, *Ciò che la storia potrebbe insegnare. Scritti di scienza politica.* [*What we can learn from History. Writings in Political Science*], (Giuffré, Milan, 1958). The bibliographical indications contained herein refer to pp. 445–549 of this edition.
CMF	*Gaetano Mosca – Guglielmo Ferrero (Carteggio 1896–1934)*, C. Mongardini (ed.), *Opere di Gaetano Mosca. Istituto di Studi Storico–Politici dell'Università di Roma*, Vol. VI, I (Giuffré, Milan, 1980).
ESP-I	G. Mosca, *Elementi di scienza politica* [*Elements of Political Science*] (Bocca, Rome, 1896).
ESP-II	G. Mosca, *Elementi di scienza politica. Seconda edizione con una seconda parte inedita* [*Elements of Political Science. Second edn with new part*] (Bocca, Turin, 1923).
ESP-III	G. Mosca, *Elementi di scienza politica. Terza edizione riveduta* [*Elements of Political Science. Third revised edn*], 2 vols (Laterza, Bari, 1939).
PM	G. Mosca, 'Encore quelques mots sur "Le Prince" de Machiavel' ['Some further comments on Machiavelli's "Prince"'], in *Revue des Sciences Politiques* (Paris), ann. XL, vol. XLVIII, October–December 1925 and ann. XLI, vol. XLIX, January–March 1926.
PP	G. Mosca, 'Pensieri inediti' ['Unpublished Thoughts'] in *Ethos* (Rome), ann. I, no. 3, December 1945, Leonardo

	Donato (ed.) Now under the title 'Pensieri postumi' ['Posthumous Thoughts'] in G. Mosca, *Ciò che la storia potrebbe insegnare*. The references contained refer to pp. 723–7 of this edition.
PS	G. Mosca, *Partiti e sindacati nella crisi del regime parlamentare* [*Parties and Trade Unions during the Crisis of the Parliamentary System*] (Laterza, Bari, 1949).
QPDC	G. Mosca, *Questioni pratiche di diritto costituzionale* [*Practical Questions of Constitutional Law*] (Bocca, Turin, 1898). Section II of this book, entitled 'Two possible ways of modifying parliamentary government in Italy', has been reproduced in G. Mosca, *Ciò che la storia potrebbe insegnare*. The references contained herein refer to pp. 337–52 of this edition.
SC	G. Mosca, 'A proposito di una recente pubblicazione di sociologia criminale' ['On a Recent Work of Criminal Sociology'], in *Il Circolo Giuridico* (Palermo), ann. XXI, vol. XXI, 1980. Now, under the same title, in G. Mosca, *Ciò che la storia potrebbe insegnare*. The references contained herein refer to pp. 607–31 of this edition.
SDP	G. Mosca, *Storia delle dottrine politiche* [*History of Political Doctrines*] (Laterza, Bari, 1974), 9th edn.
TG	G. Mosca, *Sulla teorica dei governi e sul governo parlamentare. Studii storici e sociali* [*The Theory of Governments and the Parliamentary System. Social and Historical Studies*] (Loescher, Turin, 1884).
TSL	G. Mosca, *Il tramonto dello stato liberale* [*The Death of the Liberal State*], A. Lombardo (ed.), Preface by G. Spadolini (Bonanno, Catania, 1971). This book is a collection of most of Mosca's articles published in the daily *Corriere della Sera* of Milan.
UTM	G. Mosca, 'L'utopia di Tommaso More e il pensiero moderno' ['Thomas More's Utopia and Modern Thought'] in *Scritti della Facoltà Giuridica di Roma in onore di Antonio Salandra* (Vallardi, Milan, 1928). Now under the same title in G. Mosca, *Ciò che la storia potrebbe insegnare*. The references contained herein refer to pp. 657–69 of this edition.

Other abbreviations

AP. CD	*Atti del Parlamento. Camera dei Deputati* [Parliamentary Proceedings. Chamber of Deputies].
AP. SR	*Atti del Parlamento. Senato del Regno* [Parliamentary Proceedings. Senate].

MAIC. DGSL   *Ministero dell'Agricoltura, Industria e Commercio. Direzione Generale della Statistica e del Lavoro.* [Ministry of Agriculture, Industry and Commerce. Statistics and Labour Department].

Translator's note

With regard to the passages quoted from the *Elementi di scienza politica* and *Storia delle dottrine politiche* I have, for the most part, used the already existing translations by H. D. Kahn and S. Z. Koff respectively (see bibliography), modifying them where I felt it was necessary.

Notes

Introduction

1 E. A. Albertoni, *Gaetano Mosca. Storia di una dottrina politica. Formazione e interpretazione* [*Gaetano, Mosca. History of a Political Doctrine. Its Development and Interpretation*] (Giuffré, Milan, 1978); subsequently: *Dottrina della classe politica e teoria delle élites* [*Doctrine of the Political Class and Theory of Elites*] (Giuffré, Milan, 1985), which forms vol III (Italian series) of the 'Archivo Internazionale'.

2 For a full documentation on this wide area of research which arose out of the 'International Seminars', refer to the following volumes published by the 'Archivio Internazionale Gaetano Mosca per lo studio della classe politica' [Gaetano Mosca International Archive for the Study of the Political Class], a series conceived and directed by me. It must be pointed out that the volumes indicated herein are all collected works with many international contributions, and that the basic texts are in Italian whereas those in English and French represent a re-elaboration and synthesis of essays and documents:

vol. I (Italian series): *La dottrina della classe politica di Gaetano Mosca ed i suoi sviluppi internazionali* [*Gaetano Mosca's Doctrine of the Political Class and its Development Abroad*] (Palermo, 1982 – distributed by Giuffré, Milan);
vol. II (Italian series): *Governo e governabilità nel sistema politico e giuridico di Gaetano Mosca* [*Government and Governability in Gaetano Mosca's Political and Juridical System*] (Giuffré, Milan, 1983);
vol. I (International series): *Studies on the Political Thought of Gaetano Mosca. The Theory of the Ruling Class and its Development Abroad*, (Giuffré, Milan-Montreal, 1982);
vol. II (International series): *Etudes sur la pensée politique de Gaetano Mosca. Classe politique et gouvernement* [*Studies in the Political Thought of Gaetano Mosca. The Political Class and Government*] (Giuffré, Milan-Montreal, 1984).

3 Cremona, a town in the region of Lombardy, is of considerable interest for the fact that in the nineteenth century it possessed a political class of

Notes 169

national importance, among which the predominant thinking was liberal, democratic, republican, socialist and progressive Catholic, while in the twentieth century it became the town which elected the most intransigent and extreme Fascist boss, Roberto Farinacci. See the volume, *Una città nella storia dell'Italia unita (Classe politica ed ideologie in Cremona durante il cinquantennio 1875-1925)*, F. Invernici (ed.), vol. IV, 'Archivio Internazionale' (Italian series), (Biblioteca Statale and 'Comitato Internazionale Mosca', Milan-Cremona, 1986 – distributed by Giuffré, Milan).

4 E. A. Albertoni, *La teoria della classe politica nella crisi del parlamentarismo* [*The Theory of the Political Class in the Crisis of the Parliamentary System*], (Istituto Editoriale Cisalpino-Goliardica, Milan, 1968); *Il pensiero politico di Gaetano Mosca. Valori. Miti. Ideologia* [*The Political Thought of Gaetano Mosca. Values. Myths. Ideology*]. Preface by R. Treves (Istituto Editoriale Cisalpino-Goliardica, Milan, 1973).

5 Concerning the research and study promoted by the 'Archivio Internazionale Gaetano Mosca' the authoritative German journal *Der Staat* has written:

Thus, at present, Naples has become the centre for studies on Vico (widely known and very instructive), Milan the centre for the study and diffusion of the works of G. Mosca... The papers, research reports and discussions which emerged during the congress [the journal is referring to the 'First Gaetano Mosca International Seminar'] are contained in vol. I of the '*Archivio*'; unfortunately for reasons of space it is not possible to refer to them fittingly in all their detail, but without knowledge of them any further work on Mosca must be viewed as worthless.

(See the *Review* by G. Eisermann, Professor of Sociology at Bonn University, of the first two volumes of the Italian and the International series of the 'Archivio', and my book *Gaetano Mosca. Storia di una dottrina politica. Formazione e interpretazione*, in *Der Staat* (Berlin), vol. 22, no. 3, 1983, pp. 434–5).

The *Canadian Journal of Political Science* has written that vol. I of the International series, in English, of the 'Archivio' constitutes 'an admirable guide to what has been done and what needs to be done for a better understanding of Mosca's thinking' (see the *Review* by S. A. State, Professor of Political Science at the University of Western Ontario, in *Canadian Journal of Political Science*, September 1983, vol. XVI, no. 3, pp. 637–9).

6 For the bibliographical references most easy to come by at present see:

(i) For *Mosca: Scritti politici di Gaetano Mosca* [*Gaetano Mosca's Political Writings*], G. Sola (ed.), 2 vols (Utet, Turin, 1982). These two volumes, which form part of the 'Classici della politica' series, contain the critical editions of both *Sulla teorica dei governi e sul governo parlamentare* and the *Elementi di scienza politica*.

(ii) For the quotations from Mosca contained in this present work the original editions are referred to, using the abbreviations indicated at the end of the text;

(iii) For Pareto: the selection of political writings, also published in the 'Classici della politica' series and divided up as follows: vol. I: *I sistemi socialisti* [*Socialist Systems*], G. Busino (ed.), (Utet, Turin, 1974); vol. II: *Scritti politici di Vilfredo Pareto* [*Vilfredo Pareto's Political Writings*] (vol. I: *Lo sviluppo del capitalismo (1872–1895)*) [*The Development of Capitalism*], G. Busino (ed.) (Utet, Turin, 1974); *Scritti politici di Vilfredo Pareto* (vol. II: *Reazione, libertà, fascismo (1896–1923)*) [*Reaction, Freedom, Fascism*], G. Busino (ed.), (Utet, Turin, 1974);

(iv) For Michels: the Italian critical edition of *Zur Soziologie des Parteiwesens in der Modernen Demokratie* translated from the second German edition (1925) as R. Michels, *La sociologia del partito politico nella democrazia moderna* [*Sociology of the Political Party in the Modern Democratic System*], with an extensive introduction by J. J. Linz (Il Mulino, Bologna, 1966).

7 C. B. Macpherson, *The Life and Times of Liberal Democracy*, (Oxford University Press, Oxford, 1977), p. 77:

It is pluralist in that it starts from the assumption that the society which a modern democratic political system must fit is a plural society, that is, a society consisting of individuals each of whom is pulled in many directions by his many interests, now in company with one group of his fellows, now with another. It is élitist in that it assigns the main role in the political process to self-chosen groups of leaders. It is an equilibrium model in that it presents the democratic process as a system which maintains an equilibrium between the demand and supply of political goods.

Chapter 1

1 *Atti del Parlamento. Senato del Regno* [Parliamentary Proceedings] *Sessione unica 1924–29, (I Sessione 1924–25 XXVII Legislatura) Discussioni, Tornata del 19 dicembre 1925*, p. 4374.
2 G. Mosca, *Partiti e sindacati nella crisi del regime parlamentare* [*Parties and Trade Unions During the Crisis of the Parliamentary System*] (*PS*) (Laterza, Bari, 1949), pp. 59–60.
3 *PS*, pp. 282–3.
4 G. Mosca, *Storia delle dottrine politiche* [*History of Political Doctrines*] (Laterza, Bari, 1974), 9th edn, p. 12.

Chapter 2

1 G. Mosca, *Sulla teorica dei governi e sul governo parlamentare. Studii storici e sociali* [*The Theory of Governments and the Parliamentary System. Social and Historical Studies*] (Loescher, Turin, 1884), p. 19.
2 T. B. Bottomore, *Elites and Society*, (Penguin, Harmondsworth, 1964), pp. 15–16.

3 Bottomore, *Elites and Society*, p. 16.
4 Bottomore, *Elites and Society*, pp. 18–19.
5 G. Sartori, *Dove va il Parlamento?*, in *Il Parlamento italiano (1946–1963)*, S. Somogyi, L. Lotti, A. Predieri and G. Sartori (eds) (ESI, Naples, 1963), p. 281.
6 See G. Mosca, *Elementi di scienza politica. Seconda edizione con una seconda parte inedita* [Elements of Political Science. Second edition with new part] (Bocca, Turin, 1923), pp. 24 and fol.
7 See A. Livingston, Introduction to *The Ruling Class* [*Elementi di scienza politica*] H. D. Kahn (trans) (McGraw-Hill, New York, 1939), p. xli.

Chapter 3

1 G. Mosca, *Sulla teorica dei governi e sul governo parlamentare. Studii storici e sociali* [*The Theory of Governments and the Parliamentary System. Social and Historical Studies*] (*TG*) (Loescher, Turin, 1884), pp. 8–9.
2 *TG*, p. 18.
3 *TG*, p. 19.
4 Ibid.
5 *TG*, pp. 19–20.
6 *TG*, p. 21.
7 *TG*, p. 22.
8 *TG*, p. 23.
9 *TG*, p. 22.
10 Ibid.
11 *TG*, p. 30.
12 Ibid.
13 *TG*, p. 31.
14 Ibid.
15 Ibid.
16 *TG*, p. 33.
17 *TG*, p. 34.
18 *TG*, p. 35.
19 *TG*, p. 37.
20 *TG*, p. 39.
21 *TG*, pp. 39–40.
22 *TG*, p. 40.
23 *TG*, p. 41.
24 *TG*, p. 42.
25 *TG*, p. 43.
26 *TG*, p. 44.
27 Ibid.
28 *TG*, p. 43.
29 Ibid.
30 *TG*, p. 45.
31 *TG*, p. 44, note 1.

32 *TG*, p, 46.
33 Ibid.
34 Ibid.
35 *TG*, p. 158.
36 *TG*, p. 161.
37 *TG*, p. 163.
38 *TG*, p. 164.
39 *TG*, pp. 167–8.
40 *TG*, pp. 164–5.
41 *TG*, p. 168.
42 *TG*, p. 180.
43 *TG*, pp. 176–7, note 1.

Chapter 4

1 G. Mosca, *Sulla teorica dei governi e sul governo parlamentare. Studii Storici e sociali* [*The Theory of Governments and the Parliamentary System. Social and Historical Studies*] (*TG*) (Loescher, Turin, 1884), pp. 353–4.
2 *TG*, p. 354.
3 *TG*, p. 351.
4 A. Gramsci, *Quaderni del carcere*, critical edition, V. Gerratana (ed.) (Einaudi, Turin, 1975), vol. 3, (Notebook 19 (X), 1934–35, *Risorgimento Italiano*), p. 1978.
5 *TG*, p. 346.
6 *TG*, p. 350.
7 *TG*, p. 352.
8 *TG*, p. 170.
9 *TG*, pp. 170–1.
10 G. Mosca, *Le costituzioni moderne* [*Modern Constitutions*] (*CM*) (1887), now in G. Mosca, *Ciò che la storia potrebbe insegnare. Scritti di scienza politica* [*What we can Learn from History. Writings in Political Science*] [Giuffré, Milan, 1958), p. 454.
11 *CM*, p. 455.
12 *CM*, p. 456.
13 *CM*, p. 513.
14 *CM*, p. 510.
15 *CM*, pp. 511–12.
16 *CM*, p. 532.
17 *CM*, p. 533.
18 *CM*, p. 534.
19 Ibid.
20 *CM*, p. 536.
21 Ibid.
22 *CM*, p. 548.
23 *CM*, p. 549.

Chapter 5

1 G. Mosca, *Elementi di scienza politica* [*Elements of Political Science*] (*ESP–I*) (Bocca, Turin, 1923), pp. 387–8.
2 N. Bobbio, *Saggi sulla scienza politica in Italia*, (Laterza, Bari, 1969), pp. 187–8.
3 *ESP–I*, p. 5.
4 *ESP–I*, pp.7–8.
5 *ESP–I*, p. 49.
6 Bobbio, *Saggi*, p. 180.
7 Bobbio, *Saggi*, p. 181.
8 *ESP–I*, p. 50.
9 *ESP–I*, pp. 52–3.
10 Bobbio, *Saggi*, p. 184.
11 Bobbio, *Saggi*, p. 190.
12 Bobbio, *Saggi*, p. 191.
13 *ESP–I*, p. 61.
14 *Ibid.*
15 *ESP–I*, p. 62.
16 Ibid.
17 *ESP–I*, pp. 79–80.
18 *ESP–I*, p. 35.

To put the situation in a few words, the struggle for *existence* has been confused with the struggle for *pre-eminence*, which is really a constant phenomenon that arises in all human societies, from the most highly civilized down to those which have just emerged from a state of savagery. In the struggle between different human societies, as a rule the victorious society does not annihilate the vanquished society, but subjects it, assimilates it, imposes its own type of civilization upon it.

19 *ESP–I*, p. 97.
20 *ESP–I*, p. 125.
21 *ESP–I*, p. 132.
22 *ESP–I*, p. 142.
23 *ESP–I*, p. 387.
24 See in particular *ESP–I*, ch. X, pp. 289–390.
25 *ESP–I*, pp. 60 and fol.
26 *ESP–I*, p. 123.
27 Ibid.
28 *ESP–I*, p. 124.
29 Ibid.
30 Ibid.
31 *ESP–I*, p. 124, note 21.
32 *ESP–I*, p. 389.
33 K. Marx and F. Engels, *Manifesto del partito comunista* [*The Communist Manifesto*], F. Ferri (ed.) (Editori Riuniti, Rome, 1960) p. 51. (The note 'to

the Italian reader' was published in the Biblioteca della Critica Sociale edition, Milan, 1893.)
34 Marx and Engels, *Manifesto*, p. 58.
35 *ESP-I*, p. 372, note 63.
36 *ESP-I*, p. 374.
37 *ESP-I*, p. 353.
38 *ESP-I*, p. 360.
39 *ESP-I*, p. 361.
40 *ESP-I*, p. 376.
41 Ibid.
42 *ESP-I*, p. 386.
43 *Ibidem*.
44 *ESP-I*, pp. 387–8.
45 *ESP-I*, p. 388.
46 *ESP-I*, p. 389.

Chapter 6

1 Ministero dell'Agricoltura, Industria e Commercio. Direzione Generale della Statistica e del Lavoro [Ministry of Agriculture, Industry and Commerce. Statistics and Labour Department] (MAIC. DGSL), *Statistica delle elezioni generali politiche alla XXIV Legislatura (26 ottobre e 2 novembre 1913)* (Tip. Naz. G. Bertero, Rome, 1914), p. 43.
2 *La XXIII Legislatura. 380 Ritratti di nuovi e vecchi Deputati*, in *L'Illustrazione Italiana* (Milano), ann. XXXVI, no. 12, 21 March 1909, p. 280.
3 *I 508 Deputati al Parlamento per la XXIII Legislatura, Biografie e Ritratti*, (Treves, Milan, 1910) p. 449.
4 MAIC. DGSL, *Statistica delle elezioni*, ibid. p. 43.
5 *I deputati eletti per la XXIV Legislatura*, in *L'Illustrazione italiano* (Milan), ann. XI., no. 45, 9 November 1913, p. 159.
6 See G. Mosca, *Il tramonto dello stato liberale* [*The Death of the Liberal State*] (*TSL*) A. Lombardo (ed.) (Bonanno, Catania, 1971). For Mosca's collaboration with the *Corriere* see the extensive and up-to-date essay by A. Colombo, *L'intellettuale Mosca e la classe politica dalla tribuna del 'Corriere della Sera'* in vol. II of the 'Archivio Internazionale', (Italian series).
7 G. Salvemini, *Il problema libico e la democrazia*, in *Come siamo andati in Libia e altri scritti dal 1900 al 1915* (Feltrinelli, Milan, 1963).
8 These have already been fully dealt with in E. A. Albertoni's *Gaetano Mosca. Storia di una dottrina politica* [*Gaetano Mosca. History of a Political Doctrine*]; any reader requiring further information on this subject should refer to this work. See also R. H. Rainero, *Gaetano Mosca e i problemi coloniali (Note sul realismo di Gaetano Mosca nella questione libica)*, in 'Archivio Internazionale', vol. I, (Italian series).
9 *TSL*, pp. 153–4.
10 *TSL*, pp. 154–5.
11 *TSL*, p. 199.

12 *TSL*, p. 201.
13 Atti del Parlamento. Camera dei Deputati [Parliamentary Proceedings, Chamber of Deputies] (*AP. CD*), *Sessione 1909–12 (I della XXIII Legislatura). Discussioni. 2ᵃ Tornata N del 9 luglio 1909*, vol. III, p. 4015. In this speech, one of his very first in the Chamber, Mosca states the following: 'I think that many colleagues already know that I'm a conservative, and as such I do not accept innovations unless they are fully justified'.
14 *AP. CD, Sessione 1909–12, Tornata del 7 maggio 1912*, vol. XVI, p. 19119.
15 Ibid.
16 Ibid.
17 *AP. CD, Sessione 1909–12, Tornata del 7 maggio 1912*, p. 19120.
18 Ibid.
19 Ibid.
20 *AP. CD, Sessione 1909–12, Tornata del 7 maggio 1912*, p. 19122.
21 See Luigi Albertini, *Dopo il voto*, in *Corriere della Sera* (Milan), 7 April 1914.
22 B. Vigezzi, *Da Giolitti a Salandra* (Vallecchi, Florence, 1969) pp. 74–5.
23 *AP. CD, Sessione 1913–19, Tornata del 13 luglio 1919*, vol. XVIII, p. 19778.
24 Ibid.
25 Ibid.
26 Ibid.
27 *AP. CD, Sessione 1913–19, Tornata del 13 luglio 1919*, p. 19780.
28 G. Mosca, *Feudalesimo e sindacalismo. Il pericolo presente*, in *Tribuna* (Roma), 1 February 1920, p. 1.
29 Ibid.
30 Ibid.
31 Atti del Parlamento. Senato del Regno [Parliamentary Proceedings. Senate] (*AP. SR*), *Sessione 1921–23. (Legislatura, Sessione unica). Discussioni. Tornata del 29 luglio 1921*, p. 208. See the essay by G. Cavallari, *Gaetano Mosca e il sindacalismo rivoluzionario*, in 'Archivio Internazionale', vol. II, (Italian series). See also D. Marucco, *Arturo Labriola e il sindacalismo rivoluzionario in Italia*, (Fondazione Einaudi, Turin, 1970).
32 *AP. SR, Sessione 1921–23, Tornata del 29 luglio 1921*, p. 210.
33 *AP. SR, Sessione 1921–23, Tornata del 29 luglio 1921*, p. 211.
34 See G. A. Chiurco, *Storia della rivoluzione fascista (1919–1922)*, 5 vols (Vallecchi, Florence, 1929), vol. III (1921), p. 588.
35 *AP. SR, Sessione 1921–23, Tornata del 16 novembre 1922*, p. 3999.
36 Ibid.
37 *AP. SR, Sessione 1921–23, Tornata del 16 novembre 1922*, p. 3999.
38 *AP. SR, Sessione 1921–23, Tornata del 27 novembre 1922*, p. 4241.
39 *AP. SR, Sessione 1921–23, Tornata del 27 novembre 1922*, p. 4240.
40 *AP. SR, Sessione 1921–23, Tornata del 27 novembre 1922*, p. 4241.
41 Ibid.
42 Ibid.
43 Ibid.
44 *AP. SR, Sessione 1921–23, Tornata del 27 novembre 1922*, p. 4242.
45 Ibid.

46 AP. SR, Sessione unica 1924–29, Tornata del 19 dicembre 1925, p. 4374.
47 Ibid.
48 Ibid.

Chapter 7

1   G. Mosca, Elementi di scienza politica. Seconda edizione con una seconda parte inedita [Second edn with new part] (ESP–II) (Bocca, Turin, 1923), p. VII.
2   ESP–II, p. 335.
3   See for the use of this term: ESP–II, pp. 336, 337, 338, 339, 342.
4   ESP–II, pp. 342–3.
5   ESP–II, p. 343.
6   Ibid.
7   Ibid.
8   Ibid.
9   ESP–II, p. 467.
10 ESP–II, p. 459.
11 ESP–II, p. 471.
12 Ibid.
13 E. A. Albertoni, Introduzione alla storia delle dottrine politiche. Tre saggi di ricerca, (Cisalpino-Goliardica, Milan, 1977 and 1984), p. 16.
14 P. Villari, La filosofia positiva e il metodo storico, (Tip. Cavour, Florence, 1868), pp. 31–36. (This work appeared in Il Politecnico, 1866).
15 G. Mosca, Storia delle dottrine politiche [History of Political Doctrines] (SDP) (Laterza, Bari, 1974), 9th edn.
16 SDP, p. 305.
17 G. Mosca, Pensieri inediti [Unpublished Thoughts] (PP) in Ethos (Rome), ann. I, no. 3, December 1945, Leonardo Donato (ed.), p. 732.
18 PP, p. 733
19 Ibid.
20 G. Mosca, Sulla teorica dei governi e sul governo parlamentare. Studii storici e sociali [The Theory of Governments and the Parliamentary System. Social and Historical Studies] (TG) (Loescher, Turin, 1884).
21 TG, p. 353.
22 Ibid.
23 ESP–II, p. 170.
24 Ibid.
25 For several essential references to this see: G. Mosca, Elementi di scienza politica [Elements of Political Science] (ESP–I) (Bocca, Rome, 1896), pp. 142, 157, 158, 180, 386, 387, 388, 389. 390.
26 ESP–I, p. 143.
27 ESP–I, p. 142.
28 SDP, pp. 294–305.
29 P. Gobetti, La Rivoluzione Liberale; Saggio sulla lotta politica in Italia, now in Opere Complete di P.G., vol. I, Scritti Politici (Einaudi, Turin, 1960) pp. 955–6.

30 *SDP*, p. 305.
31 See in this respect G. Mosca and G. Bouthoul, *Histoires des doctrines politiques depuis l'antiquité. Nouvelle édition complétée par Gaston Bouthoul. Les doctrines politiques depuis 1914* (Payot, Paris, 1955), p. 334 for the following comment by Gaston Bouthoul:

> I much admired the method used by Gaetano Mosca and the great critical spirit he displayed. His work represents a very precise statement. For each doctrine, he takes into account the context in which it was formulated and the dominant mentality in the period of the events that have influenced its gestation and birth. Thus his book is a true philosophy of the political history of human societies from the most remote to the most advanced. But this history is seen from the perspective of the fundamental hypotheses inspired by the doctrine with respect to the conduct of the Government and of nations . . . Each political doctrine is an attempt at a consistent conception of and explanation for these two principal phenomena: first the State and the Government, then the particular form taken by the division of labour making up the hierarchy.

32 G. Mosca, *Elementi di scienza politica. Terza edizione riveduta* [*Third revised edn, 2 vols*] (*ESP–III*) (Laterza, Bari, 1939), vol. II, p. 242.
33 Ibid.
34 *ESP–III*, vol. II, p. 243.
35 *ESP–II*, p. 111.

Chapter 8

1 G. Ferrero, *Lo Stato e la libertà secondo uno scrittore italiano*, in *Nuova Antologia* (Rome), vol. LXXXII, no. 662, 16 luglio 1899, pp. 280–96.
2 See the various essays collected in: *Guglielmo Ferrero tra società e politica*, Rita Baldi (ed.) (ECIG, Genoa, 1986).
3 G. Ferrero, *Aventure: Bonaparte en Italie. 1796–1797*, Paris, 1936 (Italian trans. Garzanti, Milan, 1947); *Reconstruction: Talleyrand a Vienne. 1814–1815*, Paris, 1940 (Italian trans. Garzanti, Milan, 1948); *Pouvoir*, New York, 1942 (Italian trans. Edizioni Comunità, 1947)
4 H. Kissinger, *Diplomazia della Restaurazione* (1957) [English title: *A World Restored*], (Garzanti, Milan, 1973), p. 365.
5 G. Mosca, *Le costituzioni moderne* [*Modern Constitutions*] (*CM*) (1887), now in G. Mosca, *Ciò che la storia potrebbe insegnare. Scritti di scienza politica* [*What we learn from History. Writings in Political Science*] (Giuffré, Milan, 1958), pp. 453–5.
6 Regarding 'juridical defence' see, as well as the exposition in ch. 5, the essay by E. A. Albertoni, 'La difesa giuridica come fondamento etico della governabilità dei sistemi politici', published as the *Introduction* in 'Archivio Internazionale', vol. II [Italian series], pp. XVI–XX and by the same author the essay: 'Formula politica e difesa giuridica nella dottrina della classe politica di Gaetano Mosca', in *Società. Norme e Valori. Studi in onore di Renato Treves*, U. Scarpelli and V. Tomeo (eds), (Giuffré, Milan, 1984).

7   *CMF*, p. 456.
8   G. Mosca, *Storia delle dottrine politiche* [*History of Political Doctrines*] (Laterza, Bari, 1974), 9th edn, p. 305.
9   See Ferrero, *Potere*, p. 23: 'One day while I was reading the Memoirs of Talleyrand, I found in the second volume seven pages (155–162) which revealed the existence of principles of legitimacy'.
10 E. Papa, *Storia di due manifesti. Il fascismo e la cultura italiana*, (Feltrinelli, Milan, 1958), p. 95.
11 Ferrrero, *Ricostruzione*, p. X.
12 See *'Power'* (*'legitimacy'*), in *The Fontana Dictionary of Modern Thought*, (Fontana/Collins, London, 1977), pp. 490–1.
13 Ferrero, *Potere*, pp. 390–1.
14 G. Ferrero, *La democrazia in Italia. Studi e previsioni* (Edizioni della *Rassegna Internazionale*, Milan, 1925), p.133: 'Political freedom and representative institutions are the vital organs of modern society because they are the citizens' defence against the increased arbitrary power of the modern State'.
15 *Dove va il mondo? Inchiesta tra scrittori italiani* (Libreria Politica Moderna, Rome, 1923), p. 31.
16 *Dove va il mondo?*, p. 32.
17 Ibid.
18 L. Ferrero, *Diario di un privilegiato sotto il fascismo* (Chiantore, Turin, 1946).

Chapter 9

1   V. Pareto, *The Mind and Society. A Treatise on General Sociology*, A. Livingston (ed.), 4 vols (Harcourt, Brace and Co., New York, 1937), new edition (Dover Pub., New York, 1963).
2   G. Busino, *Introduzione* in *I sistemi socialisti di V. Pareto* (Utet, Turin, 1974), p. 41.
3   Busino, *Introduzione*, pp. 38–9
4   See the contribution by E. A. Albertoni in *Le élites politiche*, R. Treves (ed.) (Laterza, Bari, 1961), pp. 194–200 and the same author's *Gaetano Mosca. Storia di una dottrina politica. Formazione e interpretazione*, (Giuffé, Milan, 1978) pp. 48–62.
5   L. Einaudi, *Dove si discute di Pareto, di Mosca ed anche di De Viti De Marco*, in *Riforma Sociale* (Torino), ann. XLI, vol. XLI, dicembre 1934, pp. 707–9.
6   See V. Pareto, *Manuale di economia politica con una introduzione alla scienza sociale*, (Soc. Ed. Libraria, Milan, 1906).
7   G. L. Field and J. Higley, *Elitism*, (Routledge & Kegan Paul, London, Boston and Henley, 1980), p. 18.
8   Despite the recent appearance in France of a reduced selection of chapters from Ostrogorskij's major work edited by P. Rosanvallon (Editions du Seuil, Paris, 1979), we have referred to the first French edition, *La démocratie et l'organisation des partis politiques*, 2 vols (Calman-Lévy, Paris, 1903). Not much is known about this author; even the date of his death is debatable (1917 or 1919). See also the essay by J. G. Merquior, 'Moisej Ostrogorskij

(1854–1919) and the Theory of the Professional Political Organization', in *Rediscoveries. Some Neglected Modern European Political-Thinkers*, J. A. Hall (ed.) (Clarendon Press, Oxford, 1986).
9   For a systematic analysis of these problems see E. A. Albertoni, *Storia delle dottrine politiche in Italia* (Mondadori, Milan, 1985), and the reduced French (PUF, Paris, 1981) and Spanish (Fondo de Cultura Economica, Mexico City, 1986) editions.
10 G. Mosca, *The Ruling Class*, trans. by Hannah D. Kahn, A. Livingston ed. (McGraw-Hill, New York, 1939).
11 R. Michels, *Storia del marxismo in Italia* (Mongini, Rome, 1910); *Storia critica del movimento socialista italiano dagli inizi fino al 1911*, (La Voce, Florence, 1921).
12 A. Pizzorno, 'Sistema sociale e classe politica', in *Storia delle idee politiche, economiche e sociali*, 7 vols (Utet, Turin, 1972), vol VI. p. 13.
13 James H. Meisel, *The Myth of the Ruling Class. Gaetano Mosca and the 'Elite'*, (The University of Michigan Press, Ann Arbor, 1962) 2nd edn, p. V.

Chapter 10

1   The Italian edition is: J. Burnham, *I difensori della libertà* (1943) (Mondadori, Milan, 1947).
2   For a discussion of this subject see vol. V of the 'Archivio Internazionale Gaetano Mosca per lo studio della classe politica' (Italian series) which contains a long interview with J. H. Meisel by Patrizia Tosi. This work, in two volumes, is being prepared for publication in Italian at the end of 1987.
3   On Harold Lasswell and elitism see the important study *Harold D. Lasswell on Political Sociology*, edited and with an introduction by D. Marvick (The University of Chicago Press, Chicago, 1977). See also *Politics, Personality and Social Science in the Twentieth Century. Essays in Honour of Harold D. Lasswell* A. A. Rogow (ed.) (The University of Chicago Press, Chicago, 1969).
4   J. L. Palombara, *Gaetano Mosca nelle Università degli Stati Uniti d'America*, in 'Archivio Internazionale', vol. I (Italian series), pp. 191–201; vol. I (International series), pp. 151–64.
5   See J. A. Schumpeter, *Capitalismo, Socialismo, Democrazia* (1943) [English title: *Capitalism, Socialism and Democracy*], (Etas Kompass 1967, 2nd Italian edn). For an up-to-date reading of Schumpeter's political and economic thinking see T. B. Bottomore, *Theories of Modern Capitalism* (Allen & Unwin, London, 1985).
6   C. B. Macpherson, 'Pareto's General Sociology: The Problem of Method in the Social Sciences', in *Canadian Journal of Economics and Political Science*, vol. III, 1937, pp. 458–71; 'The Ruling Class' in *Canadian Journal of Economics and Political Science*, vol. VII, 1941, pp. 95–100. In general, for Macpherson's reading of Mosca's work see the essay by F. Sabetti (Professor of Political Science at McGill University, Montreal) *Problemi*

critici e diffusione dell'opera di Gaetano Mosca nella cultura politica canadese, in 'Archivio Internazionale Gaetano Mosca', vol. I, (Italian series and International series).
7 C. B. Macpherson, *The Life and Times of Liberal Democracy* (Oxford University Press, Oxford, 1977), p.3.
8 Macpherson, *The Life and Times of Liberal Democracy*, pp. 77–92.
9 Macpherson, *The Life and Times of Liberal Democracy*, pp. 91–2.
10 Schumpeter, *Capitalismo, Socialismo, Democrazia*, pp. 244–52.
11 Schumpeter, *Capitalismo, Socialismo, Democrazia*, p. 269.
12 K. Graham, *The Battle of Democracy. Conflicts, Consensus and the Individual* (Wheatsheaf Books, Brighton, 1986).
13 R. A. Alford and R. Friedland, *Powers of Theory. Capitalism, the State and Democracy* (Cambridge University Press, Cambridge, 1965). Especially pp. 167–207 and 250–68.
14 H. Denis, *Storia del pensiero economico* (1965), 2 vols, (Mondadori Oscar, Milan, 1975), vol. II, p. 443.
15 Burnham, *I difensori della libertà*, p. 250.
16 Burnham, *I difensori della libertà*, pp. 266–7.
17 G. Stokes and B. Brugger, 'The Technocratic Challenge to Democratic Theory', in *Liberal Democratic Theory and its Critics*, by N. Wintrop (ed.) (Croom Helm, Beckenham, 1983), pp. 361–405.
18 See N. Wintrop and D. W. Lovell, *Varieties of Conservative Theory*, in *Liberal Democratic Theory and its Critics*, pp. 176–9 *(Anti-Communist Conservatives)* dealing with J. Burnham as the author of *The Struggle for the World* (1947), *The Coming Defeat of Communism* (1950), and *Suicide of the West: Meaning and Destiny of Liberalism* (1965).
19 Bottomore, *Elites and Society* (Penguin, Harmondsworth, 1964), pp. 18–19.
20 H. D. Lasswell and A. Kaplan, *Power and Society. A Framework for Political Inquiry* (Yale University Press, New Haven, 1950).
21 I. L. Horowitz, C. Wright Mills. An American Utopian (The Free Press, New York, 1983).
22 See N. Bobbio, the word 'Elites', in *Dizionario di politica*, (Utet, Turin, 1976), pp. 365 and fol.
23. G. Sartori, *Democrazia e definizioni*, (Il Mulino, Bologna, 1969) 3rd edn especially the entries: 'Democrazia', 'Sistemi rappresentativi' in the Appendix.
24 Sartori, *Democrazia e definizioni*, p. 321.
25 Sartori, *Democrazia e definizioni*, p. 333.
26 Sartori, *Democrazia e definizioni*, p. 338.
27 Macpherson, *The Life and Times of Liberal Democracy*, pp. 93–115.
28 P. Bachrach, *La teoria dell'elitismo democratico (1967)* (Guida, Naples, 1974), pp. 26–27.
29 Bachrach, *La teoria dell'elitismo democratico*, p. 33.
30 R. A. Dahl, *Polyarchy: Participation and Opposition*, (Yale University Press, New Haven, 1971). See in particular ch. 2: 'Does Polyarchy Matter?' pp. 17–20. See also by Dahl the recent works *A Preface to Economic Democracy*,

(Polity Press, Cambrdige, 1985) and *Democracy, Liberty and Equality*, Norwegian University Press, Oxford, 1986).
31   J. H. Meisel, *The Myth of the Ruling Class. Gaetano Mosca and the 'Elite'* (The University of Michigan Press, Ann Arbour, 1962) 2nd edn.
32   See J. G. Gunnell, 'Political Theory: the Evolution of a Sub-Field', in *Political Science: the State of the Discipline*, A. W. Finifter (ed.), (American Political Science Association, Washington DC, 1983). See also by this interesting writer *Political Theory: Tradition and Interpretation* (Winthrop, Cambridge Massachusetts, 1979).
33   G. Parry, *Political Elites*, (Allen & Unwin, London, 1986) p. 14.

Chapter 11

1   N. Bobbio, *Politica e cultura* (Einaudi, Turin, 1955), p. 16.
2   M. Delle Piane, *Liberalismo e parlamentarismo* (Macri, Città di Castello-Bari, 1946); *Bibliografia di Gaetano Mosca* (La Nuova Italia, Florence, 1949); *Gaetano Mosca: classe politica e liberalismo* (ESI, Naples, 1952); B. Brunello, *Il pensiero politico italiano dal Romagnosi al Croce* (Zuffi, Bologna, 1949); P. Piovani, 'Il liberalismo di Gaetano Mosca', in *Rassegna di Diritto Pubblico* (Napoli), ann. V, nos 3–4, maggio-agosto 1950; R. De Mattei, *Gli studi italiani di storia del pensiero politico (Saggio storico-bibliografico)* (Zuffi, Bologna, 1951) 2nd edn.
3   N. Bobbio, 'Liberalism old and new', in *Confluence* (Cambridge, Mass.) ann. V, no. 3, 1956.
4   E. Pennati, *Elementi di sociologia politica* (Comunità, Milan, 1961); F. Tessitore, *Crisi e trasformazioni dello Stato. Ricerche sul pensiero giuspubblicistico italiano fra Otto e Novecento* (Morano, Naples, 1963); G. Maranini, *Storia del potere in Italia* (Vallecchi, Florence, 1967).
5   Treves, *Introduzione* to *Le élites politiche*, p. XI.
6   G. Mosca, *La classe politica*, (Laterza, Bari, 1966).
7   Bottomore, *Elites and Society*, p. 44.
8   Bottomore, *Elites and Society* p. 148.
9   I. Berlin, *Marx* (La Nuova Italia, Florence, 1967), p. 13.
10   Bobbio, 'Mosca e la scienza politica', in *Saggi sulla scienza politica in Italia*, (Laterza, Bari, 1969), p. 186.
11   E. Ripepe, *Le origini della teoria della classe politica*, (Giuffré, Milan, 1971).
12   E. Ripepe, *Gli elitisti italiani*, 2 vols (Pacini, Pisa, 1971).
13   *Storia d'Italia*, Ruggiero Romano and Corrado Vivanti (ed.), 6 vols, (Einaudi, Turin, 1972–5).
14   A. Asor Rosa, 'La politica come scienza', in *Storia d'Italia*, (Einaudi, Turin, 1975), vol. IV.
15   J. Szacki, the word 'Classi', in *Enciclopedia* (Einaudi, Turin, 1978), vol. 3; G. Busino, the word 'Elite', in *Enciclopedia* (Einaudi, Turin, 1978), vol. 5; L. Gallino, *Dizionario di Sociologia*, (Utet, Turin, 1978).
16   M. Bovero, *La teoria dell'élite* (Loescher, Turin, 1975).
17   V. Pareto, *Opere Complete* [*Complete Works*], Giovanni Busino (ed.) (Droz, Geneva, 1964). The latter date is the year of publication of the first volume. So

far about fifty volumes in all have been published and the work is still in progress.

Chapter 12

1 T. B. Bottomore, *Elites and Society* (Penguin, Harmondsworth, 1964), p. 15.
2 G. Busino, the word 'Elite', in *Enciclopedia* (Einaudi, Turin, 1978), vol. 5, p. 335.
3 G. L. Field and J. Higley, *Elitism*, (Routledge and Kegan, London, Boston and Henley, 1980). See also J. Higley, G. L. Field and K. Grøholt, *Elite Structure and Ideology*, (Columbia University Press, New York, 1976); G. L. Field and J. Higley, 'Imperfectly unified elites: the cases of France and Italy', in *Comparative Studies in Sociology*, R. Tomasson (ed.), (JAI Press, New York, 1978), pp. 295–317.
4 G. L. Field, *The Syndical and Corporative Institutions of Italian Fascism* (AMS, New York, 1968).
5 J. Lopreato, *Introduction* to *Vilfredo Pareto. Selection from his Treatise* (Crowell, New York, 1965).
6 Field and Higley, *Elitism*, p. 94.
7 'Elite disunity, political instability and recurrent dictatorial rule have characterized most societies throughout history'. Field and Higley, *Elitism*, p. 119.
8 This essay by O. Stammer is entitled 'Das Elitenproblem in der Demokratie', and is contained in *Politische Soziologie und Politik. Aus Anlaß seines 65. Geburtstages herausgegeben von Mitarbeiten und Schülern*, Berlin, 1965.
9 Stammer, *Politische Soziologie und Politik*, p. 78.
10 Stammer, *Politische Soziologie und Politik*, p. 80.
11 Stammer, *Politische Soziologie und Politik*, p. 81.
12 Stammer, *Politische Soziologie und Politik*, p. 89.
13 See A. Zingerle, *La diffusione della conoscenza dell'opera di Gaetano Mosca nel mondo di lingua tedesca. (Germania, Austria, Svizzera Tedesca)*, in 'Archivio Internazionale', vol. I, (Italian series).
14 See the various essays contained in *Sonderdruck aus Politische Vierteljahrschrift* (Wiesbaden), no. 15, 1984, and in particular Klaus von Beyme, *Die Politische Theorien der Gegenwart. Eine Einführing* (R. Piper & Co Verlag, Munich and Zurich, 1984), 5th revised and supplemented edn.
15 See especially the Italian text of the 'Lezioni berlinesi' in *La democrazia nella società che cambia* (1963), R. Lowenthal (ed.) (Jaca Book, Milan, 1967). See the report by C. Offe, 'Legittimazione politica mediante decisione a maggioranza?', in *Fenomenologia e Società* (Milano), ann. IV, gennaio 1981, nos 13–14. pp. 53–64. A. Ardigò, A Giddens, R. Lowenthal, N. Luhmann, C. Mongardini, G. E. Rusconi, *La società liberal-democratica e le sue prospettive per il futuro* (Bulzoni, Rome, 1983). (Records of the Congress held in Rome on 9–11 November 1981 by the Goethe Institut and the Institute

for Historical-Political Studies in the Political Science Faculty of Rome University.)
16 H. Kelsen, *Teoria generale del diritto e dello Stato* (Comunità, Milan, 1963), 4th Italian edn, p. 296.
17 J. L. Orozco, *Darwinismo y elitismo*. Typewritten text presented at the Third International Mosca Seminar 'Clase política, elites políticas y partidos políticos', Mexico, La Trinidad-Tlaxcala, July 1984, p. 28.
18 See J. L. Orozco, *Nota introduttiva* to the Italian version of this same author's *Interpretazione critica della difesa giuridica*, in 'Archivio Internazionale', vol. II, (Italian series), pp. 407–10.
19 Orozco, *Nota introduttiva*, pp. 408–9.
20 Orozco, *Nota introduttiva*, p. 409.
21 J. L. Orozco, 'El joven Gentile y los Prolégomenos del Fascismo', in *La Palabra y el Hombre* (Veracruz), no. 31, 1979.
22 Orozco, *Nota introduttiva*, p. 408.
23 J. L. Orozco, *La Pequeña Ciencia, Una critica de la Ciencia Política norteamericana* (Fondo de Cultura Económica, Mexico, 1978); *El Testimonio político norteamericano: 1890–1980*, 2 vols (SEP/UNAM, Mexico, 1981); *Henry Adams y la tragedia del poder norteamericano* (Fondo de Cultura Economico, Mexico, 1985).
24 A. F. Bentley, *The Process of Government. A Study of Social Pressures* (University of Chicago Press, Chicago, 1908); Orozco, *Darwinismo*, p. 15.
25 P. H. Smith, *Los laberintos del poder. El reclutamiento de las élites políticas en México, 1900–1971*, (El Colegio de México, Mexico, 1981, 1st edn. in English: Princeton University Press, 1979); R. Ai Camp, *La formación de un gobernante. La socialización de los líderes políticos en el México posrevolucionario* (Fondo de Cultura Económica, Mexico, 1981). See also the interesting approach to understanding the formation and role of ruling economic–financial groups in Mexico in S. Cordero, R. Santín and R. Tirado, *El poder empresarial en México*, vol. I (Terra Nova, Mexico, 1983).
26 A. Sekulovič, *Teorija političke klase*, (Radnička Stampa, Beograd, 1982), p. 56.
27 Sekulovič, *Teorija*, p. 54.
28 Sekulovič, *Teorija*, p. 173.
29 Sekulovič, *Teorija*, p. 121.
30 Sekulovič, *Teorija*, p. 144.
31 Sekulovič, *Teorija*, p. 172.
32 Sekulovič, *Teorija*, p. 173.
33 Sekulovič, *Teorija*, p. 237.
34 Sekulovič, *Teorija*, p. 241. For studies closely relating to this field of interest in Yugoslavia and for Mosca's ethical elitism see also the essay *L'ideale etico-politico di Gaetano Mosca* by the same writer in 'Archivio Internazionale' vols I and II, (Italian series).
35 M. Gilas, *La nuova classe. Una analisi del sistema comunista* (1957) (Il Mulino, Bologna, 1957), p. 47.
36 Ibid.

37 The author of this present work has been able to observe interesting and diverse aspects of this form of elitism while studying at first hand the organization of public administration and the social and political system in the USSR, China, Cuba, Hungary, Rumania between 1970 and 1980.
38 M. Prélot, *Storia del pensiero politico* (1970), 2 vols (Mondadori, Milan, 1975), vol. II, pp. 614–15.
39 J. Touchard with the collaboration of L. Bodin, P. Jeannin, G. Lavau and J. Sirinelli, *Storia del pensiero politico* (1959) (Etas libri, Milan, 1974), 2nd ed., 3rd reprint, pp. 654–6.
40 F. Châtelet and E. Pisier-Kouchner, *Les conceptions politiques du XXe siècle* (PUF, Paris, 1981) pp. 176–8.
41 F. Châtelet and G. Maigret (eds), *Storia delle ideologie* (1978), 2 vols (Rizzoli, Milan, 1978). See for M. I. Ostrogorskij the above-mentioned work edited by P. Rosanvallon (Editions du Seuil, Paris, 1979); R. Michels, *Les partis politiques*, (Flammarion, Paris, 1971)
42 See F. Vecchini, *La conoscenza del pensiero di Gaetano Mosca in Francia nel secondo dopoguerra*, in 'Archivio Internazionale', vol. I, (Italian series). See also by F. Vecchini the important book *La pensée politique de Gaetano Mosca et ses différentes adaptions au cours du XXe siècle en Italie* (Cujas, Paris, 1968).
43 See R. Ghiringhelli, *Gaetano Mosca e la cultura politica francese degli anni venti e trenta*, in 'Archivio Internazionale', vol. I, (Italian series).
44 G. Burdeau, *Traité de science politique*, 13 vols, (LDGJ, Paris, 1982), vol. I, pp. 64–77.
45 Burdeau, *Traité de science politique*, vol. I, p. 66.
46 N. Poulantzas, *Potere politico e classi sociali* (1968) (Editori Riuniti, Rome, 1975).
47 Burdeau, *Traité de science politique*, vol. IV, 1984, p. 7.
48 G. Burdeau, *La démocratie* (Editions du Seuil, Paris, 1966); *Le libéralisme* (Editions du Seuil, Paris, 1979).
49 Burdeau, *La démocratie*, p. 9.
50 Burdeau, *La démocratie*, p. 179.
51 Burdeau, *La démocratie*, p. 296.
52 R. Aron, *La lutte de classe. Nouvelles leçons sur les sociétés industrielles* (Gallimard, Paris, 1964).
53 R. Aron, *Démocratie et totalitarisme* (Gallimard, Paris, 1965).
54 R. Aron, *Le tappe del pensiero sociologico (1965)* (Mondadori, Milan, 1972), pp. 369–445.
55 M. Duverger, *I partiti politici (1958)* (Comunità, Milan, 1961); *Introduzione alla politica (1964)* (Laterza, Bari, 1966); *I sistemi politici (1978)* (updated edition of 1st edn, Paris, 1955).
56 Z. Sternhell, *La droite révolutionnaire. Les origines françaises du fascisme, 1885–1914*, (Seuil, Paris, 1984), pp. 19, 244, 329.
57 L. Dion, *Les groupes et le pouvoir politique aux Etats-Unis* (Québec Presses Universitaires, Laval, 1965).
58 E. N. Suleiman, *Les hauts fonctionnaires et la politique* (Seuil, Paris, 1976); *Les élites en France. Grands corps et grandes écoles*, M. Meusy (trans.), (Seuil, Paris, 1979).

59 See among the many contributions: M. Dogan, *L'origine sociale du personnel parlamentaire français élu en 1951*, in M. Duverger, *Partis politiques et classes sociales en France* (Colin, Paris, 1955); 'La représentation parlamentaire du monde rurale' in J. Fauvert and H. Mendras, *Les paysans et la politique dans la France contemporaine* (Colin, Paris, 1958); 'Les attitudes politique des femmes en Europe et aux Etats-Unis', in R. Boudon and P. Lazarsfeld, *Le vocabulaire des sciences sociales* (Mouton, Paris, 1965; 'Un fenomeno di atassia politica', in *Partiti politici e strutture sociali in Italia*, M. Dogan and O. M. Petracca (eds) (Comunità, Milan, 1968); *The Mandarins of Western Europe* (Halsted, New York, 1975); (with D. Pelassy) *La comparaison internationale en sociologie politique*; (Litec, Paris, 1980); 'Come si diventa ministro in Italia. Le regole non scritte del gioco politico', in an edited book entitled *Il sistema politico italiano tra crisi e innovazione* (Angeli, Milan, 1984).
60 G. Perrin, *Sociologie de Pareto* (PUF, Paris, 1966).
61 G. Gurvitch, *Trattato di sociologia* (1958), 2 vols (Il Saggiatore, Milan, 1967).

Select bibliography

This bibliography comprises only a selection of Italian and international editions of works by Gaetano Mosca. No attempt has been made to provide an exhaustive selection. The following works have been referred to.

Delle Piane M., *Bibliografia di Gaetano Mosca* (La Nuova Italia, Florence, 1949).
Bobbio N., *La classe politica* (Laterza, Bari, 1966, 1972 and 1975).
Albertoni E. A., *Gaetano Mosca. Storia di una dottrina politica. Formazione e interpretazione* (Giuffré, Milan, 1978). (See herein the two bibliographical studies on Mosca's work in the English-speaking and French-speaking worlds by W. Abbondanti and R. Ghiringhelli respectively.)
Mosca G., *Scritti politici. (Teorica dei governi – Elementi di scienza politica)*, Sola G. (ed.), 2 vols, (Utet, Turin, 1982).
Albertoni E. A., *Dottrina della classe politica e teoria delle élites* (Giuffré, Milan, 1985).

See also the six volumes published so far in the 'Archivio Internazionale Gaetano Mosca per lo studio della classe politica', 1982–86.

Italian bibliography

1879   *L'Italia vivente: studi sociali di Leone Carpi*, Review in *Rassegna Palermitana* (Palermo), vol. I, no. 4, 16 febbraio.
1882   *I fattori della nazionalità*, in *Rivista Europea* (Florence), XIII, vol. XXVII, no. 4, 16 febbraio.
1884   *Sulla teorica dei governi e sul governo parlamentare. Studii storici e sociali* (Loescher, Turin).
1885   *Dei rapporti fra il parlamento ed il potere giudiziario in ispecie in relazione ai giudizi di costituzionalità delle leggi alla verifica delle elezioni ed al sindacato delle Camere sull'azione del potere giudiziario*, Thesis for university teaching qualification in constitutional law (Tipografia dello 'Statuto', Palermo).
1885   *Sulla libertà della stampa*, *Appunti* (Loescher, Turin). Now in *Ciò che la storia potrebbe insegnare* (Giuffré, Milan, 1958).

1886 *Studi ausiliari del diritto costituzionale*, in *Il Circolo Giuridico* (Palermo), XVII, vol. XVII. Now in *Ciò che la storia potrebbe insegnare*.
1887 *Le costituzioni moderne. Saggio* (Amenta, Palermo). Now in *Ciò che la storia potrebbe insegnare*.
1894 *Libero scambio, protezione e trasformazione agraria in Sicilia*, in *Giornale degli Economisti* (Bologna), V, vol. IX, no. 10, 1 ottobre.
1895 *Diritto costituzionale* (Rome University, Faculty of Jurisprudence), academic year 1894–5. Lectures collated by the students Caruso, G. and Marantonio A., Rome, n.d. (but 1895).
1896 *Elementi di scienza politica* (Bocca, Turin).
1897 *Nuovo corso di diritto costituzionale* (Turin University, Faculty of Jurisprudence), academic year 1896–7. Lectures collated by the students Barberis G. E., Bollati G., and Molar G. (Lit. F.lli Bertero, Turin, n.d. (but 1897)).
1897 *Il programma dei liberali in materia di politica ecclesiastica*, in *Giornale degli Economisti* (Bologna), VIII, vol. XV, no. 11, 1 novembre.
1898 *Questioni pratiche di diritto costituzionale* (Bocca, Turin).
1900 *Che cosa é la mafia*, in *Giornale degli economisti* (Bologna), XI, vol. XX, no. 3, 1 marzo.
1900 *I primi elementi di economia politica* (Popular University of Turin). Shorthand version of the course edited and published by Savonarola Lizzini C. and De Sarro E. (Tip. Lit. C. Giorgis, Turin).
1901 *Lezioni di diritto costituzionale* (Turin University, Faculty of Jurisprudence), academic year 1900–1. Lectures collated by Moretta G. B. (Tip. Lit. C. Giorgis, Turin).
1903 *Corso di economia politica* (Turin University, Faculty of Jurisprudence), academic year 1903. Lectures collated by Peccei R. and Bevione G. (Tip. Lit. Brandoni e Gili, Turin, n.d. (but 1903)).
1903 *Diritto costituzionale* (Turin University, Faculty of Jurisprudence), academic year 1902–3. Lectures collated by Della Porta G. (Tip. Brandoni e Gili, n.d. (but 1903)).
1903 *Il principio aristocratico ed il democratico nel passato e nell'avvenire*, in *Annuario dell'Università degli Studi di Torino*, academic year 1902–3 (Stamperia Reale, Turin).
1904 *Aristocrazie e democrazie*, talk recorded by Calderoni Mario, in *Il Regno* (Florence), vol. I, no. 9, 24 gennaio.
1907 *Piccola polemica*, in *Riforma Sociale* (Turin), XIV, vol. XVII, no. 4, 15 aprile.
1908 *Appunti di diritto costituzionale* (Società Editrice Libraria, Milan).
1909 *Diritto costituzionale e amministrativo* (Luigi Bocconi University, Milan), academic year 1908–9 (Stab. Tipolitografico Succ. Bruni, Pavia, n.d. (but 1909)). For the numerous writings, volumes and university textbooks by Mosca during his teaching at the Bocconi University see the many bibliographical references, most of them new, in S. Violante *Vent'anni di magistero di Gaetano Mosca nell'Università Commerciale 'Luigi Bocconi' di Milano*, 'Archivio Internazionale', vol. I (Italian series), and

especially R. Ghiringhelli *Per una lettura critica delle lezioni di scienza politica di Gaetano Mosca all'Università Bocconi (1918–1923)*, 'Archivio Internazionale', vol. II (Italian series).

1912 *Appunti di diritto costituzionale*, 2nd revised and corrected edition (Società Editrice Libraria, Milan).

1912 *Italia e Libia. Considerazioni politiche* (Treves, Milan).

1919 *Lezioni di scienza politica*, (Luigi Bocconi University, Milan), academic year 1918–19 (Tipolitografia Tenconi, Milan).

1920 *Lezioni di scienza politica*, (Luigi Bocconi University, Milan), academic year 1919–20 (Litografia P. Capra, Milan, n.d. (but 1920)).

1923 *Elementi di scienza politica*, 2nd edition with a new section (Bocca, Turin).

1923 *Il materialismo storico*, in *La Rivoluzione Liberale* (Turin), vol. II, no. 1, 11 gennaio.

1924 *Lo Stato-città antico e lo Stato rappresentativo moderno* in *La Riforma Sociale* (Turin), XXXXI, vol. XXXV, no. 3–4, marzo-aprile.

1925 *Teorica dei governi e governo parlamentare. Studii storici e sociali*, 2nd edn revised by the author (Soc. An. Istituto Editoriale Scientifico, Milan).

1927 *Saggi di storia della scienza politica*, Vol. X of the *Politeia* collection, Giannini A. (ed.), (Anonima Romana Editoriale, Rome).

1928 *Storia delle istituzioni e delle dottrine politiche* (Rome University), academic year 1927–28 (Stab. Tipolitografico V. Ferri, Rome, n.d. (but 1928)).

1929 *Corso sintetico di storia delle dottrine e delle istituzioni politiche* (Rome University), academic year 1928–29. Lectures collated by Donato L. and Fedele A., authorized edn, (Castellani, Rome).

1931 *Corso sintetico di storia delle dottrine e delle istituzioni politiche* (Rome University), academic year 1930–31. Lectures collated by Macchiarelli, L., authorized edn (Castellani, Rome).

1933 *Lezioni di storia delle istituzione e delle dottrine politiche* (Castellani, Rome). The date given, 1932, is a mistake. The correct date, 1933, is indicated in the *Preface*.

1933 *Cenni storici e critici sulle dottrine razziste, Rendiconto dell'Accademia Nazionale dei Lincei* (course in moral, historical and philological sciences), series VI, vol. IX (Accademia Nazionale dei Lincei, Rome).

1937 *Storia delle dottrine politiche*, 2nd revised and corrected Italian edn (Laterza, Bari).

1939 *Elementi di scienza politica*, 3rd revised edn, 2 vols (Laterza, Bari).

1939 *Storia delle dottrine politiche*, 3rd revised and corrected edn (Laterza, Bari).

1949 *Partiti e sindacati nella crisi del regime parlamentare* (Laterza, Bari).

1971 *Il tramonto dello Stato liberale*, Lombardo A. (ed.), Preface by G. Spadolini (Bonnano, Catania).

1974 *Gaetano Mosca e la teoria della classe politica*, edited and with an introductory essay by E. A. Albertoni (Sansoni, Florence). (Anthology chosen from *Teorica, Le costituzioni moderne, Elementi di scienza politica, Storia delle dottrine politiche, L'allargamento del suffragio e le amministrazioni locali* (1912), *Atti parlamentari* (1926)).

1983 *Giornale di un revisore*, Albertoni E. A. in 'Archivio Internazionale', vol. II, (Italian series) (Giuffré, Milan).
1986 Degree thesis (original text), *I fattori della nazionalità* Brancato F. (ed.) in (Nuovi Quarderni del Meridione; (Palermo), ann. XXIV, nos 93-94, gennaio-giugno.

International Bibliography

America and Britain

1931 Entry: *Giusti Giuseppe*, in *Encyclopedia of the social sciences*, vol. VI, (Macmillan, New York).
1931 Entry: *Machiavelli Niccolò*, in *Encyclopedia of the social sciences*, vol. IX, (Macmillan, New York).
1931 Entry: *Mafia*, in *Encyclopedia of the social sciences*, vol. X, (Macmillan, New York).
1931 Entry: *Manzoni Alessandro*: in *Encyclopedia of the social sciences*, vol. X, (Macmillan, New York).
1935 'Church sects and parties', in *Social Forces* (Chapel Hill, NC), vol. XIV, 1, October.
1939 *The Ruling Class (Elementi di scienza politica)* Livingston, A. (ed.), Kahn H. D. (trans.) (McGraw-Hill, New York).
1953 'Climate, Resources and Race', in *An introduction to Social Science*, A. Naftalin, B. N. Nelson, Q. Sibley, D. W. Calhoun, and A. G. Papandreou (eds) (J. P. Lippincot, New York).
1958 *The Final Version of the Theory of the Ruling Class*, in J. H. Meisel *The Myth of the Ruling Class. Gaetano Mosca and the Elite* (University of Michigan Press, Ann Arbor). The 'Supplement' to this book contains an English translation of the last chapter in the *Lezioni di storia delle istituzioni e delle dottrine politiche* (Castellani, Rome, 1932 (rectius 1933)) under the shortened title *Storia delle dottrine politiche*; the different versions of 1929, 1933 and 1937 are referred to in a footnote.
1960 'The Ruling Class', in C. W. Mills, *Images of Man* (G. Branziller, New York).
1961 'On the Ruling Class', in *Theories of Society*, vol. II, T. Parson, E. Shils, K. D. Naegele and J. R. Pitts (eds), 2 vols (The Free Press, Glencoe).
1962 *The Final Version of the Theory of the Ruling Class*, in J. H. Meisel *The Myth of the Ruling Class. Gaetano Mosca and the Elite*, 2nd edn, (University of Michigan Press, Ann Arbor).
1970 'Pluralism and Democracy', in *The Conservative Tradition in European Thought*, R. L. Schuettinger (ed.) (G. P. Putnam's, New York).
1970 'The Ruling Class', in *Power in Societies*, M. E. Olsen (ed) (Macmillan, New York). (Partial reprint of *The Ruling Class*, A. Livingston (ed.), 1939).
1971 'The Ruling Class', in *Political Sociology a Reader*, S. N. Eisenstadt (ed.) (Basic Books, New York and London).

1971 'The Political Class', in *Political Sociology*, A. Pizzorno (ed.) (Penguin Books, Harmondsworth).
1972 *A Short History of Political Philosophy*, S. Z. Koff (trans.) (T. Y. Crowell, New York). (Translation of *Lezioni di storia delle istituzioni e delle dottrine politiche*, 1933 with Preface and final note by Sondra Z. Koff and Stephen Koff).
1972 'Power and élites', in *The Few and the Many*, T. R. Dye and I. H. Zeigler (eds) (Duxbury Press, Belmont). (Reprint of pp. 50–3 and 335–7 of *Elementi* from the English version, *The Ruling Class*).
1975 'The Ruling Classes', in *Reflections on Inequality*, S. Andreski (ed) (Croom Helm, London).

France

1926 *Encore quelques mots sur 'le Prince' de Machiavel*, in *Revue des Sciences Politiques*, (Paris), vols. XL, XLVIII, no. 4, octobre-décembre 1925 and XLI, XLIX, 1, janvier-mars.
1927 *Formes et problèmes de l'émigration*, in *Revue des Sciences Politiques*, (Paris), vols. XLII, L, no. 3, juillet-septembre.
1928 *La crise du régime parlementaire. Causes et remèdes*, in M. J. Laski, C. Borgeaud, E. Larnaude, G. Mosca, M. J. Bonn, *L'évolution du régime représentatif. Cinq réponses à une enquête de L'Union interparlementaire* (Payot, Lausanne-Genève).
1936 *Histoires des doctrine politiques depuis l'antiquité jusqu'à nos jours*. G. Bouthoul (trans. and ed.) (Payot, Paris).
1955 Mosca G. and G. Bouthoul, *Histoires des doctrine politiques depuis l'antiquité. Nouvelle édition complétée par Gaston Bouthoul. Les doctrines politiques depuis 1914* (Payot, Paris).
1965 Mosca G. – G. Bouthoul, *Histoires des doctrine politiques depuis l'antiquité*, (Payot, Paris).

Germany

1926 *Können die Fortschritte der Politik als wissenschaftlich in Zukunft die sozialen Krisen ausschalten?*, in G. Salomon *Jahrbuch für Soziologie* (Karlsruhe). (L. Gorm, translation of 2nd part of ch. 5 of *Elementi*, edn, 1923).
1943 *Demokratisches Repräsentativsystem, Kommunismus, Bureaukratischer Absolutismus, Corporativismus*, in *Neue Zürcher Zeitung*, no. 1266, 15 August 1943. (Translation of pp. 483–9 of *The Ruling Class*, 1939, with presentation by W. Röpke.)
1950 *Die herrschende Klasse. Grundlagen der politischen Wissenschaft, mit einem Geleitwort von Benedetto Croce*, F. Borkenau (trans.) (A. Francke, Bern-München). (Translation of *Elementi* from the English edn: *The Ruling Class*, 1939.)
1962 *Endgültige Fassung der Theorie der herrschenden Klasse*, in J. H. Meisel *Der Mythos der Herrschenden Klasse. Gaetano Mosca und die 'Elite'* (Düsseldorf-Wien). (Translation of the 40th and last chapter in *Corso di storia delle*

istituzioni e delle dottrine politiche, Rome, 1932, from the English version, J. H. Meisel, in *The Ruling Class*, 1958.)

Japan

1973 *Shihaisuru – Kaikyu*, translation by Shimizu Hayao (Diamondo-sha ed., Tokyo). (Translation of *The Ruling Class* [*Elementi di scienza politica*], New York, 1939 without Preface by A. Livingston.)

Mexico

1980 *La Clase Política*, in *Revista de Administración Pública* (Mexico), 42, abril-junio. (Translation of ch. 1 of *Elementi di scienza politica*, edn, 1896.)

1984 *La Clase Política* (Fondo de Cultura Economica, Mexico). (Translation of selected anthology *La classe politica*, taken from *Elementi di scienza politica*, 3rd edn, 1939, edited and with an introduction by N. Bobbio, Italian edn, Bari, 1966.)

Poland

1938 *Historia Doktryn Politycznych od Strarozytnósci do Naszych Czasów*, translation and introduction by Stanislaw Kozicki (Trzaska, Evert and Michalski, Warszaw). (This is a translation of *Lezioni di storia delle istituzioni e delle dottrine politiche*, Rome, 1933, with an additional new chapter (ch. XLI) by the editor, S. Kozicki dedicated to Polish political writers; see the Italian translation of this chapter with notes on 55 Polish political writers edited by E. A. Albertoni in 'Archivio Internazionale', vol. II (Italian series).)

Spain

1941 *Historia de las doctrinas políticas*, translation and appendix by Legaz y Lacambra (Editorial Revista de Derecho privado, Madrid). (Translation of *Storia delle dottrine politiche*, 3rd Italian edn, 1939.)

Yugoslavia

1966 *Birokratija i tehnokratija*, V. Stanovic and A. Sojanovic (eds), Preface by J. Djordjevcic (Sedma Sila, Belgrade). (Anthology on bureaucracy and technocracy with several pages translated from *Elementi di scienza politica*.)

Name index

Agrippa, Menenio, 80
Ai Camp, Roderic, 151
Albertini, Luigi, 6
Alford, Robert, A., 123
Alighieri, Dante, 59
Aristotle, 19, 20
Aron, Raymond, 158
Asor Rosa, Alberto, 142

Bachrach, Peter, 127, 128
Basso, Lelio, 137
Bentley, Arthur F., 151
Berlin, Isaiah, 139
Bernstein, Eduard, 77
Bobbio, Norberto, xvi, 48, 49, 95, 125, 131, 132, 135, 137, 138, 140, 142
Bonomi, Ivanoe, 77, 78
Bottomore, Thomas B., xvi, xvii, 16, 125, 126, 127, 137, 138, 139, 140, 145
Bouthoul, Gaston, 156
Bovero, Michelangelo, 142
Brunello, Bruno, 135
Burdeau, Georges, 156, 157, 158
Burnham, James, 120, 123, 124, 125, 126, 145, 150
Burzio, Filippo, 141
Busino, Giovanni, 111, 142, 145, 156
Brugger, Bill, 124
Carle, Giuseppe, 6

Catlin, George G., 137
Châtelet, François, 155
Comte, Auguste, 86
Crispi, Francesco, 47, 58
Croce, Benedetto, 9, 39, 83, 90, 102, 137, 150
Czudnowski, Moshe M., xii, xvi

Dahl, Robert A., 128, 129
D'Annunzio, Gabriele, 74
Dante, see Alighieri
Darwin, Charles, 53
Delle Piane, Mario, 11, 135
De Maistre, Joseph, 101
De Mattei, Rodolfo, 135
Denis, Henri, 123
Descartes, René, 102
Diaz, Porfirio, 89
Dion, Léon, 158
Dogan, Mattei, xvi, 159, 163
Dorso, Guido, 135, 141
Duverger, Maurice, 158

Einaudi, Luigi, 6, 112
Emerson, Ralph W. 151
Engels, Friedrich, 59
Euchner, Walter, xvi

Facta, Luigi, 78
Ferrero, Guglielmo, 16, 60, 61, 98, 99, 100, 101, 102, 103, 104, 105
Ferrero, Leo, 105

Name index

Field, Lowell G., xvi, 113, 146, 147, 161, 162
Finer, Herman, 120
Firpo, Luigi, xvi
Friedland, Roger, 123

Gallino, Luciano, 142
Gentile, Giovanni, 9, 79, 137, 150
Ghiringhelli, Robertino, 156
Gilas, Milovan, 152, 154
Giolitti, Giovanni, 47, 66, 67, 69, 71, 72, 73, 77
Gobetti, Piero, 35, 40, 63, 92, 135, 141
Goodrick, Paul, xvii
Graham, Keith, 123
Gramsci, Antonio, 34, 35, 36, 132, 135
Gumplowicz, Ludwik, 86
Gunnell, John G., xvi, 129
Gurvitch, Georges, 159

Haller, Carl L. von, 101
Herzen, Alexander, 29
Higley, John, xvi, 113, 146, 147, 161, 162
Hitler, Adolf, 103
Hobbes, Thomas, 64
Horowitz, Irving L., 125
Hughes, Henry Stuart, 46

Kahn, Hannah D., 117
Kaplan, Abraham, 125, 127
Kelsen, Hans, 149
Kissinger, Henry, 99

Labriola, Arturo, 77
La Palombara, Joseph, 120, 137
Lasswell, Harold D., 120, 125, 127
Linz, Juan J., 121, 137
Lipset, Seymour M., 126
Livingston, Arthur, 17
Lombroso, Cesare, 6, 60, 65, 66
Lopreato, Joseph, 146
Loria, Achille, 60
Lovell, David W., 124

Lukacs, György, 16

Machiavelli, Niccolò, 3, 56, 64, 89
Macpherson, Crawford B., xv, 121, 122, 128
Maffesoli, Michel, xii, 159
Mairet, Gérard, 155
Mann, Thomas, 126
Mannheim, Karl, 16, 120
Marescotti, Ercole A., 15
Marx, Karl, 59, 61, 114, 123, 138, 139
Matteotti, Giacomo, 8
Maurras, Charles, 89
Mazzini, Giuseppe, 40
Meisel, James H. 16, 54, 118, 120, 126, 127, 129, 137, 138, 156
Merriam, Charles E., 120
Messedaglia, Angelo, 4
Meynaud, Jean, 157
Michels, Robert, xiv, xv, xvi, xvii, 6, 7, 86, 111, 113, 114, 115, 116, 117, 118, 120, 121, 123, 125, 126, 134, 141, 143, 148, 155, 156, 157
Mills, C. Wright, 125, 127, 129, 136, 137, 138, 152, 153
Mongardini, Carlo, 16, 105, 141
Montesquieu, Charles-Louis of Secondat, 20
Mussolini, Benito, 8, 9, 78, 79, 81, 82

Napoleon I, 27, 30, 102

Orlando, Vittorio Emanuale, 7
Orozco, José Luis, xvi, 150, 151, 162
Ortega y Gasset, José, 120
Ossowski, Stanislaw, 38
Ostrogorskij, Moisej I., 113, 114, 155

Palma, Luigi, 4
Papadopoli, Angelo, 69
Pareto, Vilfredo, xiv, xv, xvi, xvii, 7, 86, 92, 110, 111, 112, 114, 115,

116, 117, 118, 120, 121, 122, 123, 125, 126, 128, 131, 134, 136, 138, 141, 142, 143, 145, 148, 152, 155, 156, 158, 159
Parry, Geraint, 129
Passerin d'Entrèves, Alessandro, xvi, 137
Pelloux, Luigi, 47
Perez Miranda, Rafael, xvi
Perrin, Guy, 159
Piovani, Pietro, 135
Pisier-Kouchner, Evelyn, 155
Popper, Karl, xi
Poulantzas, Nicos, 157
Prélot, Marcel, 155
Prezzolini, Giuseppe, 112, 113, 121
Protonotari, Francesco, 4

Ripepe, Eugenio, 141
Roosevelt, Franklin D., 147
Rousseau, Jean-Jacques, 39, 87, 150
Ruffini, Francesco, 6, 9
Runciman, Walter G., 118

Sabetti, Filippo, xvi
Saint-Simon, Claude-Henri (Count of Rouvroy), 86
Salandra, Antonio, 4, 10, 65, 73
Salemi, Maria Giuseppa, 4
Salvemini, Gaetano, 67, 121
Sartori, Giovanni, 17, 127, 128, 129, 136, 137
Schumpeter, Joseph A., xv, 121, 122, 123, 124, 125, 126, 127, 128, 138, 145, 147, 152, 160, 161
Sekulovič, Aleksandar, xvi, 152, 153, 154, 155, 162
Sereno, Renzo, 120
Sieyès, Emmanuel-Joseph, 150
Sighele, Scipio, 13
Sola, Giorgio, 141
Solari, Gioele, 6

Sonnino, Sidney, 69
Smith, Peter H., 151
Spadafora di Policastrello, Giuseppe, 65, 66
Spencer, Herbert, 151
Stalin, 103, 154
Stammer, Otto, 147, 148
Starobinski, Jean, xii
Starrabba, Antonio Di Rudinì, 4, 5, 47, 65, 66
Sternhell, Zeev, 158
Suleiman, Ezra, 159
Sweezy, Paul M., 128
Szacki, Jerzy, 142
Stokes, Geoff, 124

Taine, Hippolyte A., 86
Talleyrand-Perigord, Charles Maurice, 99, 101
Tomasi di Lampedusa, Giuseppe, 32
Touchard, Jean, 155
Touraine, Alain, 137
Treves, Renato, xvi, 37, 137
Trotsky, 123, 154
Truman, David, 120

Umberto I of Savoy, King of Italy, 47

Vecchini, Francis, 155
Vico, Giambattista, 89
Villari, Pasquale, 89
Visconti, Luchino, 32
Vittorio Emanuele III of Savoy, King of Italy, 75

Weber, Max, 114, 152
Wintrop, Herman, 124

Zanardelli, Giuseppe, 47
Zingerle, Arnold, 148, 149
Zylberberg, Jacques, xii, 142, 159